Also by Brian Curtis

The Men of March:
A Season Inside the Lives of College Basketball Coaches

How Good Do You Want to Be?

(with Nick Saban)

Every Week a Season

Every Week a Season

A Journey Inside Big-Time College Football

BRIAN CURTIS

BALLANTINE BOOKS

NEW YORK

To Tamara,
My one and only

To Mom, Dad, Greg, and Mike,
My loving family

2005 Ballantine Books Trade Paperback Edition

Published in the United States by Ballantine Books,
an imprint of The Random House Publishing Group,
a division of Random House, Inc., New York.

Originally published in hardcover in the United States by
Ballantine Books, an imprint of The Random House Publishing
Group, a division of Random House, Inc., in 2004.

ISBN 0-345-48337-5

Printed in the United States of America

www.ballantinebooks.com

2 4 6 8 9 7 5 3 1

Text design by Mary A. Wirth

CONTENTS

FOREWORD

Since December 25, 1951, when a beloved aunt gave me a Voit football for Christmas, my life has been almost continuously intertwined with this great American game. It has been a source of some of my life's greatest moments and biggest disappointments. It has also been responsible for many invaluable lessons that could only have been learned on "the fields of friendly strife."

Like thousands and thousands of men in this country, this game afforded me the opportunity to earn a college degree, and for that I am forever grateful. And like the vast majority of those people who have played high school and college football, I have benefited from its greatest gifts. I have learned the humility that sooner or later this game teaches to almost every participant, and I have formed some lifelong friendships and relationships that have enriched and changed my life for the better.

At Riverview High School in Riverview, Michigan, I played for Coach Bud McCourt—a man we feared and respected and tried to please. Bill McCartney, who would later win a National Championship at Colorado, was there and so was Woody Widenhofer, who would become the head coach at Missouri and Vanderbilt. Rollie Dotsch was my head coach at Northern Michigan University and, had not cancer cut his life short, every football fan would know his name.

After college I was a high school teacher and coach for seven years and I loved every minute of it. But in 1976 I was offered an assistant coaching job at Eastern Michigan University, which I accepted. Two seasons later I was hired by Gary Moeller at Illinois. Then in March of 1980, the legendary Bo Schembechler hired me at Michigan. It was the greatest break of my career.

My guess is that my coaching career is similar in many ways to those of my peers. I have had some success. I have been to the summit and I know the abyss that is part of being fired. I know the incredible highs of last-second victories that are part of championship seasons, and I know the gut-wrenching despair that comes with last-second losses that end championship dreams. I know about the pressure of unrealistic expectations, and I know about the criticism that comes when things don't go well. I am also acutely aware of those critics who charge that we have lost our way in intercollegiate athletics, that we make too much money, that we have sold out to the shoe companies and the corporate influence, that we do not care about the academic mission of the universities we represent, and that we do not care about the young people we spend our lives coaching. This is the arena in which we live and work and compete, and to the degree that the arena is a negative one, some of that negativity is of our own making. Regardless, most coaches would agree, I think, that the greatest reward in coaching is watching young men struggle, grow, persevere, and mature while competing in a game that requires even the most talented to give their best effort on a consistent basis. The coach's job is ultimately to mold all of these people from all these various backgrounds into a winning team. He knows—everyone knows—that he must win, because if he fails to win, he will be replaced.

I have been in college football for a long time and I have seen the game and the world around it change dramatically. These young athletes are bigger, stronger, faster; the recruiting is never-ending; the media has become a part of our daily lives even in the off-season; and the revenue generated and the costs associated with football programs have grown to levels that are barely comprehensible.

Every Week a Season is the most accurate and compelling picture of what goes on in major college football that I have read over the years. Not only does Brian Curtis capture the rhythm of practice weeks, the logic of planning and strategy sessions, and the intensity of games, he also paints a picture of the human side of the sport. Coaches have wives and children, and some of us are blessed with grandchildren. We have a life away from the game, even if some days it doesn't seem like it.

But what is most remarkable about this book is the unparalleled access that the top college football programs in America gave Brian. As a head coach for nine years and an assistant for many more, I can tell you the inner sanctum of college football is well guarded. The fact that nine head coaches—including some of the best in America— allowed Brian to be in staff and team meetings, locker rooms, chapel services and everything else, is a testament to their trust and respect for him. As I read through *Every Week a Season*, I was fascinated by how other coaches run their programs—from the way they keep a team loose before game time to what down and distance they focus on in a Tuesday practice; from how they recognize academic achievement to how they manage their staff. I am sure that if Brian spent a week with us at the University of Michigan he would find many similar practices.

The stories revealed in these pages are similar to ones you'd hear at Michigan or any other great program. The debate about which LSU kicker would take the field in the national championship game; the silence over Boston College's pre-game breakfast, and the equally powerful silence that hung over Tennessee's practice field when fallen teammates lay motionless on the field; the pit in the stomach of Arizona State's Dirk Koetter as his team tried to salvage a difficult season; the motivational rubber bands that my friend Barry Alvarez gave his Wisconsin Badgers to remind them just what was at stake; the tension that pervaded Florida State after a loss to Clemson; Sonny Lubick's explanation of the proper technique to fresh-faced walk-ons at Colorado State—these are the things I remember from these pages. These are the things that define college football.

The truth is that every single game is important today and that is one of the strengths of our sport. There is great consequence attached to each win and loss. Coaching staffs across the country offer up their early mornings and late nights to best prepare for Saturday, knowing full well that the opponent is out there doing the same thing. I know that when we face off against Notre Dame or any of our Big-Ten rivals, their staff and fans are as revved up as we are in Ann Arbor, and that is what makes the games so great. The beauty of football, the drama, the teamwork, the character building—these things have not changed since my playing days in the 1960s. It's just that everything else has.

LLOYD H. CARR
University of Michigan
Ann Arbor, MI
June 2004

ACKNOWLEDGMENTS

As you might imagine, putting together this journey was not an easy task, and the trip and the resulting book would never have been possible without the guidance, support, and graciousness of many individuals. From the spring of 2003 when I first conceived of the idea to the unbelievable fall season to the writing of the book in early 2004, the people I met along the way and those I have known for many years made this a reality. It is hard to thank everyone, so anyone I've forgotten, please accept my appreciation.

First, I must express my gratitude and sincere appreciation to the nine exceptional men who allowed me into their inner circles. They accepted me without conditions and held true to their word, opening up their offices, locker rooms, and homes, so I could get a look into their world. They trusted me when they didn't have to. They answered my questions and took the time to explain things. Their cooperation was beyond my expectations. My thanks go out to Sonny Lubick, Mark Richt, Tom O'Brien, Phillip Fulmer, Ralph Friedgen, Barry Alvarez, Nick Saban, Bobby Bowden, and Dirk Koetter. Of course, their assistant coaches and staffs, too numerous to list here, were candid, welcoming, and helpful throughout my visits, and I know many of them will one day be head coaches themselves. I would be remiss if I also did not thank the coaches' wives and families, who were gracious in welcoming me as well.

The sports information personnel at all nine schools who helped arrange my visits and made sure they all went smoothly: Gary Ozzello, Claude Felton, Chris Cameron, John Painter, Greg Creese, Justin Doherty, Michael Bonnette, Rob Wilson, and Mark Brand. To all of you and your staffs, my gratitude and praise, as you are among the best at what you do. To the administrative assistants to the head coaches who eased the process along: Lora Borup, Mary Jo Fox, Jill Hegarty, Karyl Henry, Sharon Hudgins, Linda Krier, Ya'el Lofton, Lisa Powell, and Staci Wilkshire.

There are so many wonderful people that I met along the way. Passionate fans, wonderful administrators, and students and alumni from around the nation. A special thanks to Jack Marucci, John Burnside, Ken Robbins, Megan Maciejowski, John Schropp, and Hamed Jones for their help.

I could not ask for a better editor and friend than Mark Tavani at Ballantine Books. He believed in this project from the start and I am grateful that he could share the journey with me. His professionalism, character, and talent set him apart from the pack. To Gina Centrello and Nancy Miller, thank you for giving me the chance. To Kimberly Hovey, Christine Cabello, Avideh Bashirrad, Fleetwood Robbins, Heather Smith, and the publicity and marketing staff at Random House, my many thanks for helping get the word out.

Sam Goldfeder, you have helped me achieve my goals and have been so much more to me than simply an agent. You are a good friend and a wonderful person and I look forward to working together and celebrating life together in the future.

To my wonderful family: my parents, Marty and Shelly Mand, brothers Mike and Greg, Erin, Jeff, and my in-laws, Don and Claire Marks. Your love and support have been incredible and sharing my journey with you makes it all worthwhile. To my wife, Tamara, who unconditionally gave her support to this project, knowing that it would take me away for such a long time. Your belief in me has never waivered. You are my best friend and the world is a better place because of you.

Finally, my appreciation to all of the college football fans around the country, whose passion and support make every week a journey unto itself.

Brian Curtis
Los Angeles
April 2004

Every Week a Season

College football is not a game.

College football is a Monday at midnight, Coke cans littering a conference table, coaches bleary-eyed and buzzed with caffeine. It is eating team meals in total silence from Friday afternoon until game time on Saturday night. It is chapel leaders and priests invoking the story of David versus Goliath on a weekly basis. It is a man confronting an author in a parking lot outside of a coach's weekly booster luncheon, accusing him of stealing secrets for the opposition.

College football is 800 crazies showing up seven hours early on a Wednesday afternoon, just to get good seats for the coach's radio show. It is a coach holding practice on Sunday night instead of Monday so students in his program can attend lab classes. It is the Vol Walk, the Dawg Walk, the Tiger Walk, and Terp Alley. It is silence falling over a practice when two teammates collide and do not move. It is police escorts, charters and hotels, buffets, Powerade®, and ankle tape. It is upsets and streaks, tears in the locker room, victory laps around the field.

College football is the coach who takes time off to be at his wife's side when she is struck with cancer; the coach who spends an hour every practice with the walk-ons and scout teams—and knows their names. It is the coach who breaks down when talking about his team's seniors, the coach at a loss for words after a crushing defeat. It is pits in the stomach before kickoff. It is strategy and second-guessing, match-ups and tendencies, imaginary scenarios running through heads.

College football is not a game.

Coaches watch more film in one week than most of us do in a lifetime. They rise and go to sleep at uncommon hours. They honestly believe that the work they do is the most important thing to their school, their community, and their state in any given week. They see more of their kids in the pictures on their desks than in person. They attack each week riding high on a recent win or crawling out from under the weight of a loss. Every Sunday morning they awake, ready to do it all over again, whatever may have transpired less than twelve hours earlier. Some swear, some yell. But in them, if you look, you'll find great leaders and motivators, educators and teachers, professionals who give more than 100 percent to their jobs.

It seems almost trite to describe the year-round demands on a coach, the immense pressure that he is under to win. It seems almost unnecessary to write about just how big a business college football has become or how its coaches have become wealthy celebrities. I'll assume that my readers understand that. But the true complexity of it all is revealed only in the details.

• • •

When did every week become a season? When did each and every game become so important to coaches, players, fans, and television executives?

The Supreme Court decision in 1985 that permitted individual conferences and schools—instead of the National Collegiate Athletic Association (NCAA)—to make television deals contributed to the trend, allowing the prominent programs in major conferences to be on television every week, making household names of players *and* coaches. In 1978, the maximum number of scholarships per team was reduced from 105 to 95, and between 1992 and 1994, further reduced to 85, creating what many coaches say is the parity we see today. (Of course, at the time, many coaches believed that reducing the limits would kill college football.)

The greatest factor was the development in the 1990s of the Bowl Alliance and its successor, the Bowl Championship Series (BCS). Before the kickoff of the 1998 season, the four major postseason bowls—the Rose, Orange, Sugar, and Fiesta—made a pact with the Atlantic Coast Conference, the Big East, the Big XII, the Big Ten, the PAC-10, and the Southeastern Conference, as well as with Notre

Dame. The arrangement makes it extremely difficult for teams from other conferences to play in the big four bowl games. These games are reserved for the big boys, and that means big money. In 2003, the BCS leagues received payments close to $14 million each, with additional money (approximately $4.5 million) coming if an at-large team came from their conference.

The BCS is the closest thing college football has to a playoff, with the top teams in the nation facing off in the first days of the New Year. The compromise reached in the late 1990s allows the bowls to continue to be the showcases of college football, but ensures that the top two teams face off to determine a true national champion—supposedly eliminating the controversial split national championships of seasons past. Of course, you still have to determine who the top teams are.

The basic layout for the BCS: The winners of the six major conferences receive automatic berths and two at-large teams are added to complete the list of eight teams selected to play in the four BCS bowl games each January. Based on the final BCS rankings (explained below), #1 plays #2 in the national championship game at one of the four bowls. The bowls each claim the national championship game once every four years, sharing it on a rotating basis. The traditional bowl alignments, such as the Big Ten and PAC-10 champions meeting in the Rose Bowl, take a backseat when the national title game is slated for that bowl. In fact, even when the bowl is not hosting the title game, its traditional alliances can be affected. In a complicated formula with many deviations, the BCS somehow comes out with rankings at the end of the season—but not without controversy.

The rankings have five main components, and the lower the point total, the better.

First are the polls. The average ranking of a team in the two major polls, the Associated Press and the ESPN/USA Today Coaches' Poll, is used to determine the first point criteria. If a team is ranked #6 in one poll and #10 in another, then its poll average is eight.

The second factor in the BCS ranking is the computers. The BCS uses seven different computer polls, all of them different in formula and design, created by both amateurs and professionals. The lowest computer ranking for a team is dropped, and the remaining six rankings are averaged. The computer rankings used in the BCS are those run by Anderson & Hester, Richard Billingsley, Wes Colley, Kenneth Massey, *The New York Times*, Jeff Sagarin, and Peter Wolfe.

The third measuring stick is strength of schedule (SOS), where

66.6% of a team's SOS is their opponents' winning percentage and 33.3% is the winning percentage of their opponents' opponents. Only games played against Division I-A opponents count. The SOS figure is then ranked compared to that of other Division I-A teams and divided by 25.

The fourth component is losses, and each loss adds one point to a team's total.

The final factor is quality wins, as a team is rewarded for wins over teams that finish in the top 10 of the final BCS rankings. A win over the #6 team means a subtraction of 0.4 from the point total. But there's a catch. A team does not get additional quality win points for beating the same team twice in a season.

With so few regular season games, one loss can crush a team's hopes for a national title or even a BCS bid. With the polls and computer rankings as factors, a loss early in the season is better than a loss in November. It is critical to get a high preseason ranking so that the movement to the top, assuming you win, requires a shorter distance. Of course, with SOS as a factor, coaches and athletic directors huddle to determine what opponents can boost their SOS. The risk? The better the opponent, the more likely a loss.

So, does the system work? Well, no, if you ask many fans after the 2003 season. All season long, the drama built as teams faced off in important battles from late August until early December. When a team lost a game, the pundits all but ruled them out of the national title picture. As the season wound down, the only undefeated teams left in the country were Oklahoma and Texas Christian University. The Horned Frogs could have been a problem. If you recall, the BCS was created for the major conferences, and no team from a "mid-major" had ever played in a BCS game. If a team from outside one of the BCS conferences is ranked in the top six of the final BCS standings, it must be included. Getting an at-large bid is difficult and has never happened. Luckily for the BCS creators, TCU lost late in the season. By the end of November, it appeared that the national title game would pit Oklahoma against either Louisiana State University (LSU) or the University of Southern California, both of whom only had one loss.

In the last two weekends of the season, USC beat Oregon State, LSU defeated Georgia for the SEC title, and Oklahoma lost convincingly to Kansas State in the Big XII Championship game. Now what? Three teams all had one loss. In the previous weeks, the experts were predicting who the final two would be, counting on the Sooners to run the table. It soon became apparent that a team's SOS could be the deciding factor. That is why season-ending games like Notre Dame versus Syracuse and Hawaii versus Boise State became so important. USC had beaten both Notre Dame and Hawaii, so they needed them to win to boost the Trojans' SOS. Neither did. After a long Saturday night and Sunday morning, December 6 and 7, the final rankings were revealed. Oklahoma finished #1 with a BCS index of 5.11, LSU came in second with 5.99, and USC finished third with 6.15 points. Oklahoma and LSU would play for the national title. But USC finished ranked #1 in both polls. Uh oh.

Chaos reigned, as talk radio hosts and newspaper columnists blasted the system and labeled it a failure. The BCS did not work. It was supposed to match the top two teams in the country, and it didn't—according to the polls. But according to the BCS rankings, it did. If USC defeated Michigan in the Rose Bowl, it would surely finish #1 in the Associated Press poll. But the ESPN/*USA Today* poll, voted on by coaches, is obligated to rank the winner of the BCS national championship game #1. So there was a chance we would have a split national championship. And we did.

In today's college game, expectations are that the preeminent programs—Ohio State, Oklahoma, Miami, Florida State—will roll through their regular seasons undefeated. But for teams like Colorado State, playing in a non-BCS conference, the only shot at a BCS game is to go undefeated—and then pray that the BCS rankings favor them. During the 2003 season, there was a growing chorus of complaints from the presidents and coaches of non-BCS conferences about the lack of opportunity for their schools. Meetings were held, Congress got involved, threats were made.

In February of 2004, the presidents of BCS conference schools and non-BCS schools came together and, with the blessing of the BCS Committee, decided to add a fifth BCS game beginning in the 2006 season for two more at-large teams. The added game would not guaranatee slots for non-BCS teams but it would make it a lot easier for those nonmajor conferences to be represented.

The arrangement also calls for a change in how the BCS revenue is divided among the schools. As of June 2004, it was decided that the fifth game would follow a "double-hosting" format—informally known as the "piggy-back" plan—whereby each of the four BCS bowls would host an additional game every four years. The national title game would be held a week after the bowl hosts a BCS game.

• • •

With all of this in mind, I set out on a journey of my own, to see for myself what the world of college football is all about. Spending a season with a Top 25 powerhouse would certainly be in-depth and personal, but wouldn't reveal the tendencies, trends, and personalities of the game. I reasoned that spending an entire week with multiple prominent coaches and teams would provide me with that. So in the spring of 2003, I began the process of creating a list of the programs I wanted to observe. I received recommendations from athletic directors, conference administrators, and media members. I compared that list of 30 to the spring's preseason polls, which are based primarily on what players and coaches were returning and what went on in spring practice. Of course, I wanted every team I joined to be in the Top 25. But having experienced the fate of some of the basketball programs that I profiled in my last book, *The Men of March*, I knew well that some teams that start in the polls don't end up there.

It was time to start selecting and lining up teams. When I approached each head coach, I told him what I needed: full access for one week during the 2003 season, including staff meetings, practices, player meetings, locker rooms, offices, etc. Some of the coaches I asked to participate declined because they didn't want to let an outsider in. Two said yes, but with conditions, to which I said no. One coach said yes, but for the 2004 season.

The goal was to join eight programs that could give me diverse head coach personalities and campus environments. The end result was pleasing and surprising. I lined up nine coaches and schools: Barry Alvarez at Wisconsin, Bobby Bowden at Florida State, Ralph Friedgen at Maryland, Phillip Fulmer at Tennessee, Dirk Koetter at Arizona State, Sonny Lubick at Colorado State, Tom O'Brien at Boston College, Mark Richt at Georgia, and Nick Saban at LSU. Of the nine teams, eight were in someone's Top 25 preseason poll.

Now that I had them on board, it was a matter of picking game weeks that worked for me and for the coaches. Through numerous e-mails, phone calls, and faxes, the schedule was set—and it included some very big games: LSU and Auburn, Wisconsin and Ohio State, Georgia and South Carolina, Boston College and Miami, Maryland and Clemson, Arizona State and Arizona, Tennessee and South Carolina, Florida State and North Carolina State, Colorado State and Colorado.

The journey began in Fort Collins, Colorado, in late August and ended at the national title game in New Orleans in early January. After Colorado State, I visited Georgia, Boston College, Tennessee,

Maryland, Wisconsin, LSU, Florida State, and Arizona State, in that order. As a bonus, when Georgia and LSU faced off in the SEC Championship game in Atlanta, I was with Georgia. On top of that, I joined LSU as they played for all the marbles in the Sugar Bowl.

I sat in on offense, defense, and special teams meetings during the weeks. I stood on and off the field during practices. I ate meals with the teams, spent nights at their hotels, rode the buses to Friday night movies, and sat in on chapel services, team meetings, and pregame traditions. I spent time with the head coaches, in their offices and at their homes, met their families, and shadowed them as they spoke with the press, boosters, and players. At the start of each week, I told every coach that I would be willing to leave any meeting that was a matter of a personal nature, particularly regarding players.

The head coaches and their staffs welcomed me into their kingdoms, trusting me with scouting reports, game plans, and strategies. They answered my questions, and asked some of me. I observed them late at night, tired and cranky, watching film. I sat next to them on the bus heading to the stadium as their legs shook nervously. I was there to enjoy their elation in victory or stand in a quiet locker room after a loss. My seat to the games? Right in the middle of the coaches and players on the sidelines.

Any journey is full of amazing moments, and this one was no exception. I can hear the deafening roar of the crowd in Madison, Wisconsin, as #2 Ohio State faced a critical third down and long late in the game. I can smell the freshly cut grass on the sidelines in Neyland Stadium, as a game is being decided in overtime. I feel the sweat rolling down my cheeks under a blistering sun at Georgia as the Dawgs tried to score their first offensive touchdown against South Carolina in 11 quarters. I feel the rain pounding my face during a third-quarter rainstorm in Denver. I remember the moments that defined the games and the men in charge. Tom O'Brien refusing to let his players give up late in the game against Miami; Dirk Koetter walking over to quarterback Andrew Walter and taking the blame on a busted play call; Bobby Bowden finding kicker Xavier Beitia back near the bench, just seconds after he missed a potential game-winning field goal; Mark Richt putting an arm on the shoulder of David Greene; Nick Saban thrusting an arm high in the air as LSU poured it on Auburn; Sonny Lubick's dazed look as the season's first game ended; Ralph Friedgen accepting a huge hug and kiss from his wife on the field after a game; Phillip Fulmer sharing lunch with one of his daughters in a school cafeteria; Barry Alvarez sharing a private moment with his best friends.

The journey is over and I've had time to reflect on an amazing five months. It was quite a bit of traveling, and I now consider airports and Marriotts my friends. It was many lonely nights on the road eating meals at TGI Friday's or at a student cafeteria. I witnessed some of the games' great rivalries and had the honor of joining Florida State when they won the ACC title, and LSU when they won the BCS national title.

In games the day *before* I arrived at my nine schools, the teams went a combined 8-1. In regular season games when I was with them, they went 7-2. Overall, they went 8-3. I take no credit for the wins and no blame for the losses.

This book is simply one man's experience during one college football season. Perhaps on other weeks, at other points in the season, things would have seemed quite different. But I doubt it. So much of what coaches do on a week-to-week basis does not change, and so many programs have so much in common. What sets each one apart is the passion of the fans, the resources, the schedule, and, yes, the coaches.

A journey is just that, it comes and goes. I just wish every fan could have the privilege of coming and going as I did.

CHAPTER 1

After Sonny

Colorado State University

#23 Colorado State vs. Colorado
Fort Collins, Colorado
August 24-30

In the first preseason AP college football poll, Colorado State (CSU) is ranked and Colorado (CU) is not as they prepare to meet in the season opener on August 30th. The game will be played at Invesco Field in Denver, in front of 76,000-plus passionate fans. In recent years, CSU has made the match-up a true rivalry, winning three of the last four games, after being an afterthought for many seasons. CSU returns all-conference quarterback Bradlee Van Pelt and tight end Joel Dreessen. Colorado is unstable at the quarterback position but returns a veteran team that finished first in the Big XII North Division in 2002. Both coaching staffs know that a loss can be devastating to their team's postseason hopes, not to mention a year's worth of frustration.

• • •

"And on the seventh day, he rested." Apparently, God is no football coach.

It is shortly after noon on Sunday, August 24, when the Colorado State coaching staff assembles in a room on the second floor of the McGraw Building. A wipe board dominates one side of the room. By the middle of the week, it will be filled with columns labeled Run Game, Drop Back Pass, Play Action/Screens—this week's plan of attack. Above the board, in green and gold letters, is a slogan: "Communication—is the key to success." Another board lists the names of committed recruits, and next to this list are posters. One is titled "CSU Rates" and numerically lists if a recruit is 1) a great player,

2) a legitimate player, 3) a suspect or rejected player. There are similar rating charts for Grades and Recruitability.

On this hot Sunday afternoon, the staff sits in the air-conditioned room, huddled around a table full of sodas and coffees.

"Okay, so where do we stand with the scout teams?" asks Sonny Lubick, looking at longtime assistant coach and friend Mick Delaney. Lubick's large presence comes more from the strength of his conviction than his height. His skin is bronzed from many days in the sun and there are a few wrinkles etched into his face. He looks at his staff intently, expecting prompt and detailed responses.

Delaney explains that the scout teams could use a few walk-ons to play wide receiver, running back, and safety. The NCAA limits the number of walk-ons who can practice in preseason, but once classes begin coaches can open the doors. (Of course, most of the students who walk on are quickly disillusioned or lose confidence in their own ability to play at the Division I level.) An axiom in football is, "You are only as good as your scout team." Having a disciplined, well-prepared scout team is essential in getting starters ready for opponents.

Attention soon turns to the first game of the season: rival Colorado. "This is probably the most even we have ever been headed into the game in Colorado State history," Lubick states matter-of-factly, alluding to the level of talent at both schools. This is something he couldn't necessarily say in a press conference. "We should casually get that message across to the players during practice this week."

Lubick reminds his coaches to watch this week for penalties, poor positioning, and turnovers.

After three grueling weeks of preseason practice, it is pretty clear who the starters are, except for the punter, but all agree to give the candidates until Thursday to prove themselves. Athletic trainer Fred Oglesby walks in and hands every coach an injury report. Luckily, there is nothing major.

A final issue is special teams. Co-offensive coordinator John Benton expresses concern that so many key starters are lined up to cover kickoffs on special teams. Special teams and tight ends coach Darrell Funk, a newcomer to the CSU staff from Northern Illinois, counters that only six or seven starters are on the kickoff team. Lubick quickly interjects that the team's top four safeties are on special teams. His philosophy is to always have the best players on special teams— starters or not.

The offensive and defensive coaches split up to begin to formulate a game plan for Colorado. This week is a bit unusual. First, it is

CSU's biggest game of the year. Second, it is being played at Invesco Field in Denver, the home of the Denver Broncos—a neutral site. Third, and perhaps most important in terms of preparation, it is the season's first game. There is no game film to review from a win or loss the day before. No bad morale. No losing streaks. Plenty of time to prepare. In fact, the coaches have been reviewing Colorado film from last season and creating a game plan since spring practice. By the time game week rolls around in late August, much of the scouting, film watching, and game planning has already taken place. But this is football and these are football coaches, so it is done over and over again.

"I was so psyched to come in today, actually," says co-offensive co-ordinator Dan Hammerschmidt, "to really get going."

Hammerschmidt is joined in the offensive meeting by Delaney, Funk, and wide receivers coach Matt Lubick, the head coach's son. Benton retreats to his office to work on a strategy for combating CU blitzes. Hammerschmidt asks about Dexter Wynn, a stunningly quick and athletic cornerback who had played a little with the offense in preseason. Because he is slowed by a hip injury, the coaches decide to limit Wynn to eight plays on offense in the upcoming practice.

• • •

John Benton was a graduate assistant (GA) at CSU in the late 1980s and remembers drives to Boulder, an hour away. In those days, the only place in Colorado that could develop the game and practice film used by coaches was in Boulder, so every day at the end of practice he would race to the shop to get the film developed. Air Force and Colorado were using the same shop, so if he showed up after them, the wait could be hours. He would return to Fort Collins, mission completed, where the coaches would be waiting.

But the new millennium means computers, and the reliability, expediency, and accessibility of the new technology have changed the game for coaches. Now the standard system can spit out cut-up clips in a matter of seconds. Without much trouble, a coach can make a tape consisting only of plays from the 40-yard line on third down on the right hash at night on grass when his team is trailing. The computers can get *that* specific. The computers are hooked up to projection screens and the images are controlled by remote.

"Beware," Lubick says, "we can't get too reliant on technology. You still have to go out there and coach the team and relate to them."

But Sundays are all about film. As the offensive staff watches clips of the Colorado defense from the 2002 season, including the loss to

CSU, they search for tendencies and weaknesses. Perhaps there's a short cornerback who could be a good match-up for a CSU receiver; maybe a defensive end is small compared to his line mates so CSU could run to his side; perhaps Colorado likes to play tight man-to-man on second down. Colorado State puts in a new offensive package for the game, learning a lesson from last season when TCU and New Mexico had success playing a combination of man-to-man and zone defenses against Colorado State. They want to get standout tight end Joel Dreessen the ball and get running back Marcus Houston outside.

"This is the first game, so we try to keep things simple," Hammerschmidt acknowledges.

Benton adds, "We have had a long preparation for this game, so at this point we are just tweaking."

A few feet away in the defensive coaches' meeting room, they, too, are watching film. They're reviewing clips of the Colorado offense at work in 2002 against Oklahoma, UCLA, and, yes, Colorado State. Although the words "Keep It Simple" are posted clearly above a wipe board at one end of the room, defensive strategies are anything but. Like their offensive counterparts, the staff looks for tendencies. Lubick is a defensive guy, focusing mainly on the secondary. He spends very little time with the offense, trusting Hammerschmidt and Benton to get it done and he makes no offensive calls during games, though he may occasionally chime in through his headset, "Are we doing okay, guys?" Joining Lubick in the meeting are defensive coordinator Steve Stanard, in his first year at CSU, defensive backs coach James Ward, and defensive line coaches Jesse Williams and Tom Ehlers.

"We need to watch for backs bumping our guys outside," Lubick comments. "We should watch for trick plays like tight end or tackle eligible stuff."

That comment leads to a lengthy discussion about how CSU would counter. Sitting in a strategy meeting is like landing in a foreign country with no comprehension of the language. Terms fly across the room: *China, Boston, Black, Zeke, Zoro, Buzz, Under Pirate 57, Over 8*. The coaches throw out terms as they talk about players watching the angle of the fullback's first steps to determine if the play is a pass or a run or to call out switches so smoothly that, as Lubick points out, "It is as nice and smooth as an orchestra."

Eventually, the staff has a preliminary game plan. One board lists the numerous offensive formations that Colorado runs under columns headed "21," "22," and "10." These numbers represent the offensive personnel groups, with the first number indicating the number of backs and the second representing the number of tight ends. For each of these groups, the CSU coaches come up with a list of defensive plays that they believe will work best against the personnel groups. As the coaches debate, discuss, and decide, Lubick asks if they will have time to put all of the sets in during practice this week, to which the assistants unanimously say yes. Near the conclusion of the meeting, around 5:00 p.m., Lubick stands up and says, "We don't give a hoot what they do, we're as good as them."

The coaches all stay and work longer. The offensive staff takes a dinner break and then resumes work at 6:00 p.m., knowing they will probably be there until 10:00. On Monday morning, the entire staff will regroup at 8:00 a.m. to plan practice for the week and to meet yet again as offense and defense. After months of planning, scouting, watching film, and practicing, CSU is finally in a game week. But have they prepared enough? Have they covered every possible scenario?

Lubick is exhausted, but less tired than he was during the dawn to midnight days of the previous weeks. He retreats to his office to sign a few footballs before taking off for home. His office is not large. The walls are covered with pictures of former players who have gone on to the NFL, recent team photos, plaques from charitable foundations, a picture of Lubick throwing out the first ball at a Colorado Rockies game, a Colorado Congressional Record document acknowledging the 2002 win over Colorado. There are pictures of his daughter and two sons, as well as of his grandsons, Matthew and William. Off to the side of his desk sits a bookshelf with dozens of green notebooks full of past year's practice plans, game plans, and notes. Resting on the upper shelves are books, including *Jackie's Nine* by Sharon Robinson, *Parseghian and Notre Dame* by the legendary coach, *They Call Me Coach* by John Wooden, Tom Osbourne's *Faith in the Game*, Jim Dent's *The Junction Boys*, and *Seabiscuit* by Laura Hillenbrand. On his desk is Rick Warren's *New York Times* best-seller *The Purpose-Driven Life*.

The office reveals little about the modest man, and even less about his humble beginnings. His rise to the top of his profession is as unlikely as his escape from a small town.

• • •

Born and raised in the small enclave of Butte, Montana, Lubick was the son of a miner in a town full of them. Remarkably, Butte has produced some of the great coaches in the game, guys like Jim Sweeney and Sam Jankovich. Louis "Sonny" Lubick, named after Joe Louis and Lou Gehrig, played high school football at Christian Brothers High and played his college ball at Western Montana, where he earned a degree in History in 1960. After high school, Lubick initially worked in the mines but after an injury, he headed off to college. Butte was a blue-collar town, and for Lubick, getting a college degree was an accomplishment. He didn't want a life working underground.

He was first a high school coach, then was hired in 1970 as an assistant at Montana State while earning a Master's in Administration. He rapidly rose through the assistant ranks and in 1978 was named the head coach. His first team went 8-2 but things went downhill and, by 1981, the program had slipped to 3-7. Lubick and his staff were fired. He resurfaced a year later at Colorado State as the offensive coordinator under head coach Leon Fuller. In 1985, he joined Jack Elway at Stanford for three seasons, before heading south to Miami and joining Dennis Erickson as defensive coordinator. It was with the Hurricanes that Lubick gained a national following, helping lead Miami to two national championships while playing in four title games. When Colorado State had an opening after Earl Bruce was fired in 1992, Lubick returned to Fort Collins as the head coach. And things have never been the same.

"This is a good sports town with knowledgeable fans," says Lucky Kerig, a 30-something bar owner in town. "On game days, our place is empty. For away games, it is full." Kerig continues, "Things changed in this town when Sonny came to CSU. He built things the right way with morality, family, and community. That's why everyone wants to play for him. There wasn't much before Sonny."

Before Sonny. Before Sonny, the football program at CSU rarely won games and tried hard to pack the stadium on game days. Morale was low, losses mounted, and CSU was nowhere near the national radar. The football offices were in cramped quarters in a building next to the basketball arena, with such little space that team meetings had to be held in the bleachers of the basketball arena, sometimes during basketball practice. When the team split into position meetings, some groups were in hallways, some in the locker room, some even outside. Thoughts of a new athletic facility were never taken seriously—and considering the dismal past, the lack of enthusiasm for the football team was not surprising.

But after Lubick arrived, the Rams began winning, and with winning came a window to take the program to the next level. A new athletic center with offices, a weight room, and locker room would cost $12 million. Lubick helped raise an unprecedented $6 million in 18 months, and after the CSU students overwhelmingly passed an "athletic tax" to raise the remaining amount, the center was completed in 1998.

"It never would have happened before Sonny," notes longtime CSU sports information director (SID) and alum, Gary Ozzello. The result is the state-of-the-art McGraw Athletic Facility, complete with offices for all sports and the athletic administration, the ticket office, and more. It is connected to Moby Arena, where the weight room was tripled in size and the locker rooms revamped.

In 2002, the University raised over $30 million for its general fund-raising campaign—almost three times the amount they raised *Before Sonny*. The Rams have won six Mountain West titles and gone to seven bowl games. In the 100 years *Before Sonny*, CSU went to just two bowl games. In the previous 40 years before Lubick's arrival, they had just 10 winning seasons. Since his arrival in Fort Collins, Colorado State has entered the lexicon of college football, consistently ranked in the polls and appearing on television almost every weekend. He was the National Coach of the Year as named by *Sports Illustrated* in 1994 and the Rams rank twelfth in the nation in total victories since 1994. After just 10 seasons at CSU, Lubick is the winningest coach in school history, including nine straight winning seasons, sixth among current head coaches.

But how much farther can Lubick go with CSU? Playing in the non-BCS Mountain West Conference, the Rams would most likely have to go undefeated to be one of two at-large teams in the four BCS games. Since the inception of the modern-day BCS in 1998, no team from a non-BCS conference has ever played in the Series. This puts enormous pressure on those teams to win—all the time. But Lubick doesn't see it that way.

"I think that is a bunch of hogwash. Everybody can be out of it. A team like Colorado, or any in a major conference, faces a tough schedule and many get eliminated early. We have just as good a chance as they do," Lubick says.

There is at least one major difference between the BCS conference programs and all others: resources. Colorado State spends approximately $4.7 million on football annually, compared to a budget of $9–12 million for major programs that bring in $20 million in revenue and compared to just $3.4 million at CSU. As a result, the smaller schools cannot pay their coaches as much. Lubick's package with incentives is over $500,000 and the average assistant coach's salary at Colorado State is $77,000, both well below those at BCS conference schools. You have to wonder if that is a factor when options arise. Lubick's name continued to pop up for jobs as recently as 2000, when he was rumored to be in line for the job at Southern California.

But for now he's content in Fort Collins and the only thing on his mind is Monday's practice. How is his team going to respond after a weekend away from football?

• • •

At precisely 8:00 a.m. on Monday morning, August 25, 15 staff members, including GAs, interns, and an academic counselor, gather in the staff room for their daily meeting. The group designs practice for the day, organized into 22 five-minute periods, or about two hours worth of football. Lubick asks for suggestions for practice from the group, and tries to reach a consensus on the practice schedule. They decide to finish off Monday's practice with the first-team offense going against the first-team defense. There will be two "live game" punting situations in the afternoon session, testing the readiness of the special teams. The game is just five days away.

Defensive coordinator Steve Stanard stayed late on Sunday night. To the wipe board, he added a plethora of information including statistics about Colorado's tendencies, breaking them down into passing and running plays and numbers and percentages. For example, when Colorado lines up in the "22" personnel group with two backs and two tight ends, the Buffaloes ran the ball 82 percent of the time, telling an opposing coach a lot about how to counter.

Hammerschmidt and Benton work furiously on charts Monday afternoon, diagramming defensive formations they expect to see in the Saturday game. There are 70 offensive plays listed on the board under the Run and Pass categories. (*Thunder*) *Sink Rip/Liz Base 95 Strike. Thunder* indicates the personnel group (i.e., "21" for that play). *Sink* refers to the formation. *Rip/Liz* tells the tight end and receivers the strong side. *Base* is the protection for that play while *95 Strike* refers to the pass patterns run by the receivers. The coaches work on scout cards, diagramming the defensive plays that they want the scout defenses to run against their offense in practice. This process can take hours. The offensive scouting report lies on the table and it is almost 30 pages. It includes last year's game goals and this season's; a CU depth chart and overview; Colorado player bios taken from the media guide; diagrams of CU fronts, blitzes, and coverages. How much of this information the players absorb is questionable.

Just before noon, Lubick leaves his staff for the half mile ride to C.B. & Potts restaurant, where he holds his weekly press conference. There are beat writers, television crews, and radio guys on hand for quotes—and pizza. The walls of the place are full of CSU memorabilia: a Wheaties box with Ram alum Amy Van Dyken on the cover, CSU jerseys, pictures, the old stadium's original scoreboard from 1949. Co-owner Kevin Sheesley, who played for the Rams in the late 1970s, laments that fan support is not as strong as it should be. "Fans are still slow to come around. We are adding 4,000 seats to the stadium. We should be adding 40,000."

After a brief opening statement, the man at the mike holds court. "Ticket sales have been good for the game, so we get some money back for our video equipment . . . Preseason seemed more grueling this year, maybe because of the new rules with two-a-days . . . We still have a lot of questions to address in the next four days . . . Dexter [Wynn] will be healthy and will practice on both sides of the ball . . . Probably no true freshmen will play this week . . . What does CU have in store? I can't control it. Maybe we will send someone up there this week to look through the fence to see what they are doing."

The last statement is a reference to Colorado coach Gary Barnett's comments a few weeks earlier about someone watching their closed practice through a fence and posting details on the Internet.

Lubick answers questions for ten minutes before the hungry crowd heads to a buffet bar of pizza and salad. Sitting in the back of the upstairs room is Lubick's wife, Carol Jo, who greets reporters and CSU athletic personnel with hugs and warm smiles.

After grabbing a plate of food, Lubick heads over to a table and breaks bread with five writers. He casually answers more questions, talks about the rivalry and generally seems to enjoy lunch. It is what SID Gary Ozzello calls "the weekly 'after-news-conference news conference.' "

Tony Phifer, who has been covering CSU for close to twenty years, says, "It is much different dealing with him [Lubick] than any coach. He has learned to treat the media well in this state. He understands it." *The Coloradoan* reporter points out that Lubick has no inhibitions about letting the media know about any trouble, whether there is an injury, a player disciplined, or eligibility issues.

By being so upfront, Phifer says, it often "buys him the benefit of the doubt."

"When I started twenty-five years ago," Lubick says, "there was only one guy that would come out to practice. Now look at the numbers. Of course, talk radio and such are looking for controversies. I still read the papers but I understand that half the articles will be positive and half negative."

• • •

At 2:20 p.m., special teams coach Darrell Funk tells the players in the first-floor auditorium all about punt returns. He shows them clips from last year's CU game. Raising his ire is the fact that Colorado kick returner Jeremy Bloom hit the Rams up for huge returns in last year's CSU win, including a 75-yard punt return for a touchdown.

"He is just a guy. Go down and knock the —— out of him," Funk commands. "We are not going to make him bigger than life."

Hanging above Funk's head is a sign that reads, "Teamwork: The ability to forsake individual recognition in lieu of a common goal. Teamwork not only defines the individual but it also defines the organization." Funk clearly embraces the philosophy and expects his players to do the same.

Twenty minutes later, all of the players are in their respective position meeting rooms for 40 minutes. In these smaller groups, the position coaches show more film and begin to reveal the game plan for Saturday. Hammerschmidt sits down with his quarterbacks, including Bradlee Van Pelt, the reigning conference player of the year. Van Pelt is intelligent, brash, and obviously comfortable with himself. If you have ever seen the football movie "The Program," think Joe Cain. Van Pelt has long, blond hair, good looks, and a strong build. He asks questions of Hammerschmidt about the defenses and rapidly identifies blitzes while watching CU game film. Because Van Pelt is a scrambler, Hammerschmidt decides to show him, backup Justin Holland, and redshirt freshman Joey Kearney, film of the 2002 Colorado-Missouri game. Missouri QB Brad Smith also is a scrambler.

"One thing about Bradlee," says Hammerschmidt, "regardless of some of his antics and comments, he knows his stuff and is not afraid to ask questions."

A quick conversation with Van Pelt shows that Hammerschmidt knows his quarterback well. He is honest, wacky, and at times seems to be putting on a show. A sampling of Van Pelt, or "BVP" as he's named himself, reveals a young man unafraid to go beyond the standard sound bites most of his peers seem content to dish out.

ON NERVES: "It is tough the night before, the anticipation. Do you know the reads? You can't have a bad game. . . . Mondays there are butterflies when you know it's game week, but there are less butterflies as you get older."

ON COACHES: "You have to put all of your trust in your coaching staff. You want to trust them and hope they call a good game. Players are like chess pieces and you hope coaches put you in a position to win."

ON TEAMMATES: "When you are dealing with players' dreams, there is a passion. There is a lot of jealousy within our team."

ON FAME: "At first it's weird when kids stare at you, but you get used to it. There are more negatives with it than positives. There are rumors that you can't control. You can't be nice to everyone but when you are not, you're called on it."

ON ACADEMICS: "I think A's require too much time. Football is my priority."

ON PRESSURE: "During the game, the most pressure is on you. That's what you live for."

Van Pelt first enrolled at Michigan State, hoping to play quarterback, but was moved to defense. He had enough faith in himself to know that he could play quarterback, and he was smart enough to see that it would have to be elsewhere. He came to CSU with raw athletic talent, poor fundamentals as a signal-caller, and a heart the size of the state. He developed into a starter with formidable skills. At the start of the 2003 season, he is listed as a candidate for the Davey O'Brien Award, given to the nation's top quarterback. A few days from the start of the season, he seems prepared to go out and back up the hype. But he's been known to talk a little trash and he can expect a harsh reception from the Buffaloes.

• • •

In a typical game week, Monday is a light day for the players. The staff meets with the team, goes over the game film from the previous game, and the players jog and stretch. But with the opener on Saturday, Sonny Lubick is in no mind-set for an easy practice. They have a lot to cover in five days.

As the players run past Lubick during warm-ups, the coach yells, "You win today, you win this week. This is when you win." On a cool afternoon, the players are focused yet loose. They gather around their coach before breaking into drills. "Be alert, work hard, and let's have no mistakes today in practice," Lubick insists. With that, the horn sounds and players sprint to various parts of the three practice fields. Punters work on kicks, the wide receivers run routes, the quarterbacks take snaps from an automated snapping machine, the linemen hit each other. Defensive line coach Tom Ehlers instructs a group of six on how to block on a double team.

"It is just like that song, 'Get Down On It,' " he says.

The drills continue in smaller groups and the shouts from the coaches are punctuated every five minutes by the horn. Periods are dedicated to special teams, skellys (skeleton drills where linemen are absent), individual position drills, team versus scout, etc. A sample defensive practice plan for the linebackers looks like this:

Period 1	Special Teams	Period 10	Scout Skelly—Bronco
2	Special Teams	11	Scout Skelly—Bronco
3	Pursuit	12	11 Personnel
4	Sprint Pass/Boot	13	11 Personnel
5	Sprint Pass/Boot	14	10 Personnel
6	Sprint Pass/Boot	15	22 Personnel
7	Scout 9 on 7 (21, Slot, Pro, Black)	16	22 Personnel
8	Scout 9 on 7 (21, Slot, Pro, Black)	17	O v D (Red Zone, 3rd)
9	Scout Skelly—Bronco	18	O v D (Red Zone, 3rd)

The practice plans allow for a rhythm and build to full-team periods with the starters on both sides of the ball facing off. A typical practice has 18–24 periods, depending on the day of the week and what needs to be worked on. The longer days come in the beginning of the week.

During Monday's practice, Van Pelt rotates snaps with backup quarterback Justin Holland, working with the first-team offense. After a tight end runs a wrong route, Van Pelt, a team captain, calls for the team to get focused. On another play, a scout team defender rushes Van Pelt, his helmet knocking into Van Pelt's arm. Van Pelt cringes and holds his wrist. Hitting the quarterback is a no-no in practice. The injury is minor and he is ready to go moments later.

As practice continues, there are sounds of cars crashing—literally. The CSU practices are open to the public and media every day, and the practice fields sit alongside Shields Street, a road that is heavily congested, particularly in the afternoons. Cars often stop to gaze at the goings-on in practice, forcing the drivers behind them to slam on their brakes. Staff members say an average of three crashes per day is the norm.

Practice comes to a close at 6:00 p.m. after the team is put through long sprints down the field. Van Pelt leads the pack on almost every dash. As the players finish up and gasp for air, they gather on one knee around Lubick for some final words.

"This was not a great practice today. Our scout teams were not good. You guys need to be much better," Lubick says, removing his baseball hat and scratching the back of his head. He is frustrated especially by the punt return coverage at the end of practice. Alluding to Colorado returner Jeremy Bloom, the player that Funk referred to in the special teams meeting, Lubick says, "Let's get down field and get that guy." But Lubick does make sure to hand out compliments, even to the scout players who he has just scolded. After all, a team is only as good as its scout team.

• • •

The next day at practice, after some extra time on the field and in meetings with the GAs, the scout teams are a bit improved. Practice is dominated by the booming and forceful voice of Steve Stanard, and punctuated by the more low-key approach of John Benton. There is the occasional sound of Lubick's voice, saying something like, "Oh, gosh fellas, can we get it right?" As is typical, Lubick spends a great deal of time with the younger players, working on techniques and positioning.

"CSU is really one of the few schools that really embrace walk-ons and scouts," remarks redshirt sophomore John Spight. "They treat all the walk-ons here well, which makes us want to play hard. A lot of the freshmen are surprised when Coach Lubick works with them."

Most programs pay little attention to those who pay their way through school and who are often used as tackling dummies during the season. But, as we've seen, things are different here. At CSU, walk-ons have done good things. In fact, six of the CSU players who have played under Lubick and gone on to the NFL joined the Rams as walk-ons. Every year, there are freshmen who were told by one or more of the CSU coaches during their senior year in high school that they would have the chance to try out at CSU in the fall. So, each year, Lubick and his staff offer walk-ons an open meeting and a 30-minute tryout.

Toward the end of practice, the first-team offense and first-team defense face off for eight plays. Three plays in, linebacker Courtney Jones comes through the line and hits low on Van Pelt, knocking into his leg and throwing him off balance. Many of the players and coaches pause or let out a groan before realizing that the star is okay. Van Pelt is sharp in practice and is his usual animated self. He is Public Enemy #1 for Colorado, and not only because he torched them in the 2002 game, passing and running his team to victory. His spike of the ball in the face of a Colorado player after scoring the winning touchdown was not taken well, nor was his comment that "Colorado was the worst #7 team ever." The newspapers and Internet chat rooms buzzed of bounties on Van Pelt. What will happen Saturday night?

• • •

In the morning edition of *The Denver Post*, there is a feature article on Van Pelt on the front page. Lubick hesitates to read the story, concerned about what his brash star may have said now. Lubick knows that Brad can be Brad, and in the past, he has reminded his outspoken leader to tone it down. He thought about speaking with him on Tuesday, but has waited until Wednesday. But before he can get a hold of Van Pelt, Lubick is placed on a conference call with the ESPN announcers covering the game on Saturday.

The Wednesday afternoon position meetings move at a rapid pace. For the QBs, it is Hammerschmidt pointing out better positioning for Van Pelt; for the defensive backs, it is the head coach telling the secondary that he doubts that CU's rookie quarterback will drop back to pass, so they should expect short and quick routes; for the wide receivers, it is Matt Lubick emphasizing correct routes; for the running backs, it is Mick Delaney praising Marcus Houston for good positioning on option plays and reminding all runners to have their shoulders square to the line of scrimmage at the time of taking a handoff.

• • •

Marcus Houston is a 6'3", 207-pound running back out of Denver's Thomas Jefferson High School and was regarded as the top high school running back in the nation in 1999, topping the lists of *Parade* and *USA Today*. Houston stunned the masses by deciding to play college ball at Colorado. He was hailed as the savior of Buffalo football. In his first two games in a CU uniform, Houston rushed for 100 yards and 150 yards, respectively. But the promise was derailed when he suffered a hip flexor injury in his third game and took a medical red-shirt in 2000. Replacement Chris Brown did well with the opportunity and made many Buffalo fans forget about Houston. A groin pull hampered Houston's play in 2001, and splitting time with Brown did not help. Neither did reported clashes with running backs coach Eric Bieniemy. Year 2002 was no better with yet another injury which forced Houston to miss eight games.

In early January 2003, Houston asked for, and was granted, his release from Colorado. But where he ended up was even more shocking than where he had started out: Colorado State. On top of that, Houston was granted a waiver by the NCAA and was cleared to play in May of 2003 despite an NCAA requirement that athletes who transfer go through a full academic year. Nobody seems to know why he got the waiver.

Regardless of the reasons for the waiver, Houston looked forward to suiting up in his first game for his new school. Besides being a great athlete, Houston has incredible credentials as a student. He excels in the classroom and in community service, having created a Just Say Know campaign in eleventh grade in Denver and having traveled the globe to Ghana to aid in a redevelopment project.

"It was tough decision in January [to transfer] but I am really glad that I made it. I look forward to this season," Houston says. He refuses to compare the CU and CSU programs and refrains from speaking about his former coaches at Colorado, but is more than willing to praise his new coaches.

"I decided to take my final five official visits as a senior to Florida State University, Colorado, Texas, UCLA, and USC. Before I left, Coach Lubick called to wish me luck. . . . He is just a first-class guy." Irony of ironies, Houston's first game in a Ram uniform will be against Colorado. Many CU fans are wishing him the worst.

• • •

Every Wednesday night, Lubick does his one-hour radio show. He jogs off the field from practice, changes clothes, and heads to a nearby restaurant where a crowd that includes Carol Jo awaits. Many of the assistant coaches join him by 6:30 p.m., some with their wives and children. It is a family atmosphere as the show broadcasts live, with cheerleaders and the CSU Ram mascot wandering through the crowd. Lubick leaves shortly after his show ends, but not before making the rounds, shaking hands, giving kisses like a politician. Typically on Wednesday nights, the staff retreats to the office to make recruiting calls for a few hours. But with the recruiting period not starting until September 1, the staff has a rare night off.

"I have probably tried to find more balance between family and work as I get older, but it probably is more balanced toward football," Lubick says. "I end up spending more time with other people's kids. Often, my mind doesn't allow it. Even when I am with my family, my mind is elsewhere. Heck, my son [Matt] is next door and we don't get to talk."

For Dan Hammerschmidt, a life-altering moment in 1999 put things in perspective. "In November of 1999, my wife was diagnosed with cancer. She went to Houston to get treatment and be with her family. I would miss two days of practices a week and then fly back for Thursday, Friday, and game day. I had to take care of our kids and football stuff. It really changed my thinking." His belief now is that nothing in life is more important than family and you can be successful as a coach without sacrificing your family.

• • •

Discussion in the Thursday morning staff meeting centers on the recruitment of junior college (juco) players and the itinerary for the Friday trip to Denver. Lubick, whose program takes very few juco players, is adamant that the priority must be on high school players who can stay four or five years. "We've learned that quick fixes don't work," he reminds his staff. His son Matt, who is regarded by his colleagues as the ultimate recruiter, counters his father with the fact that they have had success in the past with a few juco players and there are some diamonds in the rough. They decide to take up the issue next week.

The staffs draw up cards for the scout teams and add a few more plays to the game plan. Of course, there is more film. Practice on Thursday is a reflection of the staff's work during the day. There are only 16 periods and the players do not wear full pads. The first 25 minutes of practice are set aside for special teams—and for Darrell Funk screaming directions at rapid-fire pace. From field goals to fake field goals, from kickoffs to kick returns, from point after touchdowns (PATs) to onside kicks. It moves fast, at times resulting in confusion as players run on and off the field. It is the longest time during the week that the entire team practices special teams. There are some holes, and from the look on Lubick's face, the head coach is not convinced that the special teams are where they should be 48 hours from kickoff. Mistakes on special teams can be costly. As Saturday night will prove.

During the 80-minute practice, there are missed routes, dropped passes, too many players on the field, and more problems with the scout teams. Yet another defensive player knocks into Van Pelt, hitting his throwing arm—the fourth such incident this week, causing much consternation for the coaching staff.

Unique to Thursdays is the postpractice meeting that Lubick holds with those on the travel team. His purpose is twofold: first, he wants to begin to get the players into a game mind-set; second, he has the players vote for team captains—a weekly ritual Lubick learned from Dennis Erickson at Miami. The method rewards seniors who have worked hard and, as Lubick indicated to his staff that morning, "the players seem to do a great job picking deserving guys." Before voting for team captains, the head coach takes 15 minutes to address his players for the first time about the meaning of the Colorado game. In addition to showing lowlights of the 1998 loss when special teams cost CSU and sensational special teams play from the 1999 win, the coach plays to the emotions of his players.

"I don't have to say much about this game," he begins. "This is the best venue in college football. You came to Colorado State to play in the big games. Everything you ever dreamed about since middle school will be there Saturday. It's all about attitude. All of this from the start of practice has been about the coaches. Now it's your baby, so go out and have fun."

And, as if the team needed even more motivation, Lubick relays an interview he had heard on the morning radio talk shows from former Colorado coach Bill McCartney. " 'No way that CSU can play with Colorado,' that guy said. He said we can't compete."

In a final summation, like a trial lawyer in court, Lubick reviews his most important points: 1) eliminate foolish penalties, 2) eliminate turnovers, 3) eliminate missed assignments, 4) stop the long run and pass, 5) be good in the red zone, and 6) do well on special teams.

Then, as he likes to do, Lubick finishes on a high note, telling his boys, "I couldn't ask for a better group of guys to take down there."

• • •

Sonny Lubick stands before 40 Colorado State boosters, dressed in slacks, a collared shirt, and a brown sport coat. It is Friday, and the Colorado State Touchdown Club has convened for lunch at a local restaurant to hear from the coach. The Club is made up of the hard-core CSU boosters, those who give enough money for great seats, cool CSU merchandise, and, of course, access to the coaches. Three or four times a year, usually on the day before a big game like Colorado, Air Force, or Wyoming, the group gathers to listen to Lubick.

"Geez, well, I am excited to be here and excited for CU tomorrow," he begins. "I thank you for your support and enthusiasm for CSU football. I know many of you have been here way before I came to town."

He goes into another rendition of what he had told his players the night before, about expectations, desire, and playing for CSU. He admits that sometimes his players speak too much. The donors nod: they, too, feel that the players spout off too much. Lubick is funny, self-deprecating, and the audience eats it up. He takes a few questions about the possibility of rain, the health of his players, and if the addition of three new coaches to his staff has changed anything. The coach is out the door before dessert is served.

By 1:30 on Friday, the coaches are in the office, most of them dressed in ties and sport coats for travel. The team assembles in the McGraw Auditorium, yet again, for some words from Lubick. The players are dressed up, most wearing a pair of khakis with a collared shirt, some in much more fashionable outfits. One sports crocodile skin shoes. "I got a call from Tokyo this morning," Lubick begins, letting his players know that former CSU players have been calling from around the world to wish the team their best. He warns the team "not to set yourselves up for the kill" and reminds them that they are playing for everybody at CSU. He then pauses, put his hand on his hip, and, without looking at anyone in particular, says: "One more thing. If anyone in this room is thinking or talking about the BCS, you need to be hit over the head. None of this stuff about the BCS and an undefeated season. Undefeated? How about just winning one? We can worry about that in the end of November."

The team walks to the practice fields for a ten-minute walkthrough. At a typical away game, the team would walk through in the opposing stadium, but due to a Denver Broncos game at Invesco Field on Friday night, the team is relegated to their own practice field. They file on to the team buses—one for the offense, one for the defense—and head to Outback Steakhouse for a meal before leaving for Denver. Lubick and Carol Jo drive down in their own car, arriving at the Downtown Marriott just before six. The players arrive shortly thereafter and the staff of the Marriott has their room keys in envelopes waiting for them. The room assignments were faxed in Thursday by Delaney, and Van Pelt and his backup, Justin Holland, room together, as do other teammates in similar positions. After settling in, some of the coaches go to the second floor workout room, some meet with parents or family members, and others retreat to their rooms for rest. Lubick meets with the ESPN crew in the lobby.

At 8:00 p.m., there is a special teams meeting in the Denver Ballroom. Darrell Funk goes through formations on punts, kickoffs, and field goals and Lubick points out to the team that Colorado will be fielding rookie kickers and punters so "we need to get after them." As he shows a film clip of CU's field goal defense—including "leapers" or guys who time a jump to block the kick—Funk instructs his players to do whatever they can to stop them, within the rules.

After the meeting breaks, the defense watches practice tape with the staff while the offense watches a highlight tape from last year's game in the banquet room next door. Hammerschmidt hands out an article from *The Daily Camera*, which relays comments made by Buffalo coach Gary Barnett to a booster group on Thursday. Included in his remarks is a comment that Colorado had "chosen to show its class," while CSU "has shown its ass." Barnett has also said, "We've got better players than CSU does right now, I can tell you that." This is what coaches call poster board material. After watching the highlight tape, the offense moves to a larger ballroom, where they walk through 20 offensive plays. A green line in the rug serves as the line of scrimmage as players, some wearing socks, others in sandals, walk through the plays. Substitutions are made and plays are signaled in from the side.

There is a late snack—turkey and cheese sandwiches, fruit, cookies, Hershey bars—and the players gobble up the food and return to their rooms in time for the 10:15 bed check. Many of the coaches stay around and talk about the game plan and the attitude of the players before heading up to do bed checks. They would need all the rest they can get.

• • •

Things are just a little different on game day. Jokes are not as funny, conversations are not as loud. Everything that Colorado State had been working for since the end of last season will culminate in a matter of hours. Players don't need the scheduled wake-up calls from the coaches, and some even beat them down to breakfast. The coaches grab a plate of eggs and fruit, pick up a copy of the *Rocky Mountain News*, and sit and read the sports page. Occasionally, a coach peeks his head up from behind a paper to see which players have arrived. Mick Delaney got out of bed around 4:30 a.m., as he does on most mornings, and took a stroll through the lobby—just to make sure everyone else was sleeping. He sips a cup of coffee and walks out the hotel three blocks to an AMC movie theater in downtown Denver. He has arranged for the team to watch *Seabiscuit* on Saturday morning, and is doing a walk-through.

Many college programs include a movie in the weekend routine to alleviate tension, fill gaps in a schedule, or create a team bond. With most Saturday games scheduled for the afternoon, movies are reserved for Friday nights. But when CSU plays a Saturday night game, as they do this week, a Saturday morning showing is Lubick's choice. *Seabiscuit*, the current hit movie based on the best-selling book by Laura Hillenbrand, is the film.

Seabiscuit is the story of an underdog who, despite many setbacks to him and to those around him, triumphs in the end. It is part *Rocky*, part *Hoosiers*, part *Bull Durham*. As the players and coaches settle in, Lubick sits in the back row with a notebook and pen in hand. As critical scenes from the movie play out, the coach jots down a few words. The movie garners the attention of most of the players for the full 140 minutes, but as the end nears, it is clear this audience has something else on their minds.

After meetings, a walk-through in the banquet rooms, and a break, there is even less noise at lunch than there was at breakfast, as the team chows down on bread, chicken, steak, green beans, potatoes, and pasta. CSU athletic director Mark Driscoll pops in to say hello to the coaches and speaks with Lubick, who is dressed in a gray suit and a black shirt. Carol Jo is upstairs in the lobby of the Marriott, dressed in green and yellow, wearing a lucky necklace. Nearby, assistant coach James Ward sits next to his wife, Marissa, as she tries to calm his nerves a bit. Matt Lubick sits alone downstairs in the offensive meeting room, going over the game plan one last time.

After lunch, for those who want to attend, chaplain Johnny Square leads a pregame chapel which is filled to capacity with players, coaches, former players, Driscoll, Lubick, Carol Jo, and even the mayor of Fort Collins, Ray Martinez.

The pastor introduces the theme for the year, "A Purpose Driven Life," and follows that with a prayer and a reading from the Scriptures about John the Baptist, Jesus' cousin, who Square points out knew exactly his purpose in life. "As for you young men, you go to practice with a purpose, you go to school with a purpose. Will you play this game with a purpose?" He makes reference to the heart of *Seabiscuit* and points out that when the horse and its jockey found purpose, they won.

Lubick, too, addresses the team. "There has been a lot of talk this week, but now the talk is over. It is great to see some of our former players here," he says, alluding to former Ram players standing silently in the back, including Pittsburgh Steeler Joey Porter and last year's star, Cecil Sapp. "You know, their coach has made some comments, the same old stuff, that they will unleash hell tonight. So I say, bring it the hell on."

The three-mile ride to the stadium takes 25 minutes due to traffic (despite a police escort), one-way streets, and oh, yes, rain. The Denver area had not seen a downpour for over a month, but the skies have opened up in the late afternoon. The die-hard fans continue to tailgate in the parking lots, clad in their school's colors, and as the buses pull into the tunnel beneath Invesco, there is no letup of the rain.

The visiting team locker room is the size of half a football field. Each locker is three feet wide and filled with a player's jersey, pads, and personal items, his name taped to the top of the locker, his helmet resting above. The coaches change out of their dress wear and put on matching collared shirts and khaki pants. The pregame schedule is written on two large boards in the locker room and on a smaller one in the coaches' room. Lubick and his assistants look over the schedule to make changes because of the weather. "There is no reason for our guys to get soaked if they don't have to," the coach says.

At 4:40 p.m., Lubick takes a walk onto the field as his quarterbacks throw the ball around. It is still raining hard and the stadium is barely 10 percent full an hour before kickoff. Lubick has put on a large green CSU weather coat, along with his trademark glasses and a baseball hat. Ten minutes later, the entire team is stretching and warming up. Lubick walks around and shakes hands with many of the players. He approaches Van Pelt and shakes his hand, looks him in the eye, and simply says, "Play hard and keep your composure. You don't need to do anything special."

Returning to the locker room, Lubick announces the captains without fanfare: Eric Pauly, Dexter Wynn, Drew Wood, and Bradlee Van Pelt. He gives them instructions for the coin flip. Some players get retaped, some fix equipment, some just sit silently. Johnny Square takes players aside and they hold hands in prayer.

Lubick has some final words: "Men, this is your time. This is what you worked for. Wear their asses down and don't expect anything to be easy. Remember the movie today, play with your heart and look into his eyes."

The captains are called to the field and shortly behind them, the team follows. On their way out of the locker room, each player taps a sign that was taken from Fort Collins and posted with duct tape on the locker-room wall: "Attitude is a little thing that makes all the difference."

• • •

By game time, the rain has eased up. The field is wet but in good shape. The stadium is nearly full, and there are plenty more fans waiting in lines to get in. After a spring, summer, and fall of waiting; after an up-and-down week of practice; and after days of trading barbs with the opponent, it all comes down to playing the game. CSU has simple goals heading into the game. On offense, don't lose any turnovers, get tight end Joel Dreessen involved, let Marcus Houston run outside. On defense, don't allow big plays and pressure Colorado's rookie quarterback Joel Klatt. On special teams, don't allow big returns. For everyone, no penalties.

CU wins the toss and elects to kick. The CSU returners, David Anderson and Dexter Wynn, wait back at their 10-yard line for the kick, finally settling into position after switching sides on instructions from Darrell Funk. The kick goes to Wynn at the goal line, who fumbles, before CSU recovers at the 24. The offense sputters out of the gate, managing only three plays before being forced to punt. Colorado's return man, Jeremy Bloom, who had torched the Rams the year before, has a return of just eight yards.

On the first defensive series, the Rams are charged with a personal foul for hitting Klatt out of bounds. For the least penalized team in Division I in 2002–2003, this is an out-of-character start. But they hold the Buffaloes and get the ball back. Defensive coordinator Steve Stanard and defensive line coach Jesse Williams have some tough words for the defense on the bench.

Four minutes into the game, Van Pelt leads the Rams down the field. He completes passes to Dreessen, and running back Rahsaan Sanders and Van Pelt run the ball. Anderson explodes with a 46-yard catch and run and then Van Pelt scores on a 10-yard keeper. The CSU bench goes wild. As Jeff Babcock completes the PAT, the offensive line sits on the bench and John Benton praises them for their work.

Lubick comes over, removes his headset. "That is the way to be strong. You need to stay strong."

The teams trade drives without scoring, and Colorado State incurs two more false start penalties when it has the ball. The defense is doing a good job of shutting down the CU running game and Klatt is doing nothing spectacular. Colorado punts the ball to the Rams' Eric Hill on his own 34-yard line. Hill fumbles. The ball bounces and rolls back to his 10, where the Buffaloes' Vance Washington recovers. Lubick's fear is being realized: poor special teams play has led to a turnover. But Klatt returns the favor just plays later, fumbling the ball on Colorado State's seven-yard line. As time winds down in the first quarter, Colorado starts with great field position at CSU's 41-yard line. Klatt makes big plays on the ensuing drive, including a 21-yard completion to D.J. Hackett, setting up Bobby Purify's six-yard touchdown run in the second quarter. The Rams' bench is suddenly quiet. Considering the CSU penalties and special teams turnover, it is amazing the score is tied.

Though Van Pelt connects on an athletic 32-yard touchdown pass to Chris Pittman three minutes into the second quarter, the period belongs to Colorado and Klatt. The Buffaloes score three straight touchdowns to take a 28-14 lead, all of them on passes by Klatt—for 82, 10, and 45 yards. So much for CSU not giving up big plays and putting pressure on the rookie. After the first of the three TDs, Van Pelt is off the CSU bench walking up and down the sidelines, slapping guys on the pads, telling them, "This is a battle, a friggin' battle."

In between the scoring drives, Lubick talks to his secondary, imploring the safeties and corners to maintain proper field positions. Stanard is not as kind, dropping a few choice words on the entire defense and focusing his ire on the defensive line in particular, asking "How can that quarterback have five seconds to make a long pass?"

Adding to the collapse, Babcock misses two field goal attempts from 32 and 47 yards, the last coming as time expires in the first half. The Rams head to the locker room down 28-14.

* * *

Colorado State's offense and defense split during halftime to get instructions from their respective coaches. The design of the visiting team locker room at Invesco is such that the two groups can meet separately, with a wall of lockers in between. Of course, it doesn't contain the voices of angry coaches. The defense settles quietly into chairs facing a wipe board on one side of the room and Lubick comes flying in. In a matter of seconds he is moving from one thought to another, pacing, taking off his cap, rubbing his head.

"I told you it is about heart. We are just going through the motions on trying to block field goals. They haven't done anything on the run. We are making that guy [Klatt] look like an All-American out there. I am going to talk straight with you. How many long plays can we give up? It's easy for me to say all this but you have to go out there and do it."

On the other side of the lockers, the offense waits for its coaches. Hammerschmidt makes his way down from the coaching box and speaks briefly with Benton, Matt Lubick, and Mick Delaney. Van Pelt does his part to fill the void by declaring that, "We have two more quarters—we can do this." Lubick walks over to the offense and praises them for controlling the ball and the offensive line for giving great protection, speaking over the screams of Stanard who is now addressing the defense. Benton speaks in a calm voice to the offensive line, Hammerschmidt pulls the QBs aside, Matt Lubick sits in a circle of chairs with his wide receivers, as does tight ends coach Darrell Funk. Sonny Lubick walks back over to the defense, interrupts Stanard, and continues with random thoughts, but in a much more encouraging manner this time around.

As the team leaves the locker room for the second half and the players again tap the sign for luck, Lubick yells to the front, "When you hit that sign, you better mean it."

• • •

As should be expected, it is only a matter of time before Van Pelt makes a difference. After the CSU defense forces a bad punt, Van Pelt and his offense take over on the Buffalo 39. It takes only two plays before Van Pelt hits Pittman again, this time for a 38-yard touchdown. There is new life on the faces of the Ram players. But as things are picking up for the Rams, the heavens open up again and a drizzle begins. Over the next eight minutes, as the teams trade drives and Rahsaan Sanders fumbles, the drizzle becomes a downpour. The players and coaches are soaked, the ball is wet, the field is a slick platform. Streaks of lightning are seen and the rumble of thunder is heard, but play continues.

Klatt is faced with first and ten on his own 23-yard line. After a one-yard loss by Purify, the rain starts coming down even harder. On the very next play, Klatt connects with Derek McCoy, who gets behind the defense on a 78-yard scoring pass, lightning striking once more outside the stadium as the Buffaloes regain the 14-point lead. After the PAT, the head official, referee Gerald Wright, confers on the field with CSU assistant athletic director Doug Max and his counterpart from CU. They agree that it is too dangerous to continue. Wright and his assistants explain the decision to Lubick and Barnett, who both agree with the decision to suspend the game.

The teams run off the field to their respective locker rooms to a chorus of boos from the crowd. With 3:11 left in the third quarter, the Rams are back in the locker room, still trailing by 14. "We still got this son of a bitch," Lubick says excitedly, despite the deficit. "I don't know what we're doing in the secondary," he tells the defense. To the offense, "All we need is three- to four-yard gains and we will do fine." As the coaches talk with players and Benton speaks on his cellphone with Hammerschmidt, who is still up in the booth, Max huddles with the officials to determine when, if at all, the game will resume. The National Weather Service tells Wright that the storm should clear in eight to nine minutes. Wright goes into both locker rooms and asks the head coaches how much warm-up time they need. Both agree that four or five minutes is plenty.

As play resumes, Van Pelt is still in warrior mode, as he runs and passes the Rams down the field before hitting Anderson on a 33-yard touchdown pass to cut the lead to just seven, nine seconds into the fourth quarter. The momentum seems to shift back to CSU—now, if they could only stop those big plays. Colorado punts twice and Colorado State punts once over the next three possessions, before Van Pelt is picked off by Sammy Joseph on the Colorado 21 with just under five minutes remaining. It does not look good. After giving up a first down, the Ram defense holds firm and forces another Colorado punt. Though he is playing stellar at corner, Dexter Wynn has not been having a great game on special teams, and the Rams need a big play. Wynn takes John Torp's punt and, after a few cutback moves that are especially impressive on a wet field, breaks free for a 40-yard return to the Colorado 38. Three plays later, the game is tied as Van Pelt eludes two tacklers and runs 30 yards for yet another touchdown with just 1:50 left on the clock.

Having come back from two different 14-point deficits, the Rams are excited to be heading to overtime (OT). All that is needed is another strong defensive effort. The rookie quarterback for Colorado does it again. On a seven-play, 75-yard drive, Klatt hits McCoy on a 25-yard pass play and Bloom on a 33-yard play, the latter setting up first and goal for Colorado. After an illegal motion penalty, Bobby Purify runs to the outside and scores the go-ahead touchdown with 40 seconds remaining.

There is still time left for BVP to work his magic. Van Pelt manages to get the Rams to midfield with a shot at the end zone, and Lubick wisely uses his time-outs to stop the clock along the way. Van Pelt drops back to pass on what could be the final play and there is a sense on the Ram sideline that they will score. It feels like destiny. All of the work and preparation since the end of last season will not fail them now. The pass to the end zone floats for what seems like an eternity, but the play ends quickly as the ball touches the ground. Game over.

Lubick is a bit dazed as he heads to midfield to shake hands with Barnett, surrounded by photographers and police. The exchange is nothing more than a hurried handshake and Lubick tries to find his way back to the tunnel as players from both teams shake hands and hug. Johnny Square leads a prayer circle at midfield.

The final statistics reveal a remarkably close game. Colorado State outrushed Colorado 246 to 102, but the victors had 402 passing yards to the Rams' 339. Klatt was 21 for 34 with four passing TDs while Van Pelt finished 18 for 38 with three TD passes and two more on the ground. Altogether, the teams combined for 1,089 yards of total offense. Marcus Houston proved that the hype was deserved, rushing for 104 yards on 15 carries. CU's big rusher Bobby Purify had only 31 yards but scored two touchdowns. The difference? CU's receivers D.J. Hackett and Derek McCoy, who between them caught 14 passes for 295 yards and three touchdowns.

Headed into the game, Lubick presented his team with simple goals: no turnovers, no penalties, no big plays, and great special teams. The message apparently got lost.

In the locker room there are tears and there is silence. The only interruption comes from an irate Van Pelt who throws a few towels and kicks a few chairs. Who can blame him? When everyone has returned to the locker room, the staff and players again take a knee, hold hands, and recite a Hail Mary. Lubick addresses them one last time before he will see them Monday afternoon at practice.

"That was a gutty performance out there the way you kept fighting back. I tell you, those guys are just damn lucky. I am very proud of you guys, and we've got a football team in this room. We made some stupid mistakes and didn't hold it together like we should have, but I tell you what: I like this team headed into the season. This was one game. Yes, it was a big one, but we have the whole schedule ahead of us."

• • •

For Sonny Lubick, any loss is difficult. He takes it personally, takes the blame for the failure of his team. He has been in the game long enough to know that you can't win them all, but that doesn't mean the losses don't hurt. His unique blend of old-school tradition, new millennium X's and O's, and compassion for his players and staff have allowed him to take a small Colorado town and make it much bigger than it looks. Lubick is respected by coaches around the country—not only for what he knows and what he does with it, but for who he is. Who says good guys can't finish first?

The loss to Colorado probably drops any hopes of an at-large BCS berth for the Rams and, obviously, an undefeated season is no more. But there are eleven more games to be played, a conference title and a bowl game to be fought for. So on the morning of Sunday, August 31, after church with their families, the coaches meet again on the second floor of the McGraw Center to do it all again. Another season is under way.

CHAPTER 2

Faith in the Game

The University of Georgia

#8 Georgia vs. #25 South Carolina
Athens, Georgia
September 7-13

This game is the SEC opener for both teams. It is a border war between two of the South's most ardent rivals. It is one of the most recognizable coaches in University of South Carolina's (USC) history, Lou Holtz, against the young wizard, Mark Richt. Georgia enters the game highly ranked despite a sluggish win over Middle Tennessee State (MTSU) the week before. South Carolina is 2-0 after a stunning thrashing of then #15 Virginia. The Dawgs are led by quarterback David Greene but might play without standout Fred Gibson, injured late in the MTSU game. The Gamecocks sport an aggressive defense, but have an untested young quarterback.

• • •

It really is quite impressive. The whole thing. As you ride up one of the two glass elevators in the University of Georgia's Butts-Mehre Heritage Hall building, the headquarters of Georgia athletics, you are struck by the neon. This in a town, in a state, in a region of the country where you would least expect such showiness. There are bright red letters on the cement walls inside the elevator shaft, spelling out a familiar phrase: "How 'bout them Dawgs?" If you take the elevator to the third floor, you are awestruck by the college's Hall of Fame, packed with trophies, memorabilia, flags, video highlights, and all else Georgia. If you get off the elevator on the second floor, the opening is even more dramatic, as you are thrust into the Larry Munson Trophy Room, where the 1982 Heisman Trophy that Herschel Walker won rotates on its platform. Surrounding the Heisman are dozens of bowl trophies and SEC Championship statues, the National Championship trophy from 1980, and engraved lists of Georgia football records, captains, and champions.

The Trophy Room serves as the lobby for the Georgia football offices, which looks more like a corporate suite than an athletic office. The suite is circular, with the coaching offices and film rooms lining the outer walls. As you walk around the hallway, your eyes turn to the pictures and plaques. Many former Georgia players now playing in the NFL are pictured playing with their pro teams; there are enough to cover most of the walls. There is a comprehensive list of every Georgia player who ever played in the NFL. Near the entrance sits a 10-foot-wide glass case displaying footballs with the logos of teams who drafted Bulldogs in the first round.

In short, there is no mistaking two things as you walk the hall: 1) Georgia has a heck of a lot of former players in the NFL, and 2) they are darn proud of it.

One set of doors is unlike the others in the hallway, both in texture and stature. While the assistant coaches' offices hide behind dark wood, the head coach's suite is guarded by a set of shaded glass doors. On one door, in white lettering, are the words "Head Coach." On the other, "Mark Richt." Take a few steps past the reception area and you are in Richt's impressive corner domain. There is an abundance of natural light, with windows dominating two walls of the office that overlooks the practice fields. A beautifully crafted conference table sits on one side of the room with four chairs. The wall to the right is covered by bookshelves that are home to many of Richt's prized possessions: pictures of his wife, Katharyn, as well as of his four children; framed writings from the Holy Bible and Scriptures; a piece of hardware acknowledging him as the 2002 SEC Coach of the Year. His desk is covered in papers and behind him rests a flat screen computer. A large screen television is nearby.

It is at this desk the head coach sits on Sunday afternoon, just 24 hours after his team improved to 2-0 after a win over Middle Tennessee State. He is on the phone for the weekly SEC teleconference, answering questions from various reporters around the South. His first question is about the injury to star receiver Fred Gibson. The potential All-American injured his hamstring late in the game against MTSU on a kick return, at a time when the end result of the game was no longer in doubt. Richt indicates that he does not know the status of Gibson (he might know by Monday) and then takes blame for not pulling Gibson from the kick return unit. He had walked over to the special teams huddle before sending them out, he explains, but never realized that Gibson was one of them. Gibson's status, it seems, will be topic #1 for the week. There are other questions about what he learned from watching the MTSU game film and what he expects from South Carolina. "We need to score touchdowns" is his response in some manner to both questions. Besides cutting down on the penalties (Georgia had 18 against MTSU), Richt believes his offense must find ways to score TDs. This is imperative, he says, because in the last two games against South Carolina, Georgia has scored exactly zero offensive touchdowns.

When the teleconference ends—or, rather, when Georgia SID Claude Felton, listening in on his cell phone in Richt's office, puts an end to it—the tall 43-year-old puts on some running shoes and hurries out the door to meet his family for dinner. He has already been at the office for five hours, watching film from yesterday's game, talking with coaches, and poring over stats from his game and from other SEC games. He returns to the office after dinner at 7:00 p.m. to do his weekly call-in radio show. The show typically runs from 8 to 9 p.m., but due to President Bush's address to the nation, it is moved up. The coaches work feverishly on Sunday night and the men won't return to their homes until near midnight.

• • •

In the shattered land of the former Soviet Union, on soil that has been battered by war, famine, and death, sits the young nation of the Ukraine. A small town one hundred miles inside the border, has an orphanage, home to too many abandoned children. There are thousands of orphans in the country, and not many takers. When visitors come through, the children yell "Mama" or "Papa" to attract attention. They know the routine.

Thousands of miles away in a Sunday school class at Celebration Baptist Church in Tallahassee, Florida, the pastor and his parishioners are talking about God's will to care for others, the ills of society, how we should give back, how to be unselfish. The Bible says to take in the hungry, the poor, and the orphans. The idea resonates with some of the churchgoers—among them, Mark and Katharyn Richt.

In late 1998, Katharyn's sister-in-law made a trek to the Ukraine to adopt an orphan. She took along a video camera to capture the journey. When she returned, the Richts watched the tape and were taken with the love on the faces of the children. They already had two sons, Jon and David. Adoption is never an easy process, and it is made even more difficult when the orphanages are on the other side of the world. There was one boy on the video, Andre, who had personality, and whom Katharyn's sister-in-law believed would fit right in with Jon and David. But in addition to Andre, someone else caught their attention. It was a small child with blond hair and a facial deformity. It was little Anya. The Richts couldn't even decipher her gender, but their hearts and souls were drawn to her.

So in July of 1999, Katharyn traveled to the Ukraine to spend time with Andre and Anya. As it turned out, Andre had been adopted by another family. During her visit, she fell in love with a second child, Ruslan (now called Zack). He was running all over the place, seemingly out of control—Katharyn figured he would fit right in with their other kids.

In late July, just a week before fall practice began, Mark Richt took a week off from his duties as offensive coordinator at Florida State and headed overseas to join his wife. He, too, was enamored with both children. After careful prayer, he and Katharyn decided to adopt them both. Richt flew back to Florida while his wife stayed behind to finalize the complex details and bring the new additions home.

Overnight, the Richt family went from four to six, but that didn't bother them. To the Richts, it was a service to God, a small gesture to help those less fortunate. "You can't just talk about wanting to save the children," Katharyn Richt said to the *Atlanta Journal Constitution* in 2000. "You have to do your part and this was our part." It is all part of a mission to serve God, a journey that began some eighteen years ago.

• • •

Mark Richt's life changed in 1986. He was a GA at Florida State, just trying to make his mark in coaching when Pablo Lopez, an offensive tackle at FSU, was shot and killed in Tallahassee. The team and staff were shaken, especially Richt. He went into head coach Bobby Bowden's office seeking comfort. What he came away with was a new life. Richt began to study the Bible, attend church more often, and live his life in the way he believed God had envisioned. Richt became a devout Christian. Since then, his devotion to God and his job have become one. "My motivation daily is to try and honor Him by working as hard as I possibly can and succeeding in whatever I do," he says.

There is no mistaking that Richt is a man of faith, from the way he carries himself to his influence on the Georgia program to his prioritization of family and his willingness to share his faith. Katharyn dedicated herself to Christ shortly after the birth of their second child. She continues her faith, not just in church, but also through weekly Bible studies with other coaches' wives.

Richt does not leave his faith at the office door. Spirituality is a big part of the Georgia football program. His brother-in-law, Kevin Hynes, serves as the team's chaplain, as an employee of the Fellowship of Christian Athletes (FCA), an international organization promoting Christianity among coaches and players at all levels. FCA leads study groups or "huddles," works with athletes and coaches to develop curriculum, and otherwise provides a spiritual aspect to sports. The book they publish, *God's Game Plan*, is part Bible, part study guide, and can be found in the locker room, players' lounge, and coaches' offices. There are references to God on strength coach Dave Van Halanger's workout room walls. Rule #7, for instance, reads, "Ask God for help." Staff meetings open with Devotion, as they do at many schools. Team chapels are held on game days. Cussing and other vices are frowned upon.

All of the FCA meetings, Devotions, and religious activities are voluntary, and a large number of players and coaches choose to attend. There have been Muslims and other non-Christians on the team and they are treated no differently. "I will not push my beliefs on anyone," Richt insists. "If they come to me, or want to accept Jesus Christ, then I will share with them. But in no way am I trying to force it on anyone." The coach's deep religious commitment came to light after a win over Auburn in 2002, when Georgia clinched the SEC title. Richt started off his postgame news conference with some surprisingly spiritual comments that made news.

Junior defensive end David Pollack admires Richt's devotion. Pollack is as devoted to God as his coach is and attempts to carry himself in the same manner. "It is very encouraging, having your coach be open about faith. That a man of God is running the program. I learn from him."

Richt's faith allows him a unique balance in life and in coaching. The minor things that may infuriate most coaches seem to roll off of Richt. He maintains a steady emotional keel, in practice, during games, and away from football, which allows him to make clear decisions and focus on the task at hand. It's as if he is constantly at peace with himself and those around him, something you don't find often in football.

• • •

A native of Boca Raton, Florida, Richt headed to the University of Miami as a quarterback in 1978, but ended up playing behind future Hall of Famer Jim Kelly. After graduation in 1982, Richt latched on with the Denver Broncos, again saddled behind a Hall of Famer— John Elway. His final stop in the NFL was back home with the Miami Dolphins, where, yep, he sat behind Dan Marino. It was clear that it was time to put his playing days behind him. His first coaching job was as a GA at Florida State, under Bobby Bowden, from 1985 to 1986. He moved into the volunteer assistant slot for one year. Word spread about a talented young coach in Tallahassee and in 1989 he became offensive coordinator at East Carolina. It was not a major program, but it was Division I and it was almost unheard of that such a young and inexperienced coach got a coordinator position.

Richt was at East Carolina for only a year when Bowden called him back to Tallahassee, where Richt became the quarterbacks coach in 1990 and added offensive coordinator duties in 1994. He had five FSU quarterbacks move on to the NFL including Heisman winners Chris Weinke and Charlie Ward. Florida State became a national power in the 1990s and Richt was largely responsible. His reputation grew, and whenever a major head coaching job opened, his name was inevitably mentioned.

When it was announced that Georgia coach Jim Donnan would not be returning after Georgia's Oahu Bowl in late December, Richt set his sights on Georgia. Things began to unfold in December 1999, weeks before Florida State was to play Oklahoma for the national title in the Sugar Bowl. "Georgia was always the school that Katharyn and I envisioned ourselves at," Richt reflects. "We wanted to be in the South and I thought it would be the SEC. Years earlier, the thought was there that FSU could be my job, but prayer and time changed that." He wanted the Georgia job so badly that he picked up the phone and called Georgia athletic director Vince Dooley to lobby. He also called Grant Teaff, the Executive Director of the American Football Coaches Association, and asked him to call his close friend Dooley on his behalf. When Dooley spoke with Bowden about Richt, the FSU coach had confidence in his knowledge and abilities but was concerned that Richt was "too nice."

Richt traveled with Weinke to the Heisman ceremonies in New York and met Dooley, who was in the city attending festivities for the College Football Hall of Fame. The two talked at the Waldorf Astoria on December 11. Dooley and Georgia president Michael Adams talked in the next week with Green Bay wide receivers coach Ray Sherman and Miami Dolphins assistant Chan Gailey. Dooley and Adams flew to Tallahassee on December 19 for a second interview with Richt. Shortly after that meeting, Richt was offered the job. Surprisingly, he did not immediately accept. "I think I just got cold feet," the coach says. "It was something we had wanted and prayed about and now it was here."

Richt asked Dooley if he could think about it and call him the next morning. After prayer and thought, he called Dooley at his home at 2:00 a.m. and accepted the job. Georgia did not want to make an announcement until after the Oahu Bowl, so the secret was kept until the day after Christmas as Richt prepared to coach FSU in the title game against Oklahoma.

"I knew that Georgia football was big," Richt says now. "I guess I didn't know how many demands on my time there are. I knew from watching Coach Bowden that he had a lot to do but I learned quickly." People stop Richt at restaurants, at the gas station, or at church to say hello, wish him luck, or ask for an autograph. "The first time I realized how big Georgia football was," Katharyn Richt points out, "was when we were looking for homes and all of the cars' license plates and stickers were Georgia. There were no other schools."

Mark Schlabach has been covering Georgia football for the past 10 years, first as a student reporter for the *Red & Black* and now for the *Atlanta Journal Constitution*. He knows what Georgia football was before Richt's arrival, and he knows what it's been like since.

"I think he [Richt] put it best when he said we need to take the lid off the program. The program had good athletes and great recruits but they just couldn't do anything once they got to Athens." What impresses Schlabach the most about Richt is his honesty and humility. "He is willing to admit mistakes and say, 'I screwed up.' " When Richt arrived in Athens, he brought back a sense of Georgia tradition, brought back former greats to talk to the team, and put "G"s everywhere. The sense of respect for the program is now so strong that the players, coaches, and staff will not step on the large "G"s on the carpets in Butts-Mehre.

"Coach Richt is just so grounded and humble," says defensive line coach Rodney Garner. "The kids need to feel safe and he creates that environment for a comfortable relationship between coaches and players."

Richt's success at Georgia in his first two years, on and off the field, convinced administrators to offer the coach a new, eight-year contract, which runs through December 2010. The total package is worth between $1.5 and $2 million. His base salary is $200,000 and television and radio bring him $600,000. He has a golf club membership and two cars. He receives $400,000 for equipment endorsements and $3,600 worth of Nike shoes and apparel each year. If Richt completes the length of the contract, he receives an additional $1.6 million. Interestingly, his contract stipulates that Richt is required to make at least twelve appearances at Bulldog Clubs and spend two days helping the president fund-raise.

· · ·

Every day, Georgia players are greeted in the training room by 25-year-old Mark Christiansen. An Athens native, Christiansen is a passionate Bulldog fan, trivia master, and two-year staff member. He suffers from cerebral palsy, which has relegated him to a wheelchair and left him with little ability for physical movement. Two years ago, he wrote letters to head trainer Ron Courson and Vince Dooley asking for a job. He has it. Every day, with the help of an aide or his mother, Christiansen splits his time greeting training room visitors at Butts-Mehre and greeting guests across the street at the basketball arena. He also counts repetitions as players rehabilitate their injuries. He needs to take breaths often and sometimes loses count, but he brings a smile to those he touches and, more importantly, as Courson points out, he reminds players that their injuries pale in comparison to what others go through. It is a far cry from the splendor and pageantry that are college football.

Next door to the training room sits the newly renovated, $2.3 million players' locker room. It is so new that workers were putting the finishing touches on it right before the players reported for camp in August. There is nothing different about what is in the locker room (lockers, equipment room, players' lounge) but what sets the Georgia facilities apart is the lavish quality. The players' lounge features a large-screen television, study tables, and workstations with phones and computers. There is also an adjacent video game room with five 32" televisions attached to Sony Playstation and X Box games. Each is situated in front of a black leather couch. On the wall of the video room are two red LCD timers. Controlled by a switch upstairs in the coaches' suite, the clocks count down from five minutes to alert the players when meetings are about to begin. When the clocks hit 0:00, the power in the room is shut off.

There is a mailbox for each player; most currently hold a copy of *Pumped: Straight Facts for Athletes About Drugs, Supplements and Training.* There is a message board and two computer screens that automatically post messages about meetings, practice dress, and other items for the players. The wooden lockers themselves are positioned in rows, organized by jersey number, with the player's name and number emblazoned above. The rows of lockers empty into a large carpeted area below a huge "G" that hangs from the ceiling. Eight-foot-high displays of past Georgia players who have won major awards or who have had their numbers retired surround the center area. Beyond that, on higher walls, are the names of all of Georgia's All-Americans. Near the exit to the locker room is a posting board, and this week it is covered with dozens of articles on Saturday's opponent, South Carolina.

All of the fancy and elaborate facilities in the world don't mean victories, but they do help you land players who can get you wins. And they do help those players continue on their path toward an undefeated season.

• • •

Most Monday mornings start with an 8:30 a.m. staff meeting in the conference room in the coaches' suite, but Vince Dooley has called a meeting of all head coaches, and Mark Richt attends. The football staff meeting finally gets under way near 10:00 a.m., with 18 staff members filling the room around the large mahogany table. One wall has a video screen, while another holds a master calendar. Two opposite walls display the depth charts for Georgia and its upcoming opponent. Many of the coaches are sitting in their chairs when Richt enters, dressed in a blue collared shirt and a pair of khaki pants.

"Who has this morning's Devotion?" he asks.

Every morning begins with a prayer and a short reading. The staff bow their heads as they ask for good health, continued success, and grace for their families. The injury report comes next, as described by trainer Ron Courson. Courson is a no-nonsense guy who oversees a staff of ten and holds enormous influence over the coaches and players because of his experience. He passes out a list of injuries, then proceeds to go over the list, one player at a time. Of course, he stops for a moment at Fred Gibson. "There is no bleeding, swelling, and he was in this morning for treatment. We will let him run a bit this afternoon and take it day by day." With more than 120 players on the team, and nearly 25 of them having some sort of injury, the injury report consumes ten minutes.

A discussion of penalties follows Courson's report. At every Monday staff meeting, secondary coach Willie Martinez goes over each penalty call from the previous game. Of course, after having committed 18 penalties on Saturday against Middle Tennessee State, there is much to discuss. Identifying the perpetrator, then giving his assessment of whether or not it was a good call, Martinez proceeds through all 18. Richt becomes engaged in the discussion, particularly on the subject of substitution penalties. "Was it my fault that we didn't get that off in time, sir?" he inquires about a delay of game penalty on a punt. (All coaches and players at Georgia refer to each other as "sir"— even Richt). "Did I take too much time to make the decision or did the players not know who was in?" In moments of self-evaluation, which are common for Richt, he takes notes on what he could do better, just as he had done the day before with the media, taking blame for having Gibson in on the play late in the game.

The meeting breaks at 11:15 a.m. with Richt rising to his feet and saying, "Let's go to work, men." South Carolina stampeded #15 Virginia on Saturday, so the Georgia staff faces a formidable foe. Perhaps without their top receiver.

* * *

Every Monday night is family night—the coaching staff's families join the team for a meal on the outside deck of Butts-Mehre overlooking the practice fields. Tonight, there are crabs, chicken, vegetables, and cookies, and the players and coaches sit together under a large tent. Many of the wives and kids have shown up, and Richt enjoys the time with Katharyn and three of his kids (his oldest is at football practice). As the wives and coaches chat, kids run around throwing the football, giving players high fives and eating more than enough cookies. As the team finishes up the meal, they head to position meetings in the first-floor meeting rooms until it is time to dress for practice.

At 7:20 p.m., the players are seated on a small hill alongside one of the four practice fields. Richt begins by announcing the players who made Academic Honor Roll, based on summer class performance, as well as the recipients of Victor Club (given to players for outstanding perfomance by their position coach) and Dawg Bone Awards (given out for exceptional plays including big hits, touch-downs, and interceptions). After each name is announced, the team claps once in unison.

"Men, I really don't know where we stand right now," he says, shaking his head. "We got all pumped for Clemson, played well, and, honestly, probably we were overinflated. Then we played like we did on Saturday." The players get the point. "I watched a television copy of the South Carolina game and I tell you what. One thing that stood out was just how intense and fired up they were from the start. They not only have a good defense, I think they have a great defense. They played like it was a national championship game, and they need to, to win every one—just like we do. We need this game. We can get our-selves in a hole this season by losing early. We need a great week of practice."

With that, the team begins its warm-ups, stretching and jogging, before doing an intense running drill called "fifths," where groups of players sprint around the outside of the field five times, each time after a 30-second break.

Richt has scheduled a light practice with 12 five-minute periods, and the players wear no pads, just helmets. They spend the first six periods on punts, field goals, and kickoffs. Special teams coach Jon Fabris is intense and reacts strongly when a player misses a blocking assignment. Richt stands off to the side observing, joking with some players and talking with Director of Football Operations Steve Greer. He is dressed in sneakers, khaki shorts, and a gray T-shirt that reads "Finish the Drill" on the back.

Periods 7–12 have the first- and second-team offenses working on scripted plays against the scout defense. The coaches want to get the offense familiar with some of the South Carolina blitzes, and they re-peat running and passing plays, rotating in quarterbacks. Offensive coordinator Neil Callaway and quarterbacks coach Mike Bobo run the plays as Richt stands eight feet back, occasionally interjecting a comment. Richt's calmness contrasts with the screams of Fabris and the booming voice of defensive coordinator Brian VanGorder. "You are not listening to what I said," VanGorder shouts to a player, who can't help but listen now.

Practice comes to a close around 9:10 p.m., but the night is not over for the coaches—they retreat to their meeting rooms to watch film on South Carolina and continue to plan. The offensive staff leaves the office by 11:00 p.m., while the defensive coaches are still hovering in the office when today becomes tomorrow.

• • •

Suffice it to say, defensive end David Pollack had a pretty good year in 2002. He had 102 tackles and 14 sacks. He was the SEC Defensive Player of the Year, a first-team All-American, and one of five finalists for the Nagurski Award, given to the nation's top defensive player. But now the secret is out. He is sure to see double-teams and extra attention from offenses.

"It is trying mentally and physically," the junior responds. "I think I am a better football player this year, in terms of knowledge, technique." Much of that growth he attributes to the coaching staff, both to Richt and VanGorder. "The coaching staff puts us in a position to do well every week. They teach great fundamentals. We probably play the hardest for four quarters than anybody in football."

Pollack not only has great respect for Richt as a coach, but also as a man. He respects the fact that Richt doesn't break rules and lives by the disciplined philosophy of "my way or the highway." "He treats us as his own sons," Pollack says. "He doesn't want you to embarrass yourself or your family."

Pollack is far from an embarrassment. It shows every day in practice, in the classroom, and in life. He is a team captain, a history major in good academic standing, a man of faith who speaks to local youth groups, and a raging terror on the field.

He knows that South Carolina will double- or triple-team him. He knows Saturday will be a battle.

• • •

Tuesday is media day, and media day at Georgia is a busy one. Richt arrives at the basketball arena for his press conference, early enough to grab lunch and sit with the 25 reporters in attendance. Eating with the press is not typical for Richt, but today he has time. Following a short opening statement by the coach, the first question is not surprising: "Coach, how did Fred look?" Richt answers candidly, telling the crowd assembled that "Gibson jogged a mile last night" and that "we're being cautious." Other issues that come up include the medical condition of running back Tony Milton and the potential redshirting of running back Kregg Lumpkin. If Milton cannot play, or is limited, Lumpkin will be called upon to fill in as one of three backs.

If Milton is out but can play next week, wasting a redshirt year for Lumpkin will be detrimental, Richt explains. The questions and answers continue for 30 minutes, and then Richt speaks individually with writers and does six television interviews outside.

By the afternoon, the coaches have a good idea what plays they will run against South Carolina, Brian VanGorder included. Based on his assessment of his own personnel, and after watching film of South Carolina, the defensive coordinator and linebacker coach knows that USC uses 11 and 12 personnel much more than 21. VanGorder passes out a 50-page scouting report on South Carolina to the linebackers and goes over a stat sheet with the seven players in his meeting. He points out that the tendency for USC is to run the ball in 12 and that when the Gamecocks face a third and short and the quarterback is in a shotgun, he is almost always going to run with the ball. "Bottom line, we need to be smart," he says.

He reviews game clips with the players, quizzing them as to what defensive call should be made based on the offensive alignment. A few minutes in, the mouse on the computer stops working, and shortly thereafter, the whole system shuts down. VanGorder is not happy, but he quickly moves on. Throwing around terms like Roger, Larry, Blizzard, Sky, Missile, and Rocket, the coach talks the players through various plays they can expect in the game. At 3:20 p.m., the group walks to the practice field to join the entire defense for a walk-through.

Practice today is intended to be the longest and hardest of the week. It is scheduled for 20 periods and the coaches warn the team that there will be a lot of "live" drills, meaning full contact and tackling. Richt walks onto the field sporting a big straw hat and the same attire as yesterday: khaki shorts, gray T-shirt, black Nike shoes. After warm-ups, the team splits into position drills and the fields fill with activity. Richt has the quarterbacks practicing snaps; Callaway has the offensive line doing "pancake drills," where a group of five linemen flatten willing participants as they surge forward; the running backs work on agility; the receivers take passes; the defensive line, with coach Rodney Garner, does grunt work on dummies and on each other; the punters take turns booming kicks from one field to another.

Richt is in a good mood and his players recognize it. He had planned on reading some South Carolina player quotes to the team at the end of practice, but he makes up some quotes supposedly from South Carolina players to get a laugh out of his guys, in particular the injured Fred Gibson, who is stretching nearby. "They said, 'Gibson? Who's he?' " Richt says, barely hiding a smirk.

As practice progresses, Richt walks around overlooking the offense, occasionally stepping in to encourage a player or to ask a coach a question. One field over, VanGorder and his staff are correcting player positioning on defense, quizzing players, giving them reminders. The practice builds from position drills to team-versus-scout drills until finally both first teams come together, working on the same things they just spent two hours doing, primarily goal line and short yardage. The clash is spirited and hardhitting. Even in practice, pride is on the line. (Monday practice focuses on special teams, blitzes, and the run game; Tuesday is first and 10, short yardage, and goal line; Wednesday is third and medium and third and long as well as red zone; Thursday is review.)

"I thought the offense had an outstanding day," Richt says at the end of practice. "I don't know about the defense, but I assume they did, too. And scouts, you played great and hard, which is what we needed." He reads a response from South Carolina cornerback Dunta Robinson to a question about Gibson possibly sitting out that has been reported in *The State*, a South Carolina newspaper. "I hope that he plays because if we end up winning and if he doesn't play, then they'll be saying, 'Well, they didn't have Fred Gibson.' "

Having finished the sandwiches they picked up from a nearby deli, the offensive coaches sit in the main conference room, the table they sit around littered with Diet Cokes and sunflower seeds. They watch film from practice, viewing plays over and over again, cracking jokes, pointing out mistakes, asking each other questions about alignments. Richt is relaxed, leaning back in his chair, eating hundreds of seeds. Ron Courson stops in and pulls up a chair to give Richt an injury update. "You know, with Fred, he ran some but it hurt a bit. I think he is probably doubtful for Saturday. We should hold him out and you should plan on not having him." Richt has been hoping not to hear that news, but there is no sign of panic in his voice or on his face. Courson adds that it looks like running back Tony Milton has a long-term problem with buildup in his leg and will not be playing. Lumpkin is in.

The staff takes a short break after 9:00 p.m., then settles in to watch South Carolina clips on third and medium and long. One of the wipe boards in the conference room is now covered with plays for every situation, with a little space left for additions. Richt points out that the staff is actually ahead of a typical week's planning because they can watch only two of South Carolina's games, since they had only played two. As the season wears on, there will be longer hours of film, and the staff will typically watch the previous four games of an upcoming opponent.

Down the hall in a much smaller meeting room, VanGorder and the defensive coaches watch practice film, jotting down things that players did wrong, noting who was "loafing" on plays, and trying to focus after a long and tiring day. Every "loaf" that is marked down means more conditioning for the defense the following day. It will be another long night.

• • •

In the quarterbacks meeting on Wednesday, quarterbacks coach and former Bulldog signal-caller Mike Bobo takes David Greene, D. J. Shockley, and Joe Tereshinski through potential defenses they will face as Richt listens in. Bobo introduces two new plays that Richt & Co. designed late last night. Both are based on pro receiving routes and attack a perceived weakness in the South Carolina defense—five to seven yards past the line of scrimmage. The play is intended for third downs in the red zone and includes four receivers. They will work on the plays in practice.

At the opening of practice, Richt relays the day's schedule, including a game situation at the end of practice: 40 seconds left, ball on the 50-yard line, third and five, a field goal wins it, and no time-outs. Then Richt reads yet another quote, this one from South Carolina's quarterback Dondrial Pinkins: " 'I don't think they can score 15 points [the current point spread] the way the defense is playing right now. We feel like if we can put up at least 20 points, we have a good chance of beating them.' " (*The State*, 9/9/03)

Injured wide receiver Fred Gibson shows up with no ice or wrapping but with a green jersey on. Players who are injured and aren't ready for contact wear green instead of red or white to indicate that they are off-limits. A few minutes into practice, Gibson takes off the green. "He must have found out we are going to hold him out," Richt says with a smile. "I wonder if Ron [Courson] knows he is out here." Gibson does sit out practice, but stands with his teammates during drills, listening, pining for the chance to play.

• • •

Hundreds of yards away, on the deck outside of Richt's office, Katharyn Richt and three of her children watch practice and work on homework. Family has always been a big part of Richt's life, and now they are a big part of Georgia football. "I would like to be more of a team mom," the tall, striking brunette says, "but it is hard juggling my kids' schedules. It was a lot easier when I just had one when we were at FSU." Katharyn was, for example, quite close with former Seminole All-American Charlie Ward and the two shared many conversations and memories. But Richt was an assistant then. Things are a bit different now that he is the head coach.

Being the wife of a football coach is not easy. "I think I was a bit naïve when we first got married, about just how much time he would be gone. It really hit me when Mark was recruiting. That is from December to February. He would be gone the whole week, come home Friday nights for a few hours, and then head over to the university to work all weekend."

For the children, there are positives and negatives to being the coach's kid. On the plus side, you get great seats, get to travel to interesting places, and get to meet cool people. Of course, your father is not home much and you may have to move often.

"Mark is very good about, when he walks in the door, whether I or one of the kids are up, he spends time with us," Katharyn says. Whether it is science experiments with his son or video dance lessons with his wife, he makes the time. Often, the Richt children will be around during practices or team events. "Mark and I never realized this but former players have come back and told us how they want to have a marriage and family like us," Katharyn says. "I think it is good that we can be together in front of the players as well." The coach's appreciation for family goes beyond his children and wife, as his father lived in a converted apartment above the family's garage while his sister and brother-in-law, the team's chaplain, lived for a long time in Richt's home.

• • •

Wednesday night is spent watching more film—but this time it's the future, not the past, that the coaches have their eyes on. Georgia, like many staffs, sets aside Wednesday nights for recruiting purposes. The entire staff assembles in the conference room and watches tape on nearly twenty high school prospects. After conducting their evaluations, the coaches retreat to their offices and make calls to recruits. Often, more than one coach speaks to the same high schooler. The lifeblood of any major football program is recruiting. The best coaches, facilities, and fans don't win you games—players do.

At Georgia, Rodney Garner, the defensive line coach, coordinates recruiting. It is a year-round effort to snare the top players in the country. Signing Day is in early February, and as soon as one class has been solidified—usually consisting of 20 to 30 players—the coaches immediately look ahead to high school juniors. By the time coaches are allowed on the road to evaluate prospects in May, the staff has created a list of 600 to 1,000 potential juniors to consider. They take recommendations from high school coaches they trust and from recruiting services. After the May travels, which at Georgia means a visit to every high school in the state, as many as six or seven visits a day, the staff whittles the list down to a "manageable" 300. It takes time but it's clearly worth it: 81 percent of Georgia's current players are from the Peach state. Players can make unofficial visits (visits they pay for themselves) during the fall on home game weekends; the Dawgs may host anywhere from 40 to 60 recruits, as well as parents and coaches, on unofficial visits.

The official visit in December is another story. Schools are allowed a maximum of 56 official visits a year, but some years they offer less. Last season at Georgia, only 38 players took an official visit; of those, 24 committed. The Bulldogs try to have no more than 15 recruits on an official visit on the same weekend, preferring more intimate gatherings.

On a typical official visit to Georgia, the recruit and his parents arrive in Athens around 5:00 p.m. on Friday and are welcomed at the Georgia Center Hotel by the Georgia Guys & Gals, the student support group for recruiting. There is a hospitality suite set up and the players' rooms are decorated with Bulldog paraphernalia. Friday night, dinner for the players, parents, and coaches is at the Athens Country Club followed by dessert at Richt's home, just minutes outside of Athens. The recruits and their hosts will then head out to a party while the parents return to the Georgia Center. Saturday morning, the wake-up call comes early. The guests are taken on a tour of the campus and the new academic center, where they meet with a professor in their area of interest. They will have lunch with a professor and then head to Butts-Mehre to watch a highlight tape, tour the weight room, locker room, and meeting rooms. At 6:30, they are taken to mammoth, 92,000-seat Sanford Stadium. They are given Georgia jerseys with their names and numbers on them and are introduced on the PA system, then given free reign to run around on the field. They walk up to the Sky Suites in the stadium for dinner. By

Sunday morning, the recruits and their parents are exhausted, but will meet with their position coaches and Richt before heading home.

Recruiting is a high-stakes competition and is one reason why Georgia is favored to win the SEC this year. Of course, Lou Holtz and South Carolina have some pretty good players, too, and they've proven it in the first two games of the season.

• • •

After devoting Wednesday night to the future, it is back to the present on Thursday. Richt is in the offensive line meeting room at 2:00 p.m. but seated in front of him are all of his seniors on the team, not just the O-linemen. They aren't watching film or talking about football. They are discussing the characteristics of leaders, having read a chapter from John Maxwell's *The 21 Indisputable Traits of a Leader.* The coach is teaching his weekly class on leadership, while Brian Van-Gorder is talking with the underclassmen about teamwork. It is all part of a development program at Georgia that Richt installed last year. Led by former NFL, college, and high school coach Bob Lankford, the character and leadership curriculum is intended to last throughout a player's years at the University.

Lankford is the CEO of Coach's Corner, an organization seeking to develop athletes mentally, physically, and spiritually. Lankford and strength coach Dave Van Halanger talk to the freshmen for 15 minutes after 6:00 a.m. lifting sessions on Monday and Wednesday mornings. The topics range from date rape to cheating on tests to treating teammates with respect. The curriculum was designed by Dr. Sharon Stoll, the director of the Center for Ethical Theory and Honor in Competition and Sport, based at the University of Idaho. The first year of the program is focused on "Winning in Life"; the second, "Fellowship, Followership and Leadership"; the third year, "Decision Making and Principled Thinking"; and the fourth year, "Men of Character in Application."

So there Richt is, sitting in a chair facing his seniors, talking about the topic for the week: generosity. After a review of the assigned story, Richt begins a dialogue of what it means to be generous, how we value giving, and why it is important. His players are not shy about sharing their personal feelings and stories. One speaks of giving his time to the rec center in his old neighborhood because most of the young kids don't have any role models. Another talks about how he often does not put others first, especially in the competitive sport of football, where it is survival of the fittest. The coach is candid, as well, contributing insights from his marriage and his life as a young student-athlete.

Character is critical to everything that Richt is trying to accomplish at Georgia. That is why when his men misstep—and they do at times—it eats at him. When nine of his players were caught selling their SEC Championship rings in the spring, the coach was more hurt and saddened than angry. He acknowledges that with over 100 young men, there will be incidents. But that's exactly why they need character-building activities.

There is more self-reflection by the players on Thursday, in the wide receivers meeting with coach John Eason. Eason reviews a weekly test, 37 questions about formations, pass routes, the game plan. And then a few other questions, like, "When did you last tell your mother that you love her?" and, "Who would you give your game ball to?" Between jokes and cutups and some serious talk about pass routes, the players share their stories of growing up, how much their mother or grandmother means to them, and who they cherish the most. The room falls silent when Fred Gibson talks about giving the game ball to his grandmother, who raised him because he never met his father and his mother gave birth to him when she was just 13.

• • •

"This is where the SEC Championship begins," says Richt in his prepractice talk. "It's going to be tough to lose this game and still win the Championship."

The players are not in pads as this will be a short practice: just 15 periods, no contact. David Greene looks sharp and is in a good mood. Gibson is on the field, running pass patterns at full speed, and starting with the first team. He believes he can play and is trying to convince the coaches. It is a far cry from the prognosis on Monday.

After the easy workout, Richt leaves his players with this thought: "You know men, we really have not been tested since Michael Johnson's catch against Auburn [in November 2002 to win the SEC]. It might be a battle on Saturday, we might be behind and have to come back. That's when we'll know what we are."

• • •

In a town that has a bar called "Gator Hater" and more Georgia "G" emblems than one can fathom, football is king. And those entrusted with the 100-year tradition are the most celebrated—and sometimes vilified—public figures in the state. How big is Georgia football? The school just spent $25 million to add 6,000 seats and 20 luxury boxes to Sanford Stadium, bringing the capacity to 92,000. The football program brought in over $35 million in revenue in 2002, with ticket sales alone bringing in close to $12.8 million. By contrast, the entire athletic department budget was $45 million. Included in the football budget are $25,000 for laundry, $485,000 for recruiting, and $15,000 for the preseason coaches' retreat. Playing in the BCS Sugar Bowl in January added $2.8 million to the coffers and playing in the SEC Championship game contributed $1 million more. Georgia football is big business. And no day is better for business than game day.

By 7:00 a.m. on Saturday, the tailgating has begun. All over campus—on sidewalks, on grass, in parking lots—Georgia fans have pitched tents, hoisted their flags, and started grilling food and drinking beer. The roads become clogged as the morning progresses and the conversations and music grow louder. Richt is in his office early enough to do his pregame radio interview with Loren Smith at 10:30 a.m. The players have not yet returned from Lake Elsinore, a resort 50 miles northwest of Athens where the team stays the nights before home games. (Richt joined them last night for dinner and for a brief pep talk before driving back to Athens.) Recruits begin to show up at Butts-Mehre with their parents and coaches and are greeted by the Georgia Guys & Gals, who are dressed in black skirts or pants and red and black striped sweaters.

After the players arrive and dress at Butts-Mehre, Athens swells around the team buses as they make their way across campus. They stop short of the stadium and the players and assistants get off. It is time for the Dawg Walk. Imagine a movie premiere's red carpet, with photographers and fans screaming as stars walk down the carpet. Now multiply that by 1,000 and you're getting close. It is a decades-old tradition, and the Georgia band, cheerleaders, fans, and police line the route. The path is at first blocked off by barricades, but as you approach the stadium, it becomes a human tunnel barely two feet wide. If you can't get pumped after that walk, good luck.

Unlike just about everything else around it, the locker room at Sanford Stadium is not impressive. It is a large room with white walls, a red carpet with a Georgia "G," a few dozen folding chairs. There are easel boards for position meetings, a small training room, a coaches' room. Since the team does not get dressed here, little is needed. Hanging above the door to the field is a tattered sign that reads: "Be worthy as you run upon this hallowed sod, for you dare to tread where champions have trod." After warm-ups, all of the players gather in the small shower area and get quiet. A manager turns off the lights. A player begins a prayer. "If God is with us, then who can be against us?" the group says in unison. The lights come back on and the team takes a knee around Richt.

"We had a great week of practice. A great night last night and today I can tell you are focused. You are ready to play. You need to out-hit, out-hustle, and out-heart them today because I know they will be fired up."

But he doesn't have to say much. The team knows what they must do.

* * *

On the first offensive series, David Greene leads the Bulldogs down the field. Michael Cooper picks up where he left off last week against Middle Tennessee State, breaking away for a huge run into South Carolina territory on the fifth play from scrimmage. Georgia gets to the red zone, hungry for their first offensive touchdown in their last 11 quarters against the Gamecocks, and Greene finds receiver Reggie Brown for a TD. Wait. A flag on the play. An illegal formation penalty is called on Georgia and the touchdown is negated. After the team committed 18 penalties the week before, Richt and his staff have emphasized discipline all week. This is not a good start. The South Carolina defense steps up and holds Georgia to a field goal.

The Georgia defense plays strong on USC's first possession, forcing them to punt. But Lou Holtz pulls a fast one, calling for a fake punt that results in a first down.

The defense digs in and South Carolina goes nowhere. After the series, on the bench, Brian VanGorder sits between his players, diagramming plays, offering them encouragement. On the field, Greene faces a third and long deep in Georgia's own territory. Split wide to his right is Fred Gibson, who, despite reports to the contrary, is ready to play. Gibson breaks free of his defender after a cut into the middle and holds on to Greene's pass as he is hit hard. The catch gets Georgia a first down, but costs them much more. Gibson does not get up. Ron Courson and his staff run onto the field as the crowd grows silent. Gibson is helped to his feet and limps off the field, takes a seat on the bench and never returns. The hamstring injury that he had suffered the week before, the subject of so much speculation, apparently has not healed. Yesterday, after learning that Gibson could go, Richt reflected, "I hope he is ready. If he gets hurt again I will feel real bad."

Greene continues to engineer on the impressive drive and this time, the end result is a touchdown. Reggie Brown hauls in the score over Dunta Robinson. The drought is over.

The Bulldog defense forces USC quarterback Dondrial Pinkins—the same Pinkins who said David Pollack would "not be a factor"—into scrambles and bad passes. Pollack is double- and triple-teamed but does manage to pressure Pinkins on numerous occasions. Georgia intercepts Pinkins late in the first quarter, but at the end of the play, a Georgia player is called for a personal foul, backing them up 15 yards. Another dumb penalty. On the sideline, Richt shakes his head and breaks a small grin. It doesn't really matter, as the Georgia drive goes nowhere.

Early in the second quarter, Richt puts quarterback D. J. Shockley in the game for a series, as he's hinted he might, but on Shockley's second play, what should have been an option shovel pass to the tailback ends up on the ground and South Carolina recovers the ball. It is Georgia's first turnover of the year. Late in the first half, Greene hits Brown again, this time on a five-yard touchdown pass. At halftime, the score is 17-0 and the crowd roars their approval.

"We cannot let up," Richt implores the team after the position coaches have met with their men. "I heard someone say that the score was 0-0. Well, it *is* 0-0. Football is a 60-minute game, not 30 minutes. I know that they have a lot of pride and will come out strong. They could score a touchdown and now it's 17-7 and they are right back in it. Maybe they take the lead. We have to stay focused and battle back."

But the second half is more Georgia—on both sides of the ball. The defense forces another turnover, as Sean Jones gets his second pick of the day. Pollack is all over the place, throwing larger offensive linemen out of the way. Michael Cooper rushes for a two-yard touchdown to make the score 24-0 and in the fourth quarter, Richt begins to rest the starters. South Carolina misses a field goal attempt but against the Bulldog reserves, they do manage a late touchdown. On the ensuing onsides kick, Bulldog receiver Damien Gary scoops up the ball and returns it 44-yards for a touchdown. The rout is complete, the final score 31-7. Greene finishes 16 of 27 for 208 yards, Brown catches seven passes for 104 yards and two touchdowns, and Cooper has 14 carries for 82 yards.

In the jubilant locker room, which is crowded with former players and coaches' kids, Richt praises the team. "Boy, we looked great out there today. Offense, defense, the special team coverage, we looked real good. I think we have something real special here, men. Don't you?"

The team responds with an emphatic "Yes, sir!"

• • •

Mark Richt manages a typical week in the coaching life with an impressive resolve and strong belief in who he is and what he is doing. The setbacks do not drain him and the successes do not change him. He has learned to be the CEO of a major college program without having to give up being a coach, or being a good man. If he turns out young men of character and loyalty with a devotion to family, then he has succeeded. Winning a few football games is just a bonus.

The win for Georgia was a rout but not all teams are on the winning side of lopsided games. Just ask Tom O'Brien at Boston College.

CHAPTER 3

Guard on the Watchtower

Boston College

Boston College vs. #2 Miami
Chestnut Hill, Massachusetts
September 14-20

Tom O'Brien and Boston College expected to be 3-0 heading into their Big East opener with Miami. After an unexpected opening loss to Wake Forest, the Eagles regrouped to defeat Penn State and Connecticut on the road. Miami rose to #2 in the national polls after starting off 3-0, including a win against rival Florida. BC is a team without superstars but with plenty of talent while the Hurricanes are loaded yet again with future NFLers. A national television audience will watch on Saturday night.

* * *

November 23, 1984, was not just another Friday after Thanksgiving with malls crowded, stomachs full, and football on televisions across the country. On a hot night in south Florida, on the field of the legendary Orange Bowl, an institution was forever changed. Unheralded Boston College and the defending national champions, the University of Miami, were in a shoot-out. With six seconds left, Miami led 45-41, and BC had the ball on Miami's 48-yard line. Behind center was a 5'9" senior with a strong arm and a lion's heart. Three receivers went deep on the play, the last of the game. As the clock wound down, Doug Flutie avoided the defensive pressure and let go a true Hail Mary. It was a prayer, but who better than a small Catholic school outside of Boston to have their prayer answered? Seconds later, receiver Gerard Phelan—Flutie's own roommate—caught the ball in the end zone, giving Boston College the upset. "The little engine that could" had put his school on the map.

The impact that Flutie's miracle had on his institution is immeasurable. But in what researchers have called the "Flutie Factor," applications increased sharply the following year. Boston College became a hot school to attend on a national scale and donations increased to the school and to the athletic department. "Flutie gave more exposure west of the Mississippi," says longtime Associate Athletic Director John Kane. In the 1980s, BC was known as a New England school, but with publicity and applications soaring, the school could be more selective in accepting students, thereby increasing the average GPA and test scores of incoming freshmen. "You can't buy magazine covers," Kane insists. "Flutie was on the *Sports Illustrated* cover three times." Alumni proudly wore their alma mater's colors around the country. Boston College was for real.

And they haven't beaten Miami since.

The program waivered between mediocrity and success for most of the 1980s and early 1990s, before being rocked by a gambling scandal in 1996. Members of the Eagles' football team were alleged to have bet on their own games and shaved points. Everything that the school stood for was shaken. Enter Tom O'Brien. A tall, lanky redhead, O'Brien brought a great offensive mind, a strong sense of discipline, and, most importantly, integrity, to a program that needed it. As the offensive coordinator at the University of Virginia under George Welsh, O'Brien had helped build UVA from a laughing stock to #1 in the nation. He coached players like Hermann Moore and Terry Kirby, who went on to the pros. His players played hard and Virginia gained a national following. It was only a matter of time before O'Brien got a head job at a prominent school.

His coaching career had started years earlier at his alma mater, the U.S. Naval Academy, after a tour of duty overseas for the Marines in Japan from 1974 to 1975. As a graduate of the U.S. Naval Academy and as a Lieutenant in the Marines, O'Brien learned to appreciate structure and came to recognize that disorganization was not good— philosophies that still dictate his life. After his tour of duty was over, he had a choice. He could continue serving and return to Japan or discharge from the military and help football coach George Welsh coach at Navy. The choice was easy. Under Welsh at Navy, and then at Virginia, O'Brien's coaching philosophy was shaped. He learned that the quality of time spent in preparation was more important than the quantity. He would put that philosophy to work in 1996.

"We all probably think we are ready before we really are," he now, looking back. "There are so many demands on a head coach th you don't anticipate." After Virginia lost to Miami in the Carquest Bowl in December, 1996, O'Brien began his head coaching career at BC. "I thought I could do it but I did not realize the depth of the problem."

"Things were in total chaos before Tom came," *Boston Herald* reporter Mike Shalin says. "It was an ultimate disaster. But Tom is a military guy. He runs a tight ship." O'Brien's current boss, Athletic Director Gene DeFilippo, says he found O'Brien to be better than advertised. "I followed Tom from a distance when he was at Virginia. His offense moved the ball at UVA. I was impressed with the way they played. He is more than I expected. He is a terrific football coach with discipline, morals, and values that are a terrific fit here."

His children opposed the move, crying about leaving Charlottesville and being forced onto the airplane to Boston. They had lived in Charlottesville for 15 years. His oldest child, Colleen, was a senior in high school at the time and was offered the chance to stay and finish out school in Virginia, but she chose to be with the family. Seven years later, she is a BC graduate and her two siblings are undergrads there.

When Colleen was at school, she would have lunch every Friday with her father. Now, it's Bridget's turn.

"I understand the demands much better now," says the 19-year-old Bridget, a junior. "When I was little, I knew he was a coach and it was neat to go to games and bowls, but now I know about recruiting and film and things." She continues, "It was Mom who raised us a lot by herself, she dished out the punishment." As for being a student at the college where your father is the head football coach, Bridget says, "It's cool, pretty normal," except when friends question her dad's play calling after a loss.

"I think people don't realize how funny my dad is. I mean, my friends are scared of him because he's the football coach and has a deep voice. I am sure he is intimidating to the football players but I see a totally different side." And when you watch O'Brien interact with his kids, he looks like a different man. He is comforting, smiling, hugging, doing the things parents do. But that doesn't mean his players see that side of him.

• • •

O'Brien runs his team from the third floor of Conte Forum in Chestnut Hill. Inside the football suite, the coaches' offices and meeting

...ted by dark wood hallways and maroon carpet. ...es on the west side overlook the stadium. On the ...s and awards—pictures of former Boston College ...f whom are now playing on Sundays, and awards for ...cellence to which the program is accustomed. Just in... ...e is a display listing the highest academic achievers on the current squad. Just outside the office suite, there are plaques commending the football program on its impressive graduation rates.

The biggest and brightest office is where Tom O'Brien resides. Windows overlooking the field fill one entire wall. Behind his desk and chair is a credenza with shelves, cabinets, and a writing area. Off to the right are huge color pictures of his three children, Colleen, Bridget, and Daniel. One picture shows O'Brien handing Colleen her diploma from Boston College, an honor the school allows staff members. There is a map of Ireland on the wall and an aerial shot of Boston. Mementos from decades spent in football line the cabinet shelves behind the desk: footballs from O'Brien's first win at BC and his victories over Notre Dame; a game ball from the 1970 Army-Navy game which Navy won 11-7; a Marine Corps glass emblem; a stack of Division I NCAA Rules Manuals dating back to 1997. His book collection includes Tom Brokaw's *The Greatest Generation* and *Wooden* by the legendary coach. There is a paper sign taped to the bookshelf which reads: "Some people spend an entire lifetime wondering if they've made a difference . . . Marines don't have that problem."

• • •

By Sunday afternoon, the Miami game is all the coaches can think about. Yes, Boston College had beaten Connecticut the day before, but not as mightily as hoped. They are 2-1 and look solid and healthy, but Miami is as tough an opponent as they'll play all year.

Sunday is typically the off-day for players around the country, as coaches begin to look ahead and players rest and heal. But Tom O'Brien runs things a little differently. Boston College practices on Sundays and the players have their mandatory day off on Monday. O'Brien likes the fact that the players are right back at it the day after the game. And he likes the fact that they can watch game film of the previously played game when it is fresh in their minds so they don't have to dwell on it on Monday. He also knows that Monday is a big class day, especially for labs, and the players can take advantage of the off-day. So on Sunday, instead of resting and watching NFL games, the players head over to Conte Forum for a workday.

Conte Forum and Alumni Stadium are so intertwined that it is hard to know where one begins and the other ends. The Forum houses the athletic department offices, as well as a weight room, sports medicine clinic, and locker rooms. On the first floor, the football team has meeting rooms, partitioned by sliding walls, with long wooden tables and chairs facing wipe boards in each section. There is video equipment and large screens in each room. Everywhere there is maroon carpet.

The luxury boxes that sit between Conte Forum and Alumni Stadium perhaps best encapsulate the unique athletic facilities. The row of suites is accessible from the upper concourse of the Forum, the home of Boston College basketball, ice hockey, volleyball, and concerts. There are windows on both sides of the suites because they overlook not only the Forum floor but also the field in Alumni Stadium. With the swirl of a chair or the twist of a head, a fan can literally watch two events at the same time.

As the day begins, some of the players receive treatments for injuries sustained during the win over Connecticut. Beginning at 2:00 p.m., the players stretch, lift weights, and do exercises in a pool. All of this is followed by position meetings that last until 5:00 p.m., when they put on their jerseys—no pads—and jog through the tunnel onto the field. O'Brien puts them through a light workout, focusing on stretching, conditioning, and special teams. Practice only goes 10 four-minute periods. At the conclusion, the coach stands near midfield in front of his team. "We put UConn behind us when we walked through that tunnel onto the field. We need to look ahead." His talk is short. They aways are. The coaches adjourn to their offices on the third floor and watch tape on Miami.

• • •

Normally, the staff meets at 7:00 a.m. in the morning on Monday, Tuesday, and Wednesday, a time the former military man is accustomed to. The staff meets on Monday afternoons as well. With no practice and few distractions, most of Monday is devoted to game planning. The offensive coordinator, Dana Bible, former offensive coordinator of the Philadelphia Eagles, leads the offensive staff in a meeting, joined by line coach Don Horton, running backs coach Jason Swepson and tight ends coach Jim Bridge. Spread out among the tables erected in the downstairs' meeting room, the group takes a little over an hour to formulate a tentative game plan. On the wipe board, Bible has already listed possible plays in various formations and personnel groupings. Words such as *Booster, Tiger,* and *Rhino* dot the board in small black and blue markers. There are periods of silence during the meeting, as the coaches rehearse plays in their minds. The Boston College offense is centered on four or five basic personnel groups that contain a few alternating formations and sets. As the week goes on and the coaches shape the game plan, plays will be removed from the board but not added, as is the case at many schools.

Miami is full of athletic players, particularly linebackers D.J. Williams and Jonathan Vilma and the team is solid at most positions every year. But with many from last year's roster now in the NFL, Bible and his staff determine that there could be some weaknesses. They know that trying to run outside will not work; the 'Canes are too quick. They know that passing success will be infrequent. They need to run early and often into the "bubbles"—the gaps between the line and the linebackers. And they need to neutralize Vilma. But most importantly, the BC players need to believe they can win. "We can't fear them. I mean, we can't be 'Miamitized' like so many teams get," Bible suggests to the coaches.

The defensive staff is upstairs in their meeting room, diagramming and planning. With the Miami offense playing well the last few weeks and quarterback Brock Berlin beginning to really learn to manage a game, defensive coordinator Frank Spaziani and his staff—Keith Willis, Kevin Lempa, and Bill McGovern—have their work cut out for them.

Monday afternoon brings a recruiting meeting. Who needs to be called? Who is coming in for official visits this weekend? Which kids are moving up the list? The coaches hold a copy of the master recruiting list in their hands. It lists names, schools, cities, heights, weights, speeds, GPAs, transcripts received, offers, offers accepted, visits scheduled, and columns indicating if the player would be admissible as determined by the football admissions liaison. If a player is not going to cut it, then it is better for the staff to know now and not waste time pursuing the recruit.

Mondays are an odd time for most football staffs to be meeting on recruiting, but then again, Boston College is unlike most schools.

• • •

Boston College was founded in the 1860s by a group of Jesuits who opened their doors to Irish Catholic kids who were denied admission to some of the prestigious colleges in New England, such as Harvard and MIT. The school was a small regional institution for most of its existence and, in fact, almost shut down in the early 1970s due to a lack of funds. Some major investors came to the rescue and the school recovered. In the eighties, following Flutie's miracle pass, the school gained national appeal and attracted applicants from every state. In 2003, the school received more applicants from California than from nearby Connecticut. Never lost in the mix though, was the fact that being a student-athlete at Boston College emphasized being a student over being an athlete. The mission of the College and the importance of academics shape everything that the football program is about.

"We need to find kids who can survive academically and also win and get us to bowl games," O'Brien notes. "If you look at the best academic schools, the admissions director makes decisions, not the football coach."

Howard Singer is an Associate Director of Admissions at Boston College and serves as the football liaison for the coaching staff. He is a one-man clearinghouse. Before coaches get serious about recruiting a high schooler, they send his transcripts, SAT scores, and grades to Singer to get an early determination if the recruit would be acceptable. The school is quite selective. The range of SAT scores for the middle half of the latest entering class is between 1260 and 1390 and their grades are A-/B+. Boston College received 22,500 applications last year for 2,200 freshmen slots. "What I do," says Singer, the former women's tennis coach at BC, "is to be an early judge, as best as I can, to judge if applicants can do the work at Boston College. If they can succeed with the demands of the school and Division I football." Based on his years of experience, by reviewing test scores, grades, and sometimes interviewing prospective students, Singer can get a fairly good idea if a student can succeed at BC.

The football team has just two academic counselors assigned to it full-time, many less than at other schools. Shena Latta works in the Learning Resource Center. "We have a relationship with the football coaches. We need their support and they need to buy into what we're doing." When student athletes arrive in Chestnut Hill, they are put through a battery of tests to determine their skill levels in reading, writing, and math. The counselors use the results to formulate an academic plan. The players are then put into levels based on the Learning Resource staff's level of concern. "There are three levels," Latta explains. "Level 3 are all freshmen and anyone else who is weak in academics. They must attend study hall and meet with us regularly. Level 2 students meet with us every other week and Level 1 are 3.5–3.8 GPA students and we don't see them very much." To show just how much the football staff cares about academics, the program will pay the spring semester tuition of a fifth-year player who is working on his graduate degree and has used up his eligibility. That bill can rise as high as $15,000.

The latest figures released in early September 2003 revealed that of all of the Division I schools playing football, this small private school had the nation's highest graduation rate—95 percent. The rates are based on the federal government's determination of who counts and who doesn't. In simple terms, the graduation rate is the percentage of scholarship players who enrolled at an institution as freshmen and graduated within a six-year period from that same school. Players that transfer out and graduate elsewhere count against schools; players who transfer in and graduate do not count for a school; players from junior colleges do not count, and, neither do non-scholarship athletes. So for 2002, the latest year figures that are available, Boston College's 95 percent rate means that 95 percent of the scholarship freshmen from the class of 1996 got their degrees from BC by 2002. The Eagles' best-in-the-nation rate is followed by Stanford, Rice, and Notre Dame.

"BC does a very good job in football, academics, and athletics," Gene DeFilippo exults. "The toughest part of my job is ensuring the balance between academics and athletics. Winning is very important but winning the right way is more important. We should never shortcut academics to be successful."

Academics is not the only thing that sets Boston College apart. When the athletic department wants to move a game time for television, they have to clear it with the Chestnut Hill neighbors, who may be inconvenienced. During game days, the football practice fields are not roped off—they are used as parking lots. "How many coaches have to deal with that?" O'Brien laments. A sparkling new football complex will open in 2005 adjacent to Alumni Stadium, giving O'Brien and his staff not only finer offices, but a leg up on recruiting. "Fans underestimate the importance of having great facilities. Just because you have great academics doesn't mean a kid is going to make a decision just based on that."

O'Brien is a football coach and knows that to get the top players you need more than just an impressive graduation rate. You need facilities, you need to be on television, and you need to beat #2 Miami.

• • •

Tuesday morning, the staff is ready to go at 7:00 a.m. Like at other schools, Tuesday is perhaps the most important day of the week in terms of planning and practice. The staff meeting takes no more than 10 minutes. Frank Spaziani and the defensive staff stay in the room and watch game film of Miami from this year and last. They spend time watching the Hurricanes' national title game against Ohio State in the Fiesta Bowl. Before splitting up, Spaziani asks his assistants if they had any problems with the defensive game plan heading into practice on Tuesday. A discussion ensues about the number of "checks" in the game plan. Checks refer to defenses beginning in one formation but quickly changing to another based on how the offense lines up. Over Sunday and Monday, the staff had put in some old and new checks as part of the plan, and the staff is worried that it might be too much for the players. "It makes me worried if you guys are worried," the coach says.

In the special teams meeting, coach Jerry Petercuskie sums up what many on the coaching staff believe when he stops the film and says to the players, "Geez, that guy looks fast just standing there." He has prepared a detailed scouting report on the Miami kickers, including kick yardage, hang time, and even diagrams of where their kicks landed. Containing the Miami speed on kick returns is critical, and Petercuskie has put in variations, including double-teams on the outside runners to slow the attack.

On Tuesday afternoons, O'Brien meets with the players alone. Since they do not practice on Mondays, he uses the Tuesday meeting to set the tone for the week. This talk is typical of O'Brien: short and devoid of emotion. "7:45, ESPN, national television. I know you guys don't need me to tell you about this game," he begins. He goes through his coaching points— no turnovers, no big plays, strong special teams play—and then makes this point: "You have to believe that you can beat them—and I think you can." The speech lasts just under three minutes. Like Mark Richt, O'Brien rarely displays emotion. His demeanor comes from a life in the military and in coaching.

In the practice's 20 five-minute periods on the artifical turf in Alumni Stadium, the pace is quick and the tension is high. When the first-team defense goes against the scout-team offense, a few scuffles break out. They are quickly broken up, but they show just how intense things are getting. Later, in the skelly drills, the first teams go against each other. "We have to get our first teams used to the speed of Miami," O'Brien says, "and the best way to do that is to have our fastest guys out there." It makes sense. No matter how talented or athletic backups or scout players are, at many programs only the starters can emulate the size and speed of an opponent and, in some cases, like this one, imitation falls short of reality.

O'Brien does not say much during practice and instead stands near midfield observing both ends, twirling a whistle in his hands. He trusts his coaching staff and doesn't coach a position himself; he learned in his years as a coordinator that it is better to just let the coaches coach. Rarely will he interrupt a drill or make a comment. He prefers to make mental notes and talk with coaches after practice.

Just before practice ends, backup defensive lineman Justin Bell goes down on the turf. The training staff immediately rushes to him. He has injured his hamstring on a routine play. With the help of a trainer, he manages to hop over to his teammates, who have gathered around the head coach at midfield. "We need more from the scout team," O'Brien says. "Faster play, more work, more intensity. If we can't get that from you guys then we won't be able to get ready for Saturday. Every play you need to go hard and finish."

The defensive staff immediately takes showers, orders food, and sits down to begin to review practice film. The offensive coaches go to the team meal before watching tape.

• • •

Derrick Knight is the type of kid that every coach wants to coach and every parent wants to claim. The 5'9", 205-pound senior running back from Westwood, Massachusetts, entered the 2003 season as the leading returning rusher in the Big East and a candidate for numerous national awards. Knight redshirted in 1999, carried the ball just 52 times in 2000, and spent much of 2001 as the second-string tailback. Year 2002 was his breakout season, when he rushed for 1,432 yards on 253 carries. It was the fifth year in a row that Tom O'Brien had a back rush for more than 1,000 yards.

Knight was not highly recruited out of high school. The major programs in the SEC and ACC were not knocking down his door. Had he given up football, he could have gone anywhere, with his excellent high school grades and strong test scores. But he chose Boston College and O'Brien. "BC was willing to give me a chance," he says. "My mother prepared me for college. I wanted to go somewhere I would enjoy myself outside of football, in case I got hurt. I thought about football. BC always had a great offensive line." His explosion in 2002 garnered him national acclaim, but playing at Boston College gives him little media exposure each week. He doesn't regret anything. "You have to be thankful for the shot that you get. Happy for the shot you get. Everything worked out fine for me."

The senior graduated last May with a degree in Business and takes graduate classes while playing his fifth year. He has been through a lot with O'Brien and understands his methods. "It's a hierarchy. You know your place. He knows what is going on in all areas. He is a guard on the watchtower." The routine of football under O'Brien can get monotonous, Knight acknowledges, but that doesn't mean it's wrong. "Sometimes, guys yearn for something different. It gives discipline. It has worked for five consecutive bowl games. It's all not done in vain." Not that Knight doesn't understand his teammates' desire for variation. "At times, I would have liked a change or two." Instead, he got an impressive degree and a shot at the NFL.

• • •

At 11:30 a.m. on Wednesday, there is a bit of a pause in the workweek as Mass is held for the athletic department and community in the downstairs team meeting room. O'Brien and his wife, Jenny, attend, as do some of the assistants. Two hours later, the special teams meeting takes place in the same room as the service for God. Petercuskie shows clips of Miami and of the Boston College kick protection from Tuesday's practice. "We must maintain the integrity of the pocket," he says on more than one occasion, pointing out breakdowns in protection or missed blocks or poor techniques. Many of the starters on both sides of the ball also play on special teams—something not uncommon at schools with smaller rosters and not much depth, as is the case at Boston College and Colorado State.

Practice is held on the grass practice fields adjacent to Alumni Stadium. One of the fields is enclosed by a green fence, while the other serves as the outfield for the Eagles' softball and baseball fields. Today's practice is shorter than yesterday's, just 18 periods, but it is equally fast-paced. The workout is not as spirited as those earlier in the week. Perhaps fatigue and homework are having an impact.

But the very next day, an excitement fills the air and the players whoop and holler as they go through drills. The receivers do a bump-and-catch drill, trying to snag balls out of the air by out-jumping and out-muscling defensive players. It is a lot like the kids' game of "500."

O'Brien is at his usual place at midfield. Wearing a black BC hat, a gray sweatshirt, and tan shorts, he stands at times with his arms crossed, other times bouncing a yellow ball on the artificial turf. Practice is 72 minutes long, and concludes with a two-minute drill, with the offense running plays wherever O'Brien spots the ball. It is just 4:45 when the players gather around the coach. "Everyone must play their best on Saturday. There simply are no excuses. Everyone must have the game of their careers, and if we play hellacious, we have a good shot. We need to get focused now." The players huddle and co-captain Augie Hoffmann stands at the center and tells his teammates that a hurricane is coming to town. "And bring it on," Hoffmann yells. His reference is to both Miami's nickname and to Hurricane Isabel, which has been a concern all week. O'Brien's office television is constantly tuned in to the Weather Channel.

Little does Hoffmann realize just how powerful the Hurriances are—both of them.

● ● ●

The head coach showers and gets in his car, heading toward the studios of WEEI for his weekly call-in radio show. O'Brien is not a "media darling": He rarely trips up, doesn't reveal much information, doesn't always provide tantalizing sound bites. "Tom won't tell the media much—only if he has to tell," says the *Herald*'s Mike Shalin.

"I read the papers, of course," says O'Brien. "I want to know what they're saying. Five years ago, it was anyone who could dial a phone could give their opinion. Now it's anyone who can type," he says, referring to the explosion of the Internet. On his radio show, hosted by Boston College color analyst Peter Cronan, the wry O'Brien has found his presence on the air. Just minutes into the show, the first caller asks O'Brien if he is a betting man, and who he'd bet on for Saturday's game. "Well, I'm not a betting guy. If I was, I wouldn't be here," an obvious reference to the BC gambling scandal of 1996, which O'Brien was hired to help the program overcome.

Another topic on the minds of callers to O'Brien's show is the future of the Big East conference. In the spring of 2003, there were tremors across the collegiate sports landscape when it became public that the Atlantic Coast Conference was actively recruiting the University of Miami and other Big East schools to join the nine-team ACC. Rumors, media reports, press conferences, and harsh words between ACC and Big East officials stirred the fire. Initially, the ACC wanted three teams to join, thus giving it 12 members and, according to NCAA rules, enough schools to hold a lucrative postseason conference football championship game. Enticing Miami, the nation's preeminent football program, was central to the ACC's plan. Syracuse and Boston College were also targets, and a group of ACC leaders toured all three campuses and met with their representatives. But then politics got in the way. The noninvitees from the Big East threatened lawsuits with the future of the conference in doubt. ACC presidents, who initially supported the candidacy of all three schools, began to waver.

The key to the ACC vote was the University of Virginia's president John Casteen. He was the swing vote, with Duke and North Carolina voting no, and the conference needing no more than two no votes to kill it. Government leaders, like Virginia Governor Mark Warner, got involved. He wanted the state's other big institution, Virginia Tech, also a member of the Big East, to be included in any expansion. Under pressure from the Governor, Casteen began to work the Miami/Virginia Tech plan, leaving Syracuse and Boston College out. Within days, the compromise plan was accepted. The ACC now had 11 schools, still one shy of the necessary 12, but now had two of the nation's football powers.

For Boston College, it was a roller coaster of a ride. From all indications, the school would have accepted the ACC invitation. Joining the ACC would have elevated all of the sports programs and brought in millions of dollars in revenue. More than that, the academic mission of the school would be enhanced by joining top academic schools such as UVA, North Carolina, Wake Forest, and Duke. "Boston College is such a great school, no matter what league it is in," says DeFilippo. "We are located in Boston, the sixth largest media market, we have strong morals and values, and we will be a success. Miami is the marquee football team in the country and they had to do what is best for them just like BC would have to do the same." The athletic director is confident that no matter how it played out, the Big East will keep their automatic BCS bid and this, in fact, could allow Boston College a better chance at a BCS game. "With no Miami and Virginia Tech for the next two years, that leaves West Virginia, Syracuse, Pitt, and BC as the power football programs," he says. [See Epilogue]

The football coach shares a similar view on the mess. In an open letter to the Boston College students printed in the student newspaper, O'Brien wrote the following:

Dear BC Fans:

I want to thank you for all of your support during our first three games and now is when we really need you—against the national power and Big East rival, Miami. It is a great opportunity for Boston College and our football program to be on ESPN prime time and we need to show what BC football is all about.

You can do your part by showing up early and being loud and proud. Alumni Stadium should be full and roaring when the cameras roll—Eagle enthusiasm for 60 minutes will give us momentum and an advantage on the field as well.

Our goal as a football team is to be champions in the classroom and the community as well as on the field and we expect our fans to be champions, too. Cheer with class, be supportive at all times and send a message to everyone watching ESPN on Saturday night that BC is a special place with even more special people.

Let's come together and beat the Hurricanes—GO EAGLES!

Sincerely,
Tom O'Brien
Head Football Coach

He had written similar letters in the past, and after some "boorish" behavior by Connecticut fans at UConn, he felt it was necessary to remind the BC students about sportsmanship. The media took the letter as a sign that O'Brien was worried about the BC fans' behavior because this was Miami's last Big East game against Boston College.

But that was the least of O'Brien's concerns about Miami.

• • •

Friday, the staff meets at 11:00 a.m. to briefly—very briefly—go over the weekend schedule. The staff is hosting one recruit on an official visit while more than 20 are making unofficial visits with their parents or coaches. O'Brien walks down the hall to his office to meet with the ESPN crew doing the Saturday telecast. Ron Franklin, Mike Gottfried, and Adrien Karsten are the talent, with Bill Bonnell producing. Gottfried starts out questioning O'Brien, inquiring about injuries and the Big East mess, which seems to be of key interest to the group. The coach tells them, as he has told many reporters during the week, that he only worries about what he can control and he can't control the conference alignments. A follow-up question from Franklin about scheduling Miami in the future elicits this response: "Sure, if they come up here in December to play it." (If you've never been to Boston in the winter, it's not like Florida.)

In an assembly room on the third floor, the development arm of the athletic department has put together a luncheon for donors who have endowed scholarships, as well as for the head coaches of the varsity sports and selected student athletes. The President of Boston College, Father William Leahy S.J., is there, as is Board of Trustees member and endower of the head football coaching position, Gregory Barber. A retired venture capitalist millionaire, Barber has been instrumental in raising money for the new football facility and for scholarships. DeFilippo is also there, serving as a co-master of ceremonies. After the athletic director delivers some thank-you's, the student-athletes in attendance each rise and introduce themselves and the donors who endowed their scholarships. Keeping in mind that tuition, room, and board at BC run about $37,500 a year, they offer their gratitude. O'Brien stops in for a few minutes.

At 3:30 p.m., the players are in position meetings going over some last minute changes and formations. The mood is light, as the hard work from the week is behind them. In the special teams meeting, Jerry Petercuskie reviews substitutions. Instead of walking through substitutions on the field, as many programs do the day before a game, BC players simply sit in their seats as Petercuskie reads off positions on his special teams list. When he calls a particular position, such as L4 on kickoffs, those players playing that position quickly stand up out of their seats and Petercuskie checks to make sure everyone knows his assignment. He goes through the process for kickoff protection, kickoff returns, punts, and field goals.

A few minutes later, the players run onto the wet field in Alumni Stadium for a walk-through. Dressed in maroon long-sleeve shirts and gold shorts, the special teams, offense, and defense line up to run a few plays. "This is the game of your life," O'Brien tells them. "Let's make history, not be history," he says, cracking a smile.

After a steak dinner on campus, the team heads four miles away to the Sheraton Hotel in nearby Needham. They arrive close to eight, and meet at 9:30 p.m. for a short team meeting and snack. O'Brien traditionally asks one assistant coach to talk to the team on the night before a game, rotating the responsibility from coach to coach. Tonight, it is Bill McGovern's turn. He talks about the importance of winning at home, reminding the players that they went into South Bend last season and knocked off Notre Dame. "Now the big game is in your backyard," he says. "Are you going to defend it?"

· · ·

Saturday morning, the wake-up call is at 9:40, in time for the mandatory team breakfast at 10:00. The players, still dressed in their travel khakis and collared shirts from last night, chow down breakfast and head back to campus with a police escort. They do light exercises, passing and catching drills, and offensive and defensive walk-throughs on the field before showering and dressing in white, Boston College short-sleeve shirts and maroon warm-up pants. They wear looks of seriousness and focus. Back at the hotel, the players sit quietly in the banquet room before O'Brien lets them eat, seniors first. They chow down on spaghetti, pancakes, chicken, and potatoes. They do not speak.

Before excusing them, O'Brien walks to the middle of the room. "I want to clear up one thing that I think I said this week and I have heard some of you say," O'Brien begins. "The line is, 'We all came here to play in games like this.' You guys, even the coaches came for this. I should clarify. We came here to *win* games like this. National TV, the place is going to be rocking tonight. We're playing the best team in the country. Heck, they've only lost two games in three years. This program," he continues, motioning with his arms over the room, "we can send a message tonight and separate ourselves. No regrets." There are some echoes of "No regrets!" as the players get up.

The pregame chapel at the Catholic school is actually two distinctly different voluntary services. In one banquet room, with 23 players and O'Brien, team chaplain Father Tony Penna leads a 20-minute Mass, complete with Communion, a homily, and a reading from the Gospel of Mark. "If you want to be first, you have to be last," the priest tells the gathering. "It is more than being humble," he says, "it is about servanthood." He tells a story about monkeys in Africa. Tribes take a pumpkin, carve out the middle, and make a very tiny hole in one side. They fill the pumpkin with peanuts and hoist it from a tree. The monkeys smell the peanuts, climb up to the pumpkin, and reach in. Of course, when they grab a handful of peanuts, they can't pull their hand back out because now their fists are too big, and they don't have the intelligence to realize it. The tribesmen capture and sell the animals. The point, according to Father Tony? "We can get stuck trying to go for the big treasure and not starting with the small one."

Next door, in a much smaller Christian service, chaplain Howard McClendon, a broad man with a gentle voice, relays the familiar story of David versus Goliath. Very appropriate, considering the match-up. It is a tale the players have heard before but with Miami looming, it seems fitting. "Remember that David had five polished stones but it only took one to bring him down."

With a police escort, the team makes its way to campus, greeted by a throng of tailgaters and fans in the parking lot outside the stadium. O'Brien is superstitious, like many coaches, and follows the same routine upon arriving at the stadium each week. He gets off the bus, shakes every player's hand as they walk into the locker room, then walks to the field to take a look at the weather, field, and atmosphere—this more than two hours before kickoff. He retreats to the coaches' locker room, where he stays until late into the warm-up period. High above the field in his third-floor office, his wife, Jenny, begins to entertain friends and family.

The players get taped up and some take turns in the whirlpool. They are quiet. Posted on a message board in the locker room is an article from *canesport.com* that quotes Miami linebacker Jonathan Vilma as saying, "I want a blowout."

By 7:10 p.m., O'Brien is on the field, wearing a white BC baseball cap, a maroon shirt, and tan pants with Reebok sneakers. He paces alone around the 30-yard line, looking from his team to the opposition. Some of the assistants are on the bench, some are talking with recruits on the field, others are talking with Miami staffers. By 7:25, everyone is off the field and back in the locker room. The players mill about and pump each other up while the coaches prepare in their adjoining locker room. O'Brien's locker has shirts hanging neatly and shoes arranged perfectly underneath the locker—unlike those of his assistants, whose lockers show no evidence of a military past.

With just under eight minutes to go before kickoff, Father Tony calls the players and coaches together and leads them in the Lord's Prayer. They line up at the locker-room exit. Before they bust out of the room, O'Brien silences them and offers these words, after encouraging them to make no mistakes: "Forget about everything. The clock, the fans, the TV. We need to play this one play at a time. Let's make one play, then another. Let's go!"

As the players hurriedly leave the room, they smack their hands above the doorway on a sign that reads, "Don't talk about it . . . Do it!"

* * *

The sold-out crowd is cheering wildly as the band welcomes the team onto the field. Miami wins the toss and elects to kick off. On BC's first possession, receiver Grant Adams catches a pass from quarterback Quinton Porter and breaks free for an electric 18-yard run. Alumni Stadium rocks. But wait. Boston College is called for illegal procedure and now they face a first and 15 from their own 31. On the next play, Miami commits a personal foul giving BC a first down. There is hope. However, Miami stifles them on the next three plays and BC is forced to punt to Miami's Roscoe Parish. The booming kick pins him in at his own eight, but within seconds he is on the BC side of the field headed for a touchdown, less than two minutes into the game. The crowd falls silent.

Mistake #1.

Jerry Petercuskie, who had worked all week on kick coverage, is dumbfounded. O'Brien walks near him on the sideline but says nothing. On its next few possessions, Boston College can muster little. Porter is hurried into throws, the backs have nowhere to run, and Miami exhibits the speed the Eagles staff was expecting.

It is 7-0, when the Eagles line up to punt from their own 29 with seven minutes left in the first quarter. The snap squibbles on the ground and the Eagles' Paul Cook falls on the ball.

Mistake #2.

After this second special teams blunder, O'Brien is furious, taking off his hat, rubbing his head, yelling at Petercuskie. "What the hell is going on, Jerry?" he screams. What is going on is the Eagles' best long snapper, Francois Brochu, had been injured all season and was sitting out. Backup Chris Miller, who never snaps, is subbing. As most great teams do, the Hurricanes take advantage of the mistake and, after a leaping catch by tight end Kellen Winslow to put the ball inside the one, Miami's running back Frank Gore scores to increase the lead to 14-0.

On the sideline, Frank Spaziani gets his defense together again after the Winslow catch. "He [Miami QB Brock Berlin] is looking for Winslow. He is looking for him the whole time and throwing it to him. It is up to us to get there." Early in the second quarter, Boston College finally seems to be putting together an impressive drive, aided by Miami penalties, behind backup quarterback Paul Peterson. But Peterson drops back and throws a pass right to Miami's Sean Taylor. Taylor intercepts and runs the ball 67 yards for another Miami TD—21-0.

Mistake #3.

At this point, the crowd is stunned and the coaches and players look dazed, as if they have been struck by a car on a deserted road. Nothing goes right for BC—even when they intercept Berlin the play is nullified by an Eagle personal foul. Miami adds a late field goal before the half expires to go into the locker room up 24-0.

• • •

Thirty minutes of football are gone and BC has little to be happy about as they make their way through the tunnel. The offense turns left into a meeting room while the defense heads into the locker room. It is quiet again. O'Brien heads right for the offense. "Look, we got to get something going here. I mean, let's play one play at a time and put something together. We can't do the mistakes either." He walks across the hallway into the locker room to talk to the defense. He praises them for their efforts, pointing out that they are playing great. In fact, they really only gave up the late field goal, not including the Gore TD run set up by the special teams' mistake. The coaching staff goes to their locker room. Spaziani and his defensive staff huddle around a small wipe board and draw up a play action that Miami is running. After Dana Bible and the other coaches who sit in the coaches' box make it downstairs, Bible takes out his reading glasses, opens up his notebook, and waits as O'Brien walks over. "I think we need to go to May Day," Bible says, indicating a change to a two-minute offense. O'Brien concurs.

With seven minutes left on the halftime clock, O'Brien walks into the players' locker room. "Three mistakes," he explains. "We made three mistakes in the half. Let a guy run back on us, mess up the snap, and throw a pick. We're not playing that bad. We can't have the mistakes. We are not going to get back in this in one fell swoop. We need to go one play at a time. We kick off. Let's cover their butts, shut them down on D, and get the ball back. Let's get one score and get rolling." The silence of halftime is broken by renewed sounds of optimism as the team shuffles out to the field.

• • •

The second half begins according to O'Brien's script. The special teams cover the opening kickoff and Miami starts on their 20. The defense comes on and stops Miami like O'Brien planned. But the offense comes on and goes three and out, forcing yet another punt deep in their own territory. This time, the snap isn't too low. It's too high. Miller sails the ball over the head of punter Jeff Gomulinski and through the back of the end zone for a safety, making it 26-0.

Mistake #4.

The blowout that Miami's Jonathan Vilma had hoped for is taking place. Miller heads to the bench in embarrassment, where he sits alone.

Miami drives on its next possession and running back Jarrett Payton scores on an outside run to increase the lead to 33-0. Many BC fans head for the exits. With 7:40 left in the third quarter, the Boston College offense faces a fourth and one and O'Brien opts for a punt.

The usually supportive home crowd, or what's left of it, begins to boo loudly, looking for something to cheer about—even just a first down.

The fourth quarter starts with Boston College driving and Porter back at quarterback. They get to the Miami six, where a sideline fade pass is called. Porter takes a few steps back and lofts the ball to the corner, where two Miami DBs await. The ball is picked off in the end zone for a touchback.

Mistake #5.

The Eagles finally manage to get on the board with 11:28 left in the game when Derrick Knight, the rare bright spot for the Eagles on the night, scores on a five-yard run set up by an interception by BC's Peter Shean.

With the score 33-7 and still four minutes left on the clock, Spaziani gets all of his defensive players together one last time. They huddle close around him. "Look, no one is more disappointed than me. Than him [pointing to defensive line coach Keith Willis]. We are competing. That is why I love you guys. You are still fighting. It is a long season and this is one game. We are BC. Let's get one more stop." Indeed, Boston College's defense steps onto the field just minutes later and Larry Lester picks off a pass to set up the offense with good field position. "C'mon, I want to score. Let's go!" O'Brien enthusiastically declares.

Much to his, and his staff's credit, they do not lose their composure during the debacle. They don't throw blame around or get in kids' faces. Like their players, the coaches compete to the end. They are realistic and most have been around the game for a long time. They knew that Miami has superior athletes and that BC would have to play a near flawless game to have a shot.

With 38 seconds left in the game, the Eagles' Horace Dodd scores on a four-yard run to make the final score 33-14.

O'Brien waits for Miami coach Larry Coker to begin his trek across the field, and then jogs to meet him. They say little. O'Brien searches out a few Miami players and congratulates them. He runs into Miami Athletic Director Paul Dee and the two share words and a pat on the back. O'Brien jogs over to the corner of the end zone, with his team trailing behind, to sing the school's alma mater as the band plays along.

If a fan didn't watch the game and simply read the stats, he might be bewildered by the final score. Miami had just three more first downs than Boston College, rushed for just 17 more yards, and had 11 penalties to BC's five. Of course, the punt return yardage was in

Miami's favor, as was the passing of their QBs who finished 20 for 33 compared to BC's eight for 26.

Back in the locker room, the players and coaches immediately take a knee and Father Tony leads them yet again in the Lord's prayer. Then it is O'Brien's time to talk. "If you want to be a good program, like Miami, you can't go out there and make mistakes. We made three in the first half and two more in the second. You can't do that. You want to separate yourselves and be considered from the rest of the pack—you had your chance. I really thought we had brought this program there. We scored a few late TDs. A moral victory or whatever. We don't need moral victories. This was a bad job by you guys and a bad job of coaching by the coaching staff. We will come in tomorrow and practice hard this week and we will win next week."

He knows that players come to Boston College to play with passion and a willingness to take on the big boys. He knows that the team will rebound. So tonight, there was no Flutie miracle. It can't happen every year. Some players showered and met their families outside. Some went to dinner. And some went back to their dorm rooms to study. This is Boston College, after all.

• • •

The discipline by which Tom O'Brien lives his life and runs his football program does not always result in victories. And the never-wavering routine that O'Brien, his staff, and his players are accustomed to may not make for dynamic weeks of preparation, but it does leave little to chance or question. It gives the players a chance to win, and at a school like Boston College, where football does not trump academics, that is all one can ask.

CHAPTER 4

Tennessee, Inc.

The University of Tennessee

#8 Tennessee vs. South Carolina
Knoxville, Tennessee
September 21-27

Tennessee is 4-0 and atop the SEC East after a convincing win over rival Florida in Gainesville. The Vols are led by Phillip Fulmer, a man who brought Tennessee a National Championship in 1998. Four-year starter Casey Clausen is at the helm with a steady supply of backs and receivers. Lou Holtz's South Carolina team was in the Top 25 before getting crushed at Georgia. The prime-time Saturday night game would provide for a stunning backdrop in Knoxville, the city ranked by many as the best sports town on game day in America.

• • •

Just off Kingston Pike, about two miles from the center of the Tennessee campus, beyond the million-dollar mansions lining the road out of downtown Knoxville, Junior Manis runs a barbershop. He's been cutting hair for the past 36 years and you can definitely call it a family business. His wife, Phyllis, has a chair right next to his. Next to Phyllis is their son, Rusty, and two down from Rusty is his wife, Cindy. They form the core of the Western Plaza Barbershop. It feels like a 1950s barbershop, even with the 1980s décor. It's a good feeling, like you're family when you walk in the door. The walls are covered with school pennants from around the country, from small Austin Peay to big-time Oklahoma. This is Knoxville, though, and Tennessee colors dominate: pictures, pennants, banners, and other orange memorabilia crowd the place. Pinned to a message board are the words to the Pledge of Allegiance. Across from Rusty's chair on the wall is a quote from George Burns that reads: "Too bad the only people who know how to run the country are busy driving cabs and cutting hair."

Rusty Manis hears a lot in his profession, even when he doesn't ask. In his father's shop, Tennessee coaches, players, trainers, and fans have come for years for a trim and some light talk. "For some reason, players like to tell us things that they probably shouldn't," the congenial Rusty reflects. "We hear things before they're in the paper. Of course, everyone wants to talk UT football."

Everyone includes 75-year-old Jim Ceiber, a longtime Knoxville resident who stops in for a cut. "Football is the topic from spring to fall, really all year, here at the shop and most places," the gray-haired gentleman says. "I'd say 60–70% of the time Tennessee football comes up in lunch conversations."

The barbershop is like hundreds in college towns across the country. But the passion of the loyal fans at the University of Tennessee ranks with the best. It is a place where football is not only a religion, it is life. There are "T" flags on cars, restaurants, backpacks, roads. If something can be painted orange, it is. Babies are made to wear Tennessee bibs, seniors wear the orange and white. It is a 365-day love affair among the school, the fans, and the city of Knoxville.

"Tennessee football is about as close to a legend as it gets," says reporter Chris Low, a writer for Nashville's *Tennessean*. "From ritzy clubs in Memphis to honky-tonk, everyone bleeds orange. Pipe fitters, lawyers, stockbrokers, those who work on the railroads in east Tennessee."

In the middle of it all is Phillip Fulmer, Sr. The 53-year-old presides over Tennessee, Inc. The money, the history, the stadium, the expectations. He is a coach, first and foremost, but also a CEO, a manager, a PR guru, a solicitor, and a politician. He has staked a claim to coaching legend in his 12 years as head coach at Tennessee, leading them to the 1998 National Championship. He resembles former senator and actor Fred Thompson but has crystal blue eyes. He is an unlikely man to be doing a job that is the best in the state to have—if you're winning.

• • •

After a modest childhood in Winchester, Tennessee, the Franklin County High graduate accepted a football scholarship to his home-state university. The offensive lineman became a Vol in 1968 and helped lead the team to a 30-5 record and a conference championship in his three seasons. After finishing school, Fulmer thought about entering law school and spending a career in courtrooms. But he accepted a GA position with Tennessee instead, coaching linebackers and serving as the defensive coordinator for the UT freshmen team. He moved on to Wichita State for five years and, after a one-year stay at Vanderbilt, returned home to UT in 1980. He's been here ever since. Tennessee rewarded his loyalty by naming him assistant head coach in 1987 and offensive coordinator in 1989.

In the middle of Tennessee's 1992 season, head coach Johnny Majors was fired and Fulmer was promoted. He was not a popular choice among UT fans. Some of the faithful thought he didn't fit the picture of the head coach at Tennessee. Yet Fulmer came on and won the four games he coached that first season. The following year, the Vols went 10-2. Over the next nine years, Tennessee maintained excellence, averaging just under 10 wins a year. The culmination of his rebuilding in Knoxville was an unbeaten season in 1998, complete with a national championship and an SEC title. He received numerous national Coach of the Year honors and established himself as one of the elite coaches in America.

Fulmer and his second wife, Vicky, have three daughters, Courtney (21), Brittany (19), and Allison (18). Phillip Jr., his son from his first marriage, is 33. He is a devoted family man and churchgoer who gives his time to various organizations and charities around the state and country. He has served as the President of the American Football Coaches Association and is on the board of directors of the Boys and Girls Club and Child & Family Services. Perhaps his most cherished volunteer activity is serving as the national spokesman for the Jason Foundation, an organization designed to educate teachers, parents, and students on the signs of teenage suicide.

Gus Manning has been associated with Tennessee since 1941 as a player, a student, an alumnus, and a booster. He has seen a lot in his half century and likes what he sees in Fulmer. "Phillip picks up more charisma as he goes along." And how does he compare to past Tennessee coaches? "I have been through eight coaches and Phillip ranks right up there with me."

Fulmer's boss, Athletic Director Mike Hamilton, who took over in 2003, after serving as an associate athletic director at the school, endorses Fulmer. "I couldn't draw up a better picture for the coach of Tennessee. He knows what Tennessee football means to the people in the state. He has a burning passion to succeed and I admire that he understands the total picture. He believes in all sports and is receptive to help other coaches. He'll visit with major donors in the locker room before a game. He'll fly to the Bahamas for a cruise with donors and fans."

The coach himself enjoys what he does, despite the pressures. "The hours are a bit better now," he says matter-of-factly. "It took me four to five years to really get a handle on this job." Fulmer is in a unique position in college football coaching. Barring unforeseen off-the-field problems, Fulmer can coach at UT until he says he is done. "I have security in my job," he concludes.

Security is not something you earn overnight but with South Carolina coming to town, it is something you can lose in one night.

Phillip Fulmer is more than a coach, and his job requires him to be. He runs a multimillion dollar corporation with stockholders. Tennessee spends $12.5 million on football but brings in a whopping $28.9 million, including $22.2 million just from ticket sales. Over his 12 years as the head coach, Fulmer has found a balance between the coaching side and the business side. He manages to work boosters, oblige the media, recruit the country, be involved in game planning, and spend time with his family—and do it all with poise. He fluidly moves from one area to another, never missing a beat, never forgetting which hat he wears.

For all of this, Fulmer is compensated handsomely, with a total package worth $1.7 million including a base salary of $275,000. He gets $729,000 for radio and television and $575,000 for endorsements and appearances. If he remains at Tennessee for three more years, he can collect a deferred compensation worth over $1 million. Tough to think of college football as just a game, isn't it?

• • •

Fulmer and his staff are done with Florida by 4:00 p.m. on Sunday. They have watched the game film and graded the players and, more importantly, done their "lessons." After each game, the staff takes meticulous notes about the opponent to be able to refer to them next season and aid in planning for games this season. It is a thorough review, made more enjoyable by the fact that they won. They turn their attention to their next opponent, South Carolina, and begin to watch film and come up with a game plan.

The staff meeting room at Tennessee more closely resembles a corporate boardroom than a coaches' meeting room. Fifteen leather chairs surround a large wooden table. There is a wipe board that bears the team depth chart, a master recruiting calendar, and the NCAA academic requirement for recruits, including the sliding GPA/SAT scale. One wall is all windows, overlooking part of campus.

It is 9:00 a.m. when Fulmer begins the Monday morning staff meeting. He starts by congratulating the coaches on their 24-10 victory over Florida on Saturday at Gainesville. He then asks Associate Director of Academics Fernandez West to go over the Volunteer academic situation. West had earlier passed out a list of players on a "concern list," as well as a team roster listing academic advising appointment times. Fulmer is concerned that too many of the players have not yet scheduled their advising meetings. When West mentions that one player has apparently been skipping class, contrary to earlier reports, the head coach is not happy. West blames the error on not having enough class checkers to monitor attendance. "Are you kidding me?" the coach asks. "We've got more people to check class than we need. That's not a good excuse." He then proceeds to list strength coaches, GAs, student volunteers, and even coaches who could do the job. "Hell, I'll go check on them," he says.

"All right, let's do the grades," Fulmer says, as he calls on defensive coordinator John Chavis to give his thoughts on the defensive play against Florida. Good overall, he indicates, but there were mistakes. Position by position, the defensive coaches give more specific reports on particular players' performances on Saturday followed by the offensive coaches. When the discussion turns to three secondary players who are not performing at the level the coaches desire, Fulmer does not accept a casual answer.

"Okay, what is the plan? Let's get it written down. What specific things are we going to do to get them playing?" Fulmer is a man of action, and all through the meeting, he asks for specifics on all issues. What is the problem? How is it going to be fixed? Who is responsible? He manages all issues the same way, whether it's about the depth chart, missed classes, or luggage tags. As the discussion continues, Fulmer stands up and makes his way to the depth chart board where he makes a few changes, moving some players above others based on their performance in the game.

Fulmer turns to the task at hand. "Again, great job last week but I am glad that you all have concerns because we have a lot to work on. We're doing okay, and now on the national scene, but we have to maintain it. It is a lot easier to get there than to stay there."

The meeting breaks after 85 minutes and the staff goes to work in meeting rooms while Fulmer looks at the kicking game with special teams coach Steve Caldwell. By 12:30, he is across the street in the

Gibbs Dorm cafeteria, eating lunch with his daughter, Brittany. The cafeteria is reserved for those students who live in the Gibbs Dormitory and for student-athletes. Fulmer and Brittany, a freshman on the swim team, get their food from the cafeteria line, sit at a table in the middle of the room, and enjoy a quiet moment together.

• • •

The College Football Hall of Fame in South Bend, Indiana, is a shrine to the game. There are national championship trophies, game balls from various historical match-ups, interactive video and audio displays, plaques of All-Americans and Hall of Famers. There are jerseys worn in the 1920s and game programs from long-gone eras. You cannot help but be drawn in by the tradition, the history, the passion of college football. Now imagine that same museum—complete with displays, videos, shrines, and memorabilia—just for the University of Tennessee.

Off Volunteer Boulevard, near Phillip Fulmer Way, blocks from Peyton Manning Drive, the Neyland-Thompson Complex is the home of Tennessee football. On the first floor of the 120,000-square-foot building completed in 1989, stands the Tennessee football shrine. The 1998 National Championship trophy, along with other bowl crystals and plaques, sits in a glass display case. There is green turf on the ground and a nearly regulation-size goalpost covered with orange padding. There are glass-enclosed displays of uniforms from yesteryear, videos of great moments in Tennessee football, and listings of UT players currently in the NFL. In one corner of the room, in front of a massive photo of a packed Neyland Stadium, stand two life-size sculptures: former Vols Peyton Manning and Tee Martin. They are dressed in jeans and Tennessee jackets and look like students hanging out on a Friday afternoon in the quad. There is a list of Tennessee All-Americans and a list of Vols who are in the College Football Hall of Fame.

Go through a set of double doors and you enter an enormous indoor facility, with a 70-yard turf field (to be expanded to 120 yards) with netting protecting the sides and numerous championship banners hanging high above. There is a goalpost at one end. Black-and-white pictures of Tennessee All-Americans line one wall behind the goalpost. One end zone wall and one sideline wall are two stories of aluminum, while the other two sides on the second floor are lined with offices, protected by glass all the way around. Just off the playing surface is the weight room. Here, on the wall, beside the lists of

Vol lifting records and above the orange and gray floor tiles, you can find a picture of the strength and conditioning staff of—believe it or not—14, including GAs and interns.

On the second floor, past the assistant coaches' offices and staff meeting rooms, Fulmer's assistant Mary Jo Fox is surrounded by plaques recognizing the coach from the state legislature and the City of Knoxville and a proclamation naming September 9, 2000, as Phillip Fulmer Day. There is a glass display that contains newspaper headlines from the championship season and coaching awards for Fulmer, including the 1998 National Coach of the Year.

Fulmer's office is really two large, connected rooms. The first room is a traditional office: a desk, furniture, lots of bookshelves. There are close to 100 books in his office, tomes on coaching and leadership—Joe Gibbs' *Fourth and One*, Bear Bryant's *Building a Championship Football Team*, Ken Canfield's *The 7 Secrets of Effective Fathers*, and *An Athlete's Guide to Agents* by Robert Ruxin. A replica of Neyland Stadium sits behind his desk, along with game balls, bobbleheads, pictures of his family, and a 2002 Masters baseball cap. A needlepoint that stands out on a wall reads: "On the Eighth Day God Created Tennessee." The adjoining back room is a lounge area with sofas, chairs, a conference table, and a screen and computer system. On the wall are numerous family pictures, most of them featuring his three daughters and son.

His oldest daughter, Courtney, is a 21-year-old junior majoring in speech communications. She has paved the way for her younger sisters, enrolling at Tennessee, applying nowhere else. "My dad would have been supportive of wherever I went but realistically, I couldn't go to another SEC school. That would not be good." Like other children of coaches, she has experienced the highs and lows—from traveling to new places to missing time with dad, from having the nice things in life to hearing angry words from strangers. "Since he has been here a long time, I am used to the pressure he and the family are under," she explains. "Our family is extremely close and I think the pressure makes it that way."

• • •

The team meets for the first time since the Florida win in the second-floor auditorium on Monday afternoon. It is just before two when all the players arrive and take seats. On the walls, painted in orange, are slogans like "Character, Above All Else" and "Expect to Win!" Fulmer stands in the front, with two large video screens behind him, as the more than 90 players sit and wait for him to begin. Dressed in a blue, short-sleeve polo shirt with a "T" logo and a pair of gray slacks, he has a commanding presence and the room grows silent.

"Congratulations on the win. It is not easy to go to some of these places in the SEC like Gainesville, Tuscaloosa, Athens, and such, and win, but you did it." He points out that the win on Saturday is due to "the work put in from January to August"—a fact that the seniors in the room can attest to. John Chavis, Steve Caldwell, and offensive coordinator Randy Sanders give brief reports on objectives met and objectives unfulfilled from the Florida game, and they recognize outstanding players from the game, who stand at their seats when they are acknowledged. A highlight tape from the Florida game is played, revealing the best plays, including the end of the half Hail Mary touchdown for UT. As the big hits roll and the celebratory dances in the end zone play, the players shout and laugh. The mood is vastly different than one that will overtake the team in a matter of hours.

"I heard some of you in the locker room at half, and I was happy to hear it, talk about obligation," the coach continues when the video finishes. "Obligation is what won us the game, as the seniors know. But obligation is not just 60 minutes on Saturday. Obligation is a seven-day-a-week, 24-hour-a-day thing. It's on the field, in practice, in the classroom. And socially, when you are out Saturday night after the game."

The coach talks about perseverance and its definition, and though they had yet to lose a game, they could face obstacles ahead. "You have set yourselves up with the win, and with Georgia's loss [to LSU], to control your own destiny in the SEC East," Fulmer says. "I think we are a *pretty good* football team. We're not a *good* football team. We need to work hard every day, from Monday on, because that is when you win the game." Fulmer tells the team that South Carolina has faster receivers than those at Tennessee and whose front seven on defense are "the best we've seen."

Shortly after in the offensive staff room, which doubles as the quarterbacks' position room, Sanders sits with the nine quarterbacks on the squad—yes, nine, but only three are on scholarship. The group includes senior starter Casey Clausen, a confident player from California with short blond hair and a small goatee. Sanders reviews the offensive plays from the Florida win on film, stopping often and asking Clausen what he was thinking before the snap at various times. Clausen is quiet in his responses as the other QBs listen in and look on.

It rained all night Sunday and all day Monday in Knoxville, and Fulmer realizes early in the day that practice will have to be inside. After the position meetings break at 4:15, the players and coaches head down the stairs to the indoor field. On the 70-yard field, more than 100 players practice for 100 minutes. There is a smooth progression to the day, beginning with position drills, skellys, and then team drills, followed by the first-team offense against the scouts and the first-team defense against the scouts. Fulmer walks between position drills and watches both sides of the field. Even when in conversation, he can pick out a misstep—a missed block, poor positioning, dropped balls—out of the corner of his eye. "Son, get your butt down!" he shouts to a scout player. On another occasion, he pulls backup QB C. J. Leak aside to instruct him on the proper way to turn on handoffs.

With so many players and so little space, practice is organized chaos. Stud punter Dustin Colquitt turns in a punting display—that is, until one of his punts hits the roof and then awkwardly bounces on the turf, barely missing Fulmer standing at midfield. The players who played more than 20 snaps on Saturday stretch at the end of practice instead of conditioning, while the second team, scout players, and starters who didn't play many snaps against Florida stay on the field to run.

Fulmer allows the press to stay for all of practice every day, but cameras cannot record after the fourth peiod, or about 25 minutes into practice. As practice nears its conclusion, reporters anxiously await the players and Fulmer, but for some reason the players and coaches on the far side of the indoor complex are not walking off the field. Instead, they huddle around two players, redshirt freshman Chris Heath and sophomore Jason Allen, who collided on the last play of practice. They are both on the ground. The players have shoulder pads and helmets on but are not in full gear. There has been no hitting or tackling in practice but there are always some collisions. Heath and Allen both went for a ball and violently collided. Momentum has flung them 10 yards apart.

The facility grows silent, word spreads, players come back from the locker room. Trainers hold both of their heads steady, fearing neck injuries. Then Allen moves his legs, and slowly begins to move his arms. He is dazed, but after 20 minutes is able to rise up and walk. He is sent to the University of Tennessee Hospital to get checked out. Heath is not as lucky. He is not moving. The team doctor arrives and performs tests on his arms and legs to see if he can feel anything. He can't. His eyes are wide open but glazed over. Trainers carefully cut off his jersey, shoes, and socks, and an equipment manager removes the shell on his helmet. EMT is called and upon arrival, they tape his head to a stretcher. The players and staff who remain behind—including Fulmer and Brittany, who had stopped by—join hands and are led in prayer by chaplain James Mitchell.

As Heath is loaded into the ambulance, Fulmer walks across the field to the throng of reporters. He gives them a brief update on the injuries but is not specific. He follows that up with 15 minutes of answers to questions about South Carolina. It seems surreal, considering what's just occurred. But life goes on: players toss a ball on the field, the cheerleading squad laughs as they practice stunts, the press asks questions.

By the time he finishes, Fulmer has been joined by his oldest daughter, Courtney. They head across the street for dinner. Lunch with one kid, dinner with another. After dinner, he hops in his car and heads to the hospital, where he checks in on his injured players. Fortunately, tests are negative and both players have feeling in their bodies. They are released by 9:00 p.m., though both have suffered concussions.

Of course, football is a dangerous game and the threat of paralysis is real. Players like Mike Utley from the Detroit Lions and Penn State's Adam Taliaferro have suffered at the hands of the game. Safer helmets and upper-body padding has reduced the risk, but too many players still do not use proper tackling techniques, which can help reduce the risk of injury. Heath and Allen are lucky, but it doesn't mean it won't happen again.

The coach returns to his office after the hospital visit to watch film. On Monday and Tuesday nights, he sits in and watches the practice film with one side of the ball. He will then go to his office and make recruiting calls, then watch practice from the other side of the ball alone, unless issues warrant time with one side of the ball. Sunday, Monday, and Tuesday nights, he does not leave until close to eleven.

• • •

There is relief Tuesday morning in the football offices as the news of the players' conditions spreads. John Chavis is in the defensive meeting with line coach Dan Brooks, secondary coach Larry Slade, defensive ends coach Steve Caldwell, and GA Shane Beamer, the son of Virginia Tech head coach Frank Beamer. They begin by scripting practice for the afternoon. Periods 7, 10, 11, and 12 are team, or 9 versus 8, drills and thus need to be scripted—meaning a list of plays to be run during the period must be created. To do this effectively, the coaches first need to determine what the South Carolina offense tends to do. Like other staffs, they break down the personnel and formations from their opponents' previous games. A computer program not only calculates frequencies of plays but also diagrams them, after the GAs input the information. The typical 11, 12, and 21 personnel charts are taped to the board. Looking over those sheets, the staff determines what defenses would work best, and Chavis goes to a board and lists seven defensive calls for each of the four periods. The others in the room work backward and follow him by writing in green ink the offensive plays the scout team will run against those defenses.

After the script is finalized, the coaches begin to draw the scout cards for practice. Each one fills in routes and positioning for their specific responsibilities and then Beamer colors in the markings. While the staff works on the cards, Chavis runs film of the South Carolina–Virginia game. Randy Sanders does much of the same with running backs coach Woody McCorvey, receivers coach Pat Washington, tight ends coach Greg Adkins, and offensive line coach Jimmy Ray Stephens.

Fulmer, meanwhile, prepares for his press conferences. By 11:15 a.m., 25 reporters are gathered in the downstairs atrium of the Neyland-Thompson Complex, waiting. At noon sharp, Fulmer appears wearing a dark blue suit, a white dress shirt, and an orange tie. He goes into the media room and speaks to the writers about South Carolina. It lasts a matter of minutes. He returns to the lobby, does some radio one-on-ones, and then, at precisely 12:30, holds another briefing in the Hall of Champions—this one for the benefit of television crews and an audience watching around the state on live satellite.

"Like any coach, I see the media as a distraction to what we do. But I now understand they have a job to do," Fulmer says. "They have, for the most part, been fair."

Chris Low writes for *The Tennessean*. "When I first started, I thought Coach Fulmer was guarded, bordering on a little paranoid, which is not unusual of most coaches," Low says. "Not necessarily terse or cryptic, just very guarded and calculating." And now? "I've gotten to know him and worked with him for seven years. Like anybody else, I think he wants to get to know you and form a relationship."

The 2:30 special teams meeting runs longer than the intended ten minutes, and the position coaches grow antsy. Caldwell shows the players clips of South Carolina punt formations. Previously this season, Holtz's team has faked punts, or had the punter run to a side and punt the ball. As Fulmer looks on, Caldwell implores the team to be ready for such trickery. He also points out on film that often, when returning punts, South Carolina does not get out to cover the flanker players out wide very fast, perhaps giving Tennessee an opportunity to run a fake.

Fifteen minutes later, Chavis, who in addition to being coordinator is also the linebacker coach, has the attention of his linebacker corps in their position meeting. "They are fast and strong and experienced on the outside of the lines," the coach says about the SC offensive line, "but their middle is soft." It is an area he wants his backers to attack. Watching film, Chavis points out that when the South Carolina running back raises his hands in front of his face before a snap, a running back or quarterback draw always follows. "I don't know why he does it, but read it," he says.

At the start of practice on a hot Tuesday, Fulmer calls everyone together. Players, coaches, managers, and trainers all gather around him on the main practice field. "We did a good job yesterday putting the Florida game behind us and we had a good practice. Second, we are all grateful that Chris and Jason are okay. Safety comes first. I am all for playing hard and getting after it, but there's no need in practice for fourteen guys to dive on the ground for a ball. Save it for Saturday. Managers, you need to keep things off the field and away from the sidelines. Safety is critical. You get out what you put in," the coach continues, "and we need another strong practice. South Carolina is a good football team. What I'm saying is that we need to focus. All we can worry about today is Tennessee."

The Tennessee staff arranges practices around down and distance. On Monday, the focus is short yardage, goal line and "backed up" plays, on both the offensive and defensive fronts. They will only show film to the players on those situations. Tuesday is set aside for inside runs and play action passes. Wednesday is drop back passes, screens and draws. Thursday, they put it all together.

As practice gets underway on Tuesday, the first teams meet up for a 9 versus 8 drill, with wide receivers and corners absent. There is a noticeable upswing in the noise, tenacity and enthusiasm from players and coaches. There is hitting and tackling and yelling, and calls of encouragement from players on the side. It is an intense competition between the offense and defense. But as quickly as it starts, it stops, and the sides go back to work against South Carolina scout teams. Just a moment later, looking on as the defense goes against the scouts, secondary coach Larry Slade stops a defensive drill. "This was a great practice until now!" he yells, as players are out of position and fail to get to the ball fast enough.

The first team units go against each other again later in practice, and the offense gets the defense to jump offsides on more than one occasion. As practice concludes, Fulmer briefly talks to the team. "There were a lot of mistakes today out there. We did not have a good day."

A little over an hour later, the staffs watch practice film. In the offensive room, around a desk cluttered with pretzels and ice cream wrappers, they meticulously watch the footage of the team drills. Yes, there are missed assignments and poor routes, but it is not as bad as they thought. Tonight is Fulmer's night to sit in with the defense. He points out mistakes but constantly looks at the bigger picture about personnel, often adding constructive comments like "He could make a good safety." Their meeting is briefly interrupted when Slade, who has a prized recruit on the phone, hands the phone to Fulmer.

• • •

On Wednesday, Fulmer pops in and out of the meeting rooms, asking questions, giving suggestions, keeping abreast before practice. The practice fields are hot, but the players are only wearing chest and shoulder pads. In fact, Tuesday was the only practice when Tennessee players wore full pads—typically they are in full pads Monday and Tuesday. As he usually does, Fulmer calls in his troops after the flex period. "Look, South Carolina is a darn good football team," he begins. "If we play our best and they play their best, we can beat them. I don't know how many points we will score, but our focus needs to be there. You know, you guys have a great attitude. When it's practice time, you are all business. Some of the great teams of the past had that same attitude. Now we need to keep it going today. We need to correct our mistakes, probably late in practice so tomorrow will just be a dress rehearsal. Is that a deal?" The players respond with enthusiasm and off they go.

Practice is not as up-tempo as earlier in the week, perhaps because of the heat, perhaps because the coaches have to stop drills often and correct players. When the first-team defense goes against the South Carolina scout team, Chavis has the scouts rerun many plays because he is not happy with the defense. The mistakes get corrected but they slow the rhythm of practice. Fulmer walks between the offensive and defensive fields, surveying from afar, occasionally shouting out instructions to a player or stopping a drill. He is always aware.

• • •

In 2001, the Volunteers had a secret weapon. It wasn't a freshman quarterback or a secret blitz package. It wasn't help from General Neyland. Their secret weapon was a middle-aged woman named Judy Jackson. A longtime employee of the University, Jackson moved over to athletics in the early 1990s to work with the sports programs on recruiting and student welfare. She helped coordinate recruiting visits and kept up with advisements as well. She grew close to the coaching staff and the players, serving as an advisor, mother, and friend, going to practice every day, eating meals with the players.

In 2000, after assistant Mark Bradley was let go in December, Jackson's boss had a suggestion for Fulmer: Since Jackson knew the recruits' families so well, why not send her out on the road recruiting? Fulmer thought about it, then gave her his blessing. So Jackson took the mandatory tests required by the NCAA and was certified to go on the road. For three weeks in Janaury 2001, she hit the road with various assistants and crisscrossed the nation. She had met many of the recruits and their families already on their visits to Knoxville. Having her visit the homes brought "comfortability to the families," she says, and sent a clear message that Tennessee was more than just football—it was family. Jackson still works with the football team but no longer recruits.

Recruiting at Tennessee is similar to most major programs—madness, numbers, and persistence. Tennessee spent $931,748 on recruiting in 2002. Director of High School Relations Scott Altizer keeps tabs on recruits and helps organize visits and coaches' travel. Starting with 650–800 recruits in the early spring, the list is brought down to 300 or so after coaches watch film on players and evaluate them in May. As things become serious in the fall, Altizer takes a closer look at the grades, transcripts, and test scores of potential recruits. "After doing this for such a long time, I have a pretty good idea of what it takes," he says. "We can eliminate a lot of guys who simply couldn't get in. If they get cleared by the NCAA Clearinghouse though, they will probably be admitted."

Each of the nine assistant coaches who go on the road recruiting are responsible for a geographical area of the country, as well as for all players who play their position. They each may have 50 players they are actively working on but that number dwindles by late fall. Most of the official visits to UT take place after the season and include the usual meals, jerseys with player names, stadium sound effects, and time with the head coach. When current Vol Constantin Ritzmann, who hails from Berlin, Germany, took his visit, Fulmer wrote a letter welcoming him to Knoxville, then had someone in the language department translate it for him in German, then rewrote the letter in German, and left it in Ritzmann's hotel room.

Fulmer has a national reputation as a tenacious recruiter and enjoys a part of the game that many coaches despise. Last year, he made approximately 75 home visits, an incredible amount for a head coach. He traveled the country, often stopping in two cities a day. During bowl practice weeks, he would leave after practice, fly to a nearby city for a visit, and then return later that night. The assistants all want Fulmer to visit their particular recruits, and many want the coach to visit right before signing day in early February for maximum impact.

At a school like Tennessee, no day goes by without the coaches doing something to win the school recruits. But even more so than at most other schools, at Tennessee, the effort starts with the man at the top.

• • •

There is a different mood in the office on Thursday, perhaps because the coaches spent last night at home, making recruiting calls and getting to bed early. As the week progresses, the distractions increase. There is evidence of that during the defensive staff meeting on Thursday morning, when the coaches' cell phones and the phone in the meeting room ring constantly. Some callers are friends or family, some are high school coaches, some are folks looking for tickets. In between the interruptions, the coaches are able to script the practice plays for the afternoon. For Fulmer, after the morning staff meeting, it is time to be alone in his office. He takes care of some correspondence and phone calls, makes recruiting calls, and works on his notes for the game and for the traditional Thursday meeting with the team—he leaves little to chance. Around 11:30 a.m., Brittany comes by the office and the two get into Fulmer's Lexus and head down to the river for lunch.

Janie II is docked just a stone's throw from Neyland Stadium, the grandest and most elegant ship in the "Volunteer Navy," the armada of boats that park themselves just outside the Stadium as game day approaches. In perhaps the most unique setting in college sports, fans and alumni come from all over down the Tennessee River, with Tennessee flags flying high, barbeque grills ready for tailgating and signs asking visitors to remove their shoes before boarding. *Janie II* is in dock, as close to the Stadium as vessels can get. The 136-foot boat—which has five staterooms, a permanent crew of seven, 6,000 horsepower and more gadgets than most electronic stores—was originally built for the King of Spain. After its current owner purchased the boat "for many millions," it underwent a five-month renovation and paint job. It has played host to celebrities from all walks of life, from entertainers to athletes, and on occasion is chartered by families or groups for excursions. On this day, the ship, named after the owner's wife, is playing host to a select group of guests. Seated around the table on the back deck eating lunch are Phillip Fulmer, Tennessee athletic director Mike Hamilton, a few associates and friends, and the host, Alan Jones.

Jones is a multi-millionaire businessman who has made his fortune through payday advance businesses around the nation. Worth an estimated $300 million, Jones has expansive homes in Jackson Hole, Wyoming, and in his hometown of Cleveland, Tennessee, to go along with the boat and two private airplanes. His estate in Cleveland now boasts a state-of-the-art football field. He has donated money to build complexes at two local high schools in Cleveland; he gave money to UT—Chattanooga for its wrestling program; he donates undisclosed amounts anonymously to various schools and organizations around the country.

His friends are coaches, politicians, businessmen, and neighbors. Jones himself is a former high school wrestler and "average football player," so it is no accident that his boat is parked along the Tennessee waters. He has contributed millions to the University over the years, including a large gift in 2002 to help construct a swimming and aquatics center, one in which Brittany Fulmer will soon be competing. He has given money to the football program, basketball program, and the University. He's not an alum and has no kids at the school. "Athletics taught me as much as schooling," the 50-year-old says while reclining on a sofa on the main deck. "I learned a lot about character. Winning is easy, it's losing that's tough. Sports teach you tenacity and how to win."

He is just the kind of donor that school development people love, having deep pockets and big ideas. But he really can't tell you much about the Tennessee football team, its players, or its history. But he can tell you how much he admires his friend Phillip Fulmer, a guy who "carries the weight of the state on his back." "After the win over Florida last week, it lifted the whole state," he says. "Everyone is in a better mood, the economy is better." He continues to praise Fulmer, gushing, "For a guy with that much pressure on him he is just so nice and sensitive to other people."

On Saturday, Jones will be hosting a fund-raiser on his boat for Senator Bill Frist. But today, Fulmer enjoys lunch during a busy Thursday, and the fact that he is there should tell you how important Jones is to UT athletics.

• • •

Thursday afternoon, the players return to the team auditorium and sit in front of Fulmer, exactly where they were on Monday. Dressed in a blue blazer and short-sleeve orange shirt, Fulmer quiets the crowd. In the next 10 minutes he reiterates many of the points he's been emphasizing all week: 1) South Carolina is a very good football team and should not be overlooked and 2) Tennessee has the leadership, attitude, and ability to get "where we want to go"—traits he had seen before in championship teams. "We must look forward," he emphasizes. "We have not played our best football yet." What he wants most for the guys in the room is for them to get a championship—something none of them have experienced.

The players don't face a physically demanding practice, but the day does hold mental challenges. Thursday is a day to put everything into place and the coaches have high expectations. They were not pleased with Wednesday's practice and tell the team so. Most of Thursday is spent in team drills, working against the South Carolina scouts. The offense is clicking behind Casey Clausen, and he connects on most of his passing attempts. On the defensive field, however, the screams from John Chavis say it all. He is not happy.

Late in practice, a loud and constant roar comes over the practice fields. No, it is not the marching band, as Mark Richt experiences at Georgia. It is piped-in crowd noise broadcast on loud speakers around the field. Intended to create a game atmosphere and to force the offense to communicate with signals, the tactic is most often used before a team visits a hostile stadium. Practice concludes with a two-minute drill, with the offense running plays without a huddle, culminating in a field goal attempt from 20 yards. For the first time this week, Fulmer runs a drill, blowing the whistle, placing the ball down and shouting encouragement. Kicker James Wilhoit misses the field goal try. It wouldn't be his only miss of the week.

The receivers and quarterbacks stay on the field after practice to listen to "Coach" Clausen. Three weeks ago, Clausen kept one receiver after practice to review hand signals. A week later, the one became some. Now it is mandatory for all the QBs and wide receivers. Clausen lines up players and spends 10 minutes going over the routes and hand signals, even quizzing the players on the signs.

• • •

The orange and white football helmet gives it away. Twenty minutes south of Knoxville, in a town called Maryville, down Route 129 and off the beaten path a bit, there is a private lane that dead-ends after a few hundred yards. At the end of the drive sits a sprawling 35-acre piece of land, just yards from the Maryville Greenway, an 18-mile walking and running path through the countryside. To the left of the driveway is a garage and office complex. When the home was built in 1995, the garage was intended as a barn to house tractors and equipment. Now, it holds a car, work shelves, a custom-painted Harley Davidson motorcycle, two unused offices, and an attic for storage. Proceed further along the drive to the cul-de-sac driveway, and in front of you will appear a home that could be featured in *Better Homes & Gardens*. There is a large white flag with an orange "T" proudly waving from the front porch.

The Fulmer home is built on land where a broken-down farmhouse once stood, where a creek still flows and where railroad tracks cross the premises. The Fulmers lived in Knoxville for many years when Fulmer was an assistant, but decided to build a home and move to the country after he became the head coach. The house is filled with period furniture and the home feels warm and inviting. Family pictures and sports practice schedules abound. There are paneled walls and wooden furniture, and a large deck overlooking the backyard—which runs for thousands of feet in most directions and includes a 10-foot wide creek that flows to the Tennessee River. The creek is stocked with trout that Fulmer feeds on a regular basis.

A few yards from the main house is Boys Town, a guest home that resembles a sports bar. It is the ultimate man's playpen. There is a large-screen television, a pool table, a cigar cabinet, and tons of Tennessee memorabilia on the walls. There are newspapers and pennants, as well as pictures of Fulmer as a Tennessee player and even one of his old jerseys. He has a signed picture of himself with Joe Paterno and a cherished letter from former Nebraska coach Tom Osbourne. Osbourne was Fulmer's idol and, in January of 1998, the Nebraska coach sent Fulmer a short, typed letter encouraging him to keep doing well and assuring him that good things would come. It was less than 12 months later that Fulmer won the national title.

On Friday morning, Fulmer and his wife, Vicky, get up early and go for a walk along the Greenway. They return to the house, where landscapers and carpenters are hard at work, and Fulmer makes coffee, eggs, and toast. Around 8:45 a.m., ESPN's Adrian Karsten arrives with a camera crew for a prearranged interview. After spending some time setting up, Kartsen does the one-minute interview out back by the stream. Fulmer even feeds the trout for the cameras. Dressed in a black Adidas wind suit, the coach gets a haircut before heading to the office.

At noon, he meets with a group, including close friend and Tennessee basketball coach Buzz Peterson, for a Bible study that lasts an hour.

"I like this team," Randy Sanders says in the offensive players' meeting on Friday afternoon. "You are good people. I will tell you what, this weekend will test our maturity. We care about each other. That means something. And most of all, let's have some fun."

The players exit the meeting, which they had attended with their overnight bags in tow, and walk down the street to Neyland Stadium for the walk-through. As the players play around on the field, with linemen tossing balls and kickers running pass routes, the groundskeepers are finishing painting the large orange "T" at midfield. Fulmer watches the offense run through their plays and swings a whistle around his fingers. At the conclusion, his youngest daughter, Allison, arrives, and she and Dad share some hugs as he walks over to talk to the crowd of media.

The players and head trainer Keith Clements board three buses outside the stadium and head to the Radisson Hotel in downtown Knoxville. They eat dinner quickly and reboard the buses to go to the movies. The Regal Cinemas has nine screens, so there are a number of options, and the players can choose any movie that starts between seven and seven thirty. It is an activity to keep the players occupied rather than a team-bonding event. By 10:00 p.m., more than 60 players have assembled in a downstairs banquet room at the Radisson for a voluntary team chapel. Curfew is not until eleven, so some of the players visit with family, friends, and, of course, girlfriends. Two UT police officers stay at the hotel, helping to make sure the players are where they ought to be.

They'll need the rest, as tomorrow they'll be up later than they expect.

• • •

Fulmer and the coaching staff arrive at the hotel in the morning and join the players for breakfast. Fulmer walks in and out of the room and hotel guests ask for pictures with the coach, and he gladly obliges. By ten, the players are mingling on the second floor, most dressed in their orange Adidas warm-up suits. They follow Fulmer downstairs and, despite some light drizzle, trail him on a walk. It is now Tennessee tradition that on game mornings the team and Fulmer take a short walk around the block. So there they are, close to a hundred strong, coaches and trainers included, walking around the Radisson. Fans driving by take notice: it is odd to see so many large men clad in orange.

Steve Caldwell reminds the special teams players that they have worked 40 to 50 kicking snaps in practice this week, which should tell the players just how crucial the kicking game is to victory. The offensive and defensive meetings follow and the position coaches sit with their players in different areas of their respective rooms so they can speak directly to them. Fulmer sits in the front row in the defensive meeting. As Chavis cues up a play on film, a number of conversations break out around the room. There are three red laser pointers aimed at the screen at the same time, as each coach points out something different to his guys. An observer is forced to wonder if different colored lasers might work better.

The meetings end before eleven and the players have the afternoon off before the team dinner at 3:45 p.m. Like most teams' pregame meal, the Vols' is quiet as they chow down on steak, chicken, and pasta. At each seat setting, there is a bright orange place mat with black lettering that reads: "Reach forward to those things which are before you . . . PRESS TOWARD THE MARK . . . forgetting those which are behind. This is one thing I do. Phillipians 3:13."

They board the orange buses waiting outside. Fulmer stands on the first bus with many of the seniors seated behind him, and points the way when the bus driver is about to take a wrong turn, despite the police escort heading in the right direction. The buses make their way down by the river and the Vol Navy is in full force, despite the rain. UT fans along the route shout their support and one South Carolina fan shows his displeasure with a hand gesture.

• • •

"I thought you would be sleeping," the coach says to the team once they're gathered in the team auditorium at the Neyland-Thompson Complex. "I am surprised you're not sleeping. Cause, you know, you are supposed to be asleep after last week's win and not ready for South Carolina."

Having their attention, he continues with a story. When the team was unloading at the Complex just minutes earlier, there was a line of geese flying over the buses in a "V" formation and Fulmer took notice. "You know why geese fly in that formation?" he asks the team. "Because the strongest one goes in front and blocks the wind for the others. When he gets tired, someone else goes to the front." It's quickly clear that they get the point.

Outside, thousands of Tennessee fans line the route from the Complex to the stadium for the traditional Vol Walk. Up a few hills, down a few hills, in the street and on the sidewalk, the path takes the players and coaches a quarter-mile to the stadium. Fulmer leads the way, followed by the team, with the assistants and managers bringing up the rear. Along the route are young and old—a grandmother in a wheelchair with an orange sweater and a young girl, no more than four, fully dressed in a Vols' cheerleader uniform. Halfway through, Vicky Fulmer and her three daughters stand cheering, each getting hugs and kisses from Fulmer as he passes by. The band plays, the cheerleaders cheer, and traffic stops. If you didn't know just how big Tennessee football really is, the walk tells you all you need to know.

• • •

Neyland Stadium may be big, recognizable and legendary, but it is old. There have been renovations over the years, of course, bringing additional seats, a new press box, new concessions, luxury suites, and elevators. The field is in mint condition, having been used only a few times over the course of each year. But the stadium, opened in 1921, shows its age in its bowels, in the concourses, and in the rooms beneath the stands.

Behind one end zone is the newly constructed Wolf-Kaplan Center, a large dining facility opened for the 2002 season. With numerous flat-screen televisions, intricate lighting fixtures, colorful pictures, and expensive furniture, the room serves as a hosting area for recruits, as well as a luncheon room for special events. It is so modern that it feels out of place in the decades-old stadium. Just down the concourse from Wolf-Kaplan is the Tennessee locker room. There are coaches' quarters, a media room, and a training room. The locker-room area consists of two rooms. One is the dressing room, where open wooden lockers with wooden pegs are aligned in rows. Inside of each locker, bronze plaques recognize former Vols who were All-SEC or All-American. The carpet is gray and the walls are white. The second room is a team meeting room, a simple space that holds a hundred folding chairs.

The coaches and players change in the locker room and many wander onto the field to begin warm-ups. Trainers stretch out some players inside. Fulmer, dressed in khaki pants, an orange sweater vest, and a warm-up top, makes his way to the field. He walks over to Seth Andrews, a high school student who once played football but was paralyzed in a tragic accident. His mother wrote Fulmer a letter and the coach invited Andrews and his family to attend a game. Now he is here, in his wheelchair in the end zone, eyes as wide as moons as he watches the Vols warm up. As Fulmer talks to the young man, he strokes Andrews' hands, which rest immobile on the chair's arms. During the game, Andrews will sit in a skybox and get the royal treatment, and he will serve as an honorary team captain.

In the locker room before kickoff, the team, as is custom, shouts General Neyland's maxims written in chalk on the board. In unison, they recite phrases like, "The team that makes the fewest mistakes will win," and, "Protect our kickers, our QBs, our lead, and our ball game." There are seven in all and the players know them by heart. As the team bursts out of the locker room, they each slap a sign in the shape of the state of Tennessee that reads, "I will give my all for Tennessee today."

* * *

Since there was so much emphasis placed on special teams during the week, it is only fitting that a special teams player sets the tone. After the Vols kick off, the defense stops South Carolina and forces a punt. Tennessee's Marvin Mitchell comes from the outside and blocks the sprint-punt from South Carolina's punter Josh Brown and Derrick Tinsley recovers the ball on South Carolina's 10-yard line. Lou Holtz had Brown catch the snap, run to a side, and then kick on the run. The Tennessee coaches had scouted it well and thought they could get a piece from the outside. They did. The crowd gets louder. Two plays later, Casey Clausen hits C. J. Fayton for a nine-yard touchdown pass with just under two minutes gone in the game.

South Carolina fights back on a long drive, behind the sensational running of freshmen backs Demetris Summers and Daccus Turman. Starting from their own 28, the two rush for 50 yards and lead the Gamecocks down the field. Dondrial Pinkins completes a 14-yard pass to Troy Williamson and South Carolina gets a break when, on a third and six from Tennessee's 10, the Vols are called for pass interference. The penalty gives SC first and goal from the two. The Vols stop Summers on his attempt to score, but after a time-out, Turman finishes the drive with a one-yard plunge. The drive goes 72 yards on 10 plays and takes 5:03. Fulmer's face remains expressionless and he simply turns and walks down the sideline, clapping his hands.

The Vols' Corey Larkins returns the kickoff from his goal line to the 33 and the Tennessee drive belongs to Cedric Houston and Casey Clausen. Houston runs and Clausen passes the Volunteers down the field and it's fitting that Houston scores the touchdown on a three-yard run, putting Tennessee ahead 14-7 with 4:40 remaining in the first quarter. After the scoring drive, Clausen is greeted on the sidelines by Randy Sanders, who wants to know what Clausen sees out there.

South Carolina begins its next drive deep in its own territory, but manages to get a first and goal at Tennessee's one and a touchdown looks imminent. But wait. On three consecutive plays, Vol linebacker Robert Peace stops Turman and now the Gamecocks face fourth and goal early in the second quarter. The crowd is going crazy and even Fulmer gets into the act, throwing his hands in the air to encourage yet even more noise. Holtz decides not to kick a field goal, as his kicker is 1 for 5 on the year. Tennessee thinks run. They're wrong. Pinkins rolls to his right on a bootleg and throws a TD to a wide-open Hart Turner. 14-14.

Over the next four possessions, neither team's offense does much. Tennessee moves the ball 18 yards on one possession, then punts. South Carolina manages a quick three-and-out, then punts. Starting with great field position at their 48, Tennessee picks up just two yards in three plays and Dustin Colquitt punts again. South Carolina is no better, gaining just four yards on their next drive. They punt. The four drives last just under seven minutes. Clausen is impatient on the sideline, rarely sitting for more than a few seconds and rarely speaking to anyone. He doesn't seem to panic; rather, he appears to be focused and wants no distractions.

Sanders goes back to the formula that worked on Tenneesse's last scoring drive: run Houston and pass Clausen. Houston gains 26 yards on three carries before Clausen runs for four. Clausen does damage through the air, too, finding Tony Brown for 21 yards, James Banks for 14, and Troy Fleming for 14. With first and 10 from South Carolina's 15, Houston and Brown are stopped on the ground and Clausen's third-down pass attempt to C. J. Fayton is incomplete. James Wilhoit kicks a field goal with under two minutes remaining to give the Vols a 17-14 lead. On the Gamecocks last drive of the half, they manage to get to midfield but Pinkins' last-second Hail Mary is intercepted by Brandon Johnson and the half comes to a close.

• • •

In the locker room, it is as if the team is behind by 21, not up by 3. There is concern on the faces of coaches and players as they settle in. The offensive coaches and Fulmer meet in a hallway in front of a wipe board, where Sanders drew up plays before the game. The Tennessee offense was not able to move the ball well except for the one touchdown drive, and Fulmer is concerned. Tight ends coach Greg Adkins indicates that there is real room behind the left side of the South Carolina defensive line. The linebackers are quick to their right, not their left. Sanders and Fulmer talk about options and decide to try to exploit the space and open up the offense with three or four receiver sets, forcing South Carolina to choose between stopping the run and stopping the pass.

The defensive coaches talk to their players in separate areas on one side of the team room. Chavis is none too pleased with the lack of tackling by his acclaimed defense. Summers, the freshman running back for South Carolina, has over 100 yards in the first half alone. Fulmer walks around to the various small groups on both sides of the ball.

With five minutes before the end of the half, the team gathers in front of the chalkboard. "The first five minutes are critical," Fulmer intones. "This is an old-fashioned SEC East battle."

On its first possession of the second half, the Vols go three-and-out as Clausen can't reach the first-down line on a third-down rush. Dustin Colquitt booms a punt, pinning South Carolina down at its own two. Colquitt punts again on their next posession. This one is downed at South Carolina's one-yard line. Colquitt is the best thing Fulmer has going for him.

Summers takes over for South Carolina, as Houston did for Tennessee in the first half, and the freshman makes some impressive moves rushing for 10, 8, -1, 7, 2, and -6 yards. Pinkins completes a 43-yard pass to Mikal Goodman, and South Carolina kicks a field goal with 5:15 left in the third quarter, tying the game at 17-17. There is tension on the Tennessee sideline. Some of the players are frustrated, others seem startled.

The fourth quarter starts with Tennessee driving at midfield. Houston gets the call on five straight plays but a Vol holding penalty kills the drive. Clausen is forced into a third and 15 and his pass to Jayson Swain is incomplete. With fourth and long at South Carolina's 28, Fulmer calls in Wilhoit for a field goal attempt. He misses wide right and the score remains 17-17.

The Vols commit a personal foul and pass interference on South Carolina's ensuing drive, helping the Gamecocks move from their own 29 to Tennessee's 33. But the Gamecocks hurt themselves with a delay of game. Holtz elects to punt instead of trying a field goal and Bowers gets his punt to go out of bounds at the Vols' eight. Tennessee manages just nine yards and is faced a fourth and one deep in their own territory; the crowd boos as Fulmer sends out the punt team. From a coach's perspective, it is the only call. Colquitt punts again and Summers fumbles the kick but manages to recover on his own 21. Fortunately for Tennessee, the defense steps up late in the game. South Carolina's drive is stopped when an apparent 24-yard catch by Goodman is nullified because he is called for offensive pass interference.

Tennessee has the ball back with 2:49 left in the game, starting from its own 33. SC stops the Vols on three downs. Colquitt—again—rises to the occasion, nailing a punt that is downed at South Carolina's four-yard line. He gets a hug from Fulmer on his way off the field. With just over a minute left, South Carolina runs a few plays and lets the clock expire.

Overtime.

Tennessee wins the coin toss before the extra period and decides to go on defense first—so the offense would know what they had to do when they got the ball. Dondrial Pinkins is sacked for a loss of four yards on the first play of overtime. The second play is an incomplete pass to Troy Williamson but Tennessee is called for pass interference.

South Carolina manages to get to the six and, faced with a fourth and two, Holtz kicks the field goal.

Clausen is calm as he jogs onto the field. He has been in this position before. He hands the ball to Houston on consecutive plays and the back does not disappoint, gaining a critical first down and moving the ball closer to the end zone. On a third down and three from the four, Fulmer and Sanders face a decision—run or pass. A running play is called for Houston but when Clausen spots wideout James Banks isolated in man coverage, he changes the play at the line. He takes three steps back, throws a fade pass to the corner of the end zone, and Banks pulls the ball in. Game over.

Banks is mobbed by teammates in the end zone. Fulmer does not crack a smile, just jogs across the field to meet a stunned Holtz. Brittany Fulmer, who had been standing on the sidelines during the game, reaches over and gives her dad a big kiss and hug. Fulmer goes to the middle of the field where he is joined by Tennessee and South Carolina players for a postgame prayer. As Fulmer walks off the field, holding hands with Brittany, Banks approaches him and gives him a hug.

In the Tennessee locker room, there is joy and relief. The players sit in rows of chairs, with Athletic Director Mike Hamilton looking on. Fulmer begins to speak, then stops, as the Tennessee fight song breaks out, and all of the players stand and sing loudly.

"You have to win games like that," Fulmer says in a hoarse voice. "This was not our best game and I am sure we will have a lot to work on after watching film. Hey, our hats off to South Carolina."

He awards the game ball to Colquitt and many of the players stand up and cheer. The team moved forward tonight, the coach tells them, but reminds them that "all they [the games] do is get bigger."

Everyone in the room, managers, players, coaches, and visitors, kneel and say a prayer. Most of the players head to the showers, some do radio and television interviews in an adjoining room. When Chavis walks in, Fulmer grabs him and gives him a bear hug and proclaims, "I love this guy." But Fulmer's work is not yet quite over. He walks back into the meeting room and greets many of the recruits and guests whom he had met earlier. Next is his press conference, where he admits that the Tennessee performance wasn't great, but asserts that the end result is.

After the last question, all four of his kids and his wife join him on the podium. They give each other hugs and kisses. It is as if no one else is around. All that matters is them.

· · ·

Presiding over the Tennessee empire could make an emperor out of a man, but Phillip Fulmer has resisted the temptation. He leads by remembering where he comes from, by acknowledging that he doesn't have all of the answers, and by understanding the demands of the position. His approach as a grassroots CEO works. The fact that he has survived—and won—at Tennessee for over a decade proves it. His job is safe. For now.

CHAPTER 5

Breakfast with the Fridge

The University of Maryland

**Maryland vs. Clemson
College Park, Maryland
September 28–October 4**

The season did not start out the way Ralph Friedgen and the Terrapins had hoped, nor how the pollsters had predicted. Maryland was ranked 15th to start the season but immediately dropped after being upset by Northern Illinois on the road and losing to Florida State. They regrouped and have won three in a row. Led by quarterback Scott McBrien, they now face Clemson at home, their season hanging in the balance.

• • •

It was a long wait. Almost 30 years.

Ralph Friedgen grew up in the working-class town of Harrison, in upstate New York, the son of a football coach. In high school, football, basketball, and baseball consumed him. He accepted a football scholarship to the University of Maryland, where he entered as a quarterback and left as an offensive lineman with a degree in Physical Education in 1970. During the 1969 season, Friedgen worked as a student coach/GA and stayed on until 1972 in that capacity. His first full-time coaching job was at The Citadel, where he worked with the defensive line before becoming the offensive coordinator under Bobby Ross. In 1980, he spent a year as offensive coordinator at William & Mary, followed by a year as the assistant head coach at Murray State.

Destiny brought Friedgen back to Maryland, where he again worked under Ross, and helped lead his alma mater to unprecedented success as the offensive coordinator. During Ross's tenure at Maryland, the Terps won three straight ACC championships. When Ross moved down south to Georgia Tech, Friedgen followed. When Ross moved to the NFL and the San Diego Chargers, Friedgen went along, working as an assistant coach for running backs and tight ends and then as offensive coordinator. In 1994, the Chargers advanced to the Super Bowl. Friedgen and his family returned to Georgia Tech in 1997 where he served as the offensive coordinator for the next three years as he continued to impress athletic directors and his peers.

By the early 1990s, Friedgen was prepared to be a head coach and made no secret of his desire to be one. But no one would hire him. Among the head jobs that he went for over the years were those at Clemson, Duke, South Carolina, Virginia, North Carolina State, Connecticut, and Maryland—this last one he went for three times. He was a finalist for some of them, for others he didn't even get a call back. At one point, after missing out on the job at N.C. State, the coach thought "maybe it was not in the cards" for him to be the head man, though he admits he "probably wouldn't be fulfilled" unless he got a head job. Friedgen and his wife, Gloria, decided to build a lake house outside Atlanta, where it looked like they would stay. But destiny—and Maryland—beckoned.

When Gloria talks about her husband, she swells with pride, trying hard to hide frustration at how long he waited to become a head coach. What eats at her more than anything is the fact that her husband did not get a head job offer—and not because he wasn't qualified. "It upset me the most because people were judging Ralph on his physical appearance. He wasn't on the phone looking for jobs and he isn't flashy or great with the press." But as it turns out, that's not what Maryland's athletic director was looking for.

Toward the end of the 2000 season, Georgia Tech traveled to Maryland. At the time, it was no secret that Maryland's coach, Ron Vanderlinden, was on the hot seat and probably on his way out. With less than 20,000 in attendance at the game, Friedgen headed out onto the field for pregame warm-ups as usual. Vanderlinden approached him and spent 15–20 minutes telling him all about Maryland and the players on the team. "I thought it was a little weird," Friedgen recalls. After the game, which Tech won, Vanderlinden was fired and the speculation began. Terp athletic director Debbie Yow had Friedgen on her radar as Georgia Tech prepared for a huge game against rival Georgia. But the coach had gotten accustomed to getting his hopes up and he knew his alma mater had rejected him twice before. But this time was different. "I felt like I knew him," Yow says.

On the Thursday after Vanderlinden's firing, Yow and Friedgen finally spoke on the phone. "I'm seriously interested if you're interested," the coach told Yow, "but don't waste my time." On Sunday, Yow flew down to Atlanta and met with Friedgen at a suite at the Airport Marriott. The two hit it off. Before answering a question, Friedgen turned the tables and asked a simple one: "Why haven't you guys won since I left Maryland?" Yow's response took nearly an hour. When she finished, the coach had another question: "What does a good football program mean to you?" Friedgen was prepared and must have made an impression, because at one point, Yow leaned over and said, "You're my guy."

Yow still had to conduct further interviews to satisfy others, but there was no doubt that Friedgen was indeed her guy. They discussed a visit to Maryland on Monday. Upon Friedgen's return to his house in Atlanta, a prominent Georgia Tech booster was waiting. He knew. Whatever it would take to keep him at Tech, they were willing to do it, he said. "This decision isn't about the money," the coach replied.

Monday morning, the Friedgens flew to College Park, where Gloria was shown around campus as Friedgen met with the school president, Dr. C. D. Mote. He was impressed that Mote appeared to be committed to football and seemed to understand what it was going to take to build a national program. The coach met with members of the administration and with a player committee. One player, Aaron Thompson, asked the coach, "So coach, what are you going to do to make us win that other coaches haven't done?" Friedgen succinctly summarized his philosophy: He'd teach them to avoid beating themselves; he'd teach them how not to lose; he'd teach them to believe that they can win. After the interviews concluded, Yow formally offered Friedgen the job. "I'm a perfectionist, impatient yet professional," he told her. "I don't lie don't ever lie to me. If you want me to be the coach, then I run the show," he said, though he promised he would consult with her on major matters. The Friedgens flew back to Atlanta, without giving Yow an answer. She said she would call the next morning and expect one. After so many years of striving for a head job, Friedgen finally had an offer but didn't take it right away.

The coach stayed up deep into Monday night. At 6:00 a.m. on Tuesday morning, Friedgen's phone rang. Yow wanted an answer and Friedgen gave her the one she wanted: "Yes." Friedgen informed Georgia Tech coach George O'Leary Tuesday morning and packed up his office. O'Leary did not want him to have a team meeting to say good-bye to the players and didn't want Friedgen to coach in the Peach Bowl against LSU. In a matter of hours, Friedgen was on his way to College Park. "Athletic directors hope for the best," Yow reflects. "I have an obligation to Maryland. I knew about his coaching and phi-losophy but I didn't know how smart he is. He is savvy, intelligent, with critical thinking skills. I had no way of knowing his work ethic."

An assistant for 30 years before finally getting a head job, Ralph Friedgen had the chance—at his alma mater, no less. And he's not the only one in town that's excited he's here.

"People are excited about Coach Friedgen," Alpha Epsilon Phi so-rority president Gail Sweeney says. "Before Coach Friedgen, students went to games for the social atmosphere. Now they go for the game." And what a game Saturday is shaping up to be.

• • •

The Maryland coaching staff is at work at 7:30 sharp on Monday morning. Ralph Friedgen has been in the office since seven, watch-ing film of Clemson and reviewing statistics from Saturday's win at Eastern Michigan, which put Maryland at 3-2 on the year. As he walks into the offensive meeting room, which also doubles as the staff room, his assistants are seated around the oval table, awaiting his arrival. On the walls are two sets of wipe boards and a three-month master calendar with key recruiting dates. In the middle of the table sits a box of Maryland football stationery, which the assistants are using to write letters to recruits as the staff meeting gets under way.

The coach passes out the practice schedule for Monday night's session. It follows the familiar pattern of individual skill work, group work, skellys, and team drills. Like some other schools, Maryland practices on Monday nights to allow the coaching staff more time to work on the upcoming game plan and allow the players more time to recover from Saturday's game. Next in the meeting, the coaches re-view the scout personnel to make sure that the right scout players are assigned to impersonate the right Clemson players to give the starters the most accurate look at the Tigers' plays.

It is not yet 8:00 a.m. when the meeting ends. Friedgen stays in the room for the offensive meeting this morning, joined by offensive coordinator Charlie Taaffe, offensive line coach Tom Brattan, re-ceivers coach James Franklin, running backs coach Bill O'Brien, and

tight ends coach Ray Rychleski. Friedgen, GAs, and everyone in between make a collaborative effort to break down the Clemson film.
The comments are informal and so are the salutations—assistants
refer to Friedgen as "Ralph." As they watch film, they notice that the
Clemson corners play soft on receivers, meaning they play many
yards off the line, and as a result short passes might come easy. There
is not much blitzing by the Clemson defense and, in fact, not a lot of
pressure on the quarterback. But none of these facts mean much if
the Terps can't execute.

• • •

The heart of Maryland football is the Gossett Team House on the
south end of Byrd Stadium. The building is surrounded by a chain-
link fence, dirt, cranes, and metal. The construction is a sign of things
to come. Crews are in the middle of a multiphase expansion, adding
a cafeteria, team meeting room, Hall of Fame, and new entranceway.
The coaches' offices have recently been redone and an academic center for the football team has already been built. Covers of Maryland
game programs line the walls just inside the glass double-doors at the
second-floor entrance. Down a flight of stairs is a large black-and-
white photograph of Byrd Stadium from a game in November 1961.
A hallway is lined with pictures of past teams and painted portraits
of Maryland All-Americans. Inside the red and black weight room,
painted slogans on the walls include "Strength punishes, speed kills"
and "Today's preparation determines tomorrow's achievement." The
phrase "Iron Terps" is painted on a wall. On the far side of the room,
doors lead directly onto the playing field in Byrd Stadium.

An ACC Champion sign, close to eight feet in length, hangs outside the locker room. It reads, "Think It, Believe It, Make It Happen."
Across the hall, there are progress charts and a spring practice awards'
list. The lockers are arranged in rows, with a large open space of carpet in the back of the locker room, in front of the exit to the field. The
carpet is gray and bears a large "M" logo in the middle. Former All-
American and All-ACC players' names are attached to the front of
the lockers. Above the locker-room door is a simple sign: "What you
see here, What you say here, Stays here." A chart headed with "2003
Terrapin Team Goals" includes winning the ACC and the national
championship.

Upstairs on the second floor, between the position meeting
rooms, pictures from last season's Peach Bowl victory over Tennessee
hang on the walls. Deeper into the office suite are the assistant

coaches' offices. Friedgen's office is in between, across the hall from the offensive and defensive staff rooms. His office is expansive and has an impressive view of the stadium field, as it sits 20 feet above the end zone. There is a television, microwave, and refrigerator in the office, as well as a private bathroom. A large "Terps" logo is on the floor. There are pictures of the coach's wife, his children, and the coach with various players and dignitaries, including one of Friedgen and his wife with President Bush at a recent White House correspondents' dinner. There are plaques on the wall, most of which are awards for service or for his phenomenal 2001 season when he received most of the postseason Coach of the Year awards.

With a 3-2 start to the 2003 season, it doesn't look like the coach will be adding another one this year. Or will he?

• • •

The staff works through lunch on Monday and before they know it it's 2:00 p.m. The defensive players meet with their position coaches and spend over an hour watching the Eastern Michigan game film. Many of the players read grade sheets of their performances along the way. A floor below, the offense is in the weight room getting in a lift. At 3:15, the players switch, and the offense meets with their coaches as the defense lifts. In the offensive line meeting, Tom Brattan hands out a complete grade sheet, detailing every offensive play, and each player's grade on that play—0,1, or 2.

"Congratulations on the win, guys," he begins. "Now we're 3-2 and above average. We still didn't play great. And this next game is going to be war."

Brattan spends the next hour showing the players every play from the Eastern Michigan game, starting and stopping the film to show the mistakes. The players are attentive and sharp in their self-criticism, and in answering Bratton's questions. The coach doesn't get all the way through because the team meeting is set for 4:15. The players get up, turn their chairs around, and push aside the partition wall that separates their meeting room from the main team room.

"Congratulations on the win," Friedgen tells the team before reading off the offense, defense, and special teams goals that were set for the EMU game and whether or not the team had met them. Then he turns to Clemson. "This is a big, big, big, big game. It's on TV and if you want to climb in the polls you have to play well on TV. This is the third straight game we will have 50,000-plus out there."

The players head to dinner. Special teams meet at 5:45 and coach

Ray Rychleski rapidly shows them the kicks, returns, and coverages from Saturday's game. He compliments some, corrects others, and warns everyone about the Tigers. "They have the best kick return in the country. They are good."

Clemson is #1 in kick return in the ACC. Maryland is #2 in kick coverage. Who will win the battle?

* * *

The new $3 million practice complex boasts three fully lighted fields 200 yards from the Team House. One field has Field Turf with goalposts, the other two are grass. There is a portable electronic clock and a 25-second clock, a permanent viewing tower, and cranes for video cameras. Sled dummies are built into the ground off to the side and speakers are attached to posts to provide music and crowd noise. Music? "After the Florida State game, I thought our guys were a little too tight and I wanted to loosen them up," says Friedgen. So now during warm-ups and conditioning at the end of practice, a variety of music, from hip-hop to country, blasts from the speakers.

Just as the team stretch begins, Friedgen arrives in a golf cart. After a hip replacement in the spring, he still cannot stand or walk for long periods. Wearing tan pants, a sweatshirt, a red jacket, and white baseball cap, he surveys the team stretch from the 50-yard line.

Though it is Monday and the players are not in full pads, it is an intense practice as the coaching staff exposes the players to Clemson. Defensive line coach Dave Sollazzo is particularly fired up and his voice echoes across the fields as he "encourages" his linemen. The offense works on skelly drills; Friedgen stands off to the side making notes. The coach's philosophy is to have much of the game plan in place by Monday night. The offense runs over 120 scripted plays during practice. Practice ends with a two-minute drill, this one starting on the offense's own 33, with two time-outs and 1:23 to go in the game. The drill does not go as hoped, as the first-team offense is picked off twice trying to move the ball down the field. After kick coverage and full-field sprints, practice comes to a close at 9:00 p.m. The coaching staff goes inside and begins the task of analyzing the practice film.

Unfortunately, it won't be the worst practice of the week.

* * *

Sophomore linebacker Shawne Merriman did not have to go to Maryland. Yes, he was from Frederick Douglass High School in Upper

Marlboro, Maryland, just 20 minutes from College Park, but he was good enough to go almost anywhere. As a high school senior, rated the top linebacker in the state and #14 nationwide, Merriman had interest from Florida, Notre Dame, North Carolina State, South Carolina, and many more. But the 6'3", 246-pounder chose Maryland. "I wanted to go to Maryland the whole time. I wanted to play early and I knew I could do that at Maryland." Did Friedgen play a role in Merriman's decision? "The coach, he let me know the ins and outs. I could tell he wanted to win so badly."

In his freshman season last year, Merriman played in all 14 games and even started one, almost unheard of for a true freshman. He had 5 sacks on the year, third highest on the team. He is a physical specimen with a vertical leap of 41½ inches, a 365-pound bench press, and a 565-pound squat. But Merriman has done more than bulked up physically—his football knowledge has improved, as well. "I knew that he [Friedgen] was a pretty good coach. I didn't know how much he put in the extra effort. There is no way this is not going to be a great program."

The super sophomore was a standout tight end in high school and wanted to play both sides of the ball for the Terps. Friedgen convinced him otherwise. "I wanted to play more positions than one. I wanted to play tight end. But Coach Friedgen said that great athletes only improve over time and to focus on linebacker. It was the positive way to go about it. He's like a football father."

Though he has been in the college game for only two years, Merriman understands that the things he learns on the football field translate into life lessons. "College football brings out great discipline. It is the closest thing to life. School, great athletes, competing for starting positions. It makes you a better person."

• • •

Before the sun is up on Tuesday, Friedgen has parked his Cadillac Escalade outside the offices and sits behind his desk. He normally arrives before six, when the office is empty, no matter what time he left the previous night. He constructs the practice plan for the afternoon, having talked to his coordinators last night before determining if they want time for anything specific. The defensive staff spends the morning watching film, including clips from last year's Maryland-Clemson game, a 30-12 Maryland victory at Death Valley. Occasionally, defensive coordinator Gary Blackney stops the film, approaches the wipe board, and draws plays as assistants Dave Sollazzo, Tim Banks, and Al Seamonson chime in.

Just feet away, the offense is doing the same thing. Friedgen, dressed in suit pants, a blue-and-white-striped dress shirt, and a white sweater vest, leads a discussion on an offensive blocking scheme. The coaches are trying to figure out how they should block the secondary, the line, and the linebackers on certain plays. The trick is for them to find the best scheme to block it without having to make a lot of changes to the Maryland offense—to "keep their rules in place." All of the coaches contribute to the discussion, which lasts longer than Friedgen plans.

Sports Information Assistant Director Greg Creese is waiting for the head coach in Friedgen's office for a conference call with Clemson reporters. Friedgen excuses himself from the offensive meeting and takes a seat behind his desk. There are only two reporters on the call, so Friedgen anticipates a quick conversation. The first questions are about Friedgen's long wait to become a head coach, pointed particularly at some of the ACC jobs he wanted but didn't get. "I just kept persevering and I guess good things happen," the coach remarks. In response to another question about the long wait, he says that there are many people out there wanting jobs who think that "if you have a hat and a whistle, you are qualified to coach."

When the call is over, Friedgen and Creese head up to the press box in Byrd Stadium where the coach tapes his pregame radio interview with play-by-play man Johnny Holiday. He holds his weekly press conference, where he talks about injuries, Clemson, and the fortitude of past Terp teams before a crowd of 20 reporters and six television cameras. With major metropolitan markets Washington, D.C. and Baltimore sandwiching College Park, there is no shortage of media interest in Maryland football.

In the running backs meeting Tuesday afternoon, coach Bill O'Brien instructs the backs on the changes that the staff made earlier in the day to the blocking schemes. He thinks some of the players are not fully attentive, but his opinion changes when they are able to answer his "pop quiz" questions. "It's going to be a great practice today," he says.

Wishful thinking.

Tuesday is the week's longest practice. It is a sunny, crisp day, perfect for football in College Park, and the players seem ready to go. The 3 versus 3 drill is one of Friedgen's favorite. It really is not three players versus three players. Four linemen plus a tight end and a backfield line up against different defenses and run through running plays. Two sets of these groups run plays side by side, one right after the other. They get in 28 reps in six minutes of work. But today, Friedgen is not thrilled with the pace of the drill, and the position coaches—particularly Bill O'Brien, who thought it would be a good practice—are not thrilled with their players.

By the time practice gets to the first and second teams going against the scouts, things have gone from bad to worse. The offensive line cannot stop the scout team, the running backs cannot hold on to the ball, the scout team lines up incorrectly, the 25-second clock in the end zone malfunctions. Friedgen is infuriated. He turns red, raises his voice for the first time all week, and walks as if his hip is 100 percent. He calms down a bit before addressing the team.

"Winners win the big games, losers lose the big games. Are you winners or are you losers?" he asks. He points out the poor performance by the offense, who got their "butts kicked" by the scouts and shakes his head as he thinks out loud, "I just don't know right now. I just don't know." After practice, Friedgen acknowledges that things are not always as bad or as good as coaches think once they sit down to look at the practice film, which the coaches do Tuesday night. There are some bright spots, particularly the receivers, but the offensive line does not look any better on film, nor does the second team offense.

The work has just begun.

• • •

There are yawns and tired eyes. With Friedgen sitting in, Taaffe, O'Brien, Franklin, Brattan, and Rychleski watch film of Clemson's defense. Third down and long, red zone, and two-minute offense dominate conversation for the staff on Wednesday, as goal line, second and long, and normal down and distance dominated on Tuesday. For the offense, it is a matter of figuring out what to do—or, actually, figuring out what Clemson will do. The thinking goes like this: Clemson will be watching film of the Terps' last four games, trying to come up with a scheme to prevent success; Friedgen and his staff will attempt to guess what they think Clemson will do in response to what Maryland has done and then create a game plan based on that. Got it? At times in the discussion, there are long pauses as the coaches stare at a board or into space, trying to visualize the multiple moves in a play, trying to picture what the defensive reaction will be.

Next door, the defensive staff is trying to eliminate plays. There are dozens written on the board as part of a tentative game plan. Defensive GA Greg Sesny comes in around 11:00 so that he can input the plays into his computer, which will spit out player wristbands for the afternoon practice. Once the plan is set Thursday night, the bands will be redone. But a wristband is only so big and Blackney and the assistants attempt to get the list down.

"Let me remind you of this," defensive line coach Dave Sollazzo starts his position meeting on Wednesday afternoon, "our last game against Clemson they had the ball five times in the red zone and came away with four field goals—12 points. That's what won us the game." He speaks in a booming voice and his message gets across. On every play he reviews on film with the players, he points out who is too high in his stance and takeoff. He wants players' backs so flat that, "I can eat a turkey sandwich off that back." Getting to Clemson's quarterback Charlie Whitehurst is critical to the Terps' effectiveness on defense.

The music accompanying Wednesday's warm-up is the Clemson fight song, followed by heavy metal. Tuesday and Wednesday are NFL scout days, and the scouts on hand seem amused by the music. Representatives from the Redskins, Colts, and Cardinals are among those in attendance, all armed with notepads and roster charts. The scouts are asked to leave after six periods. Practice is steady and up-tempo. Friedgen watches carefully as the offense runs plays off the script and makes notes for which plays he wants redone at the end of each period. He is pleasantly pleased with the play on offense. The defense, however, does not get high praise from Blackney, who says the first-team defense is "above average" while the second team "stinks." It is 6:15 when Friedgen blows his whistle and concludes practice.

"This was a good practice today, certainly better than yesterday. I am interested in some comments by [Clemson] Coach Bowden. He said, 'They wanted to be where we are and we have a target on our backs.' Well, I disagree. But this is going to be real battle. You guys need to get in here this week and watch film and study the game plan so on Saturday you are reacting, not thinking."

He drives the golf cart back to his office to do a live satellite interview with Comcast SportsNet from behind his desk. After that, four reporters come into his office to ask questions. The hot topic is the tentative ACC schedule for the next two years, which was released just hours earlier. A few minutes after his interviews conclude, a prized recruit arrives with his high school coach and Friedgen goes to work.

• • •

Ralph Friedgen knows football. The 2003 college football preview issue of *Sports Illustrated* recognizes him as having the best football mind. His playbook consists of hundreds and hundreds of pages, thousands of variations on running and passing plays. But beyond his ability to grasp X's and O's, Friedgen's is a mind with a vision. He has a clear picture of what it will take to get Maryland football to the elite level. Yes, it takes millions of dollars to build nice facilities like the new practice complex and additions to the Gossett Team House. But it takes more than that. It takes an attitude and a mind-set—for the players, coaches, and fans—that, indeed, they are capable of joining the elite. So how do you take a decent program and make it into something special?

"First, you need to know what the problems are," Friedgen insists. For him, the problems at Maryland were fairly obvious. "Nobody was in the seats," the coach recognized. "People want to watch exciting football with an explosive offense and an attacking defense." They had to win—and win "pretty"—to attract fans. You have to "go to the people," and Friedgen has done plenty of that in his first three seasons. From speaking engagements to media interviews, from alumni golf outings to his community breakfast on Friday mornings, Friedgen does whatever it takes to get his face, and his program, to the masses.

There is the money game, as well. "We need to get more people actively involved. We have 7,500 people in our Terrapin Club, but we should have 25,000 with all of our alumni base." There is a gala event and auction in the spring that raises money. With plans to add seats to Byrd Stadium now in the works, donations become even more crucial.

The coach recognizes that you must have a plan, a vision of where you want to go, even if it changes yearly. "It's not just about wins and losses, though we better win. It's about getting better recruits, increasing the graduation rate, getting more people to buy season tickets." There is much left to accomplish, but Friedgen has already narrowed the gap between his vision and reality and he has convinced his bosses to do the same. "Since Ralph's hiring," Yow points out, "we have pumped an extra $14 million into the athletic program. We have one of the highest paid staffs in the conference."

As he has built the program, Friedgen has done more than just win football games. He brought to life Terp Alley, a new game day tradition where the players and coaches walk through crowds of fans en route to the stadium, à la the Vol Walk or Dawg Walk. He invites the community to breakfast on Friday mornings before home games, planning and hosting the program himself. He reaches out to academia, striving to bridge the wide gap between athletics and academics, inviting deans to his house, to practices, and to games. He makes subtle changes to the football program. When the team sits to eat a meal together, the pecking order for the buffet is determined by grade point averages. When the dorm lottery is held each spring to determine rooming assignments for the fall, those with the highest GPAs get to choose first within their class level. Players with high GPAs are allowed to miss some of the daily mandatory breakfasts. Motivation, Friedgen believes, is in the details. The coach instituted a council of 11 players consisting of representatives of all the classes, that meets regularly with the coach to express the players' concerns and provides him with a sounding board for his ideas.

Friedgen's vision for Maryland football plays a role in every decision he makes, from recruiting to facilities to fund-raising. His eye is always on the future. His unique football mind garners attention from outsiders, but perhaps his most precious gift is his ability to understand the culture that surrounds him. After all, he did wait years for the opportunity, and that is a long time to spend crafting a vision.

• • •

Coaches James Franklin and Bill O'Brien stand up and demonstrate a blocking move for backers Thursday morning during the offensive staff meeting. They are watching film from yesterday's practice and are conflicted about which is the proper technique. Friedgen has excused himself to meet with a player. Apparently, the player has not been performing up to standards and has been lazy in practice. When the coach confronts him, the player denies taking plays off. That's when Friedgen goes to the tape. He shows him 12 plays from practices during the week where he clearly did not go hard. The coach tells him to step up or be replaced. Discussion over. When Friedgen returns to the staff room, he runs the film from the Clemson–Georgia Tech game, a blowout win for the Tigers and their best game so far in the season. Before each snap, Charlie Taaffe calls out the play that the Terps would run in that down-and-distance scenario—it is a rehearsal of the game plan, to see how things match up. Friedgen has done this before, but not since last year. After watching film alone very early in the morning, he wants to make sure the coaching staff is ready for all possibilities.

On Thursday, as is now a weekly tradition, Friedgen spends two hours meeting with individual players. Each week, he asks a group of six or seven players, some newcomers, some veterans, to meet with him in his office. For a few, it is a time for a reprimand or a stern warning; for others, the coach levels praise and encouragement. By the end of the season, every player has made the visit at least once. Some of the meetings are warm, some are chilly.

After a solid practice with minimal errors, Friedgen recognizes players who have done well on tests and papers in Kinesiology and Family Studies classes. After hearing his name called, each player walks to the front of the team and shakes hands with the head coach. Next, Friedgen recognizes the scout team players of the week and announces the captains for Saturday. Now, for Clemson. "This is a very big game for us. Being 4-2 and having momentum is a lot better than 3-3 and starting over." After a brief pause, he asks, "Are you tired of wearing rings? Do you still remember that our goal is the ACC Championship? You get what you put in. If a championship is what you want, then you have to put in the work on Saturday."

Reporters are waiting in Friedgen's office after practice, as well as students from the student radio station to tape a pregame interview. It is a quick session, and Friedgen hurries off to a local high school to watch one of his daughters play in a volleyball match, as he promised he would. By the time he arrives, the match is over.

• • •

Friday morning, Ralph Friedgen has breakfast with some friends. About 350 of them.

In what has become a Maryland tradition, Friedgen invites the entire Maryland community—students, fans, alumni, boosters, and family—to the University of Maryland Inn & Conference Center on the southwest side of campus, for a free continental breakfast and some football talk on the Fridays before home games. Many head coaches stop in to a booster luncheon during game weeks, though usually only for a few minutes. But Friedgen's breakfast, or "Breakfast with The Fridge," is his idea and he hosts the program. It started out in 2001 as a small gathering but grew to as many as 900 during the 2001 and 2002 seasons. The coach talks about the previous game and the next day's opponent, and answers questions for more than

45 minutes on topics from game day parking to concession food to nickel defenses to his wife's tailgate party.

There are many people in the crowd wearing red this morning, from silver-haired alums to a 10-year-old boy, who probably should be in school. The coach begins promptly at 7:30 a.m., talking about the win over Eastern Michigan. He talks about the Clemson game, how the outcome could dictate the season, how critical special teams will be, especially kick coverage. He adds a unique feature to the breakfast on this day—an 11-minute video presentation by defensive line coach Dave Sollazzo. Sollazzo taped a segment on Thursday on signaling in plays, before hitting the road to recruit on Friday. Friedgen warns the audience about Sollazzo's standard decibel levels and then introduces the segment in which Sollazzo explains how plays are signaled in to players during games.

(It's also worthy of mention that Friedgen greatly surprises this author by inviting him on stage to explain this book project and answer questions.)

Afterward, the coach makes some comments and takes questions from the audience. "This has been a tough team to coach . . . There is true parity in college football . . . I've had discussions with [running back] Bruce [Perry] about the NFL and I told him, 'They want to see you practice and play, even with some injuries.' " The coach is candid with his words, as if speaking to three close friends over a late-night beer. It is part of his charm but a habit that has gotten him, and will get him, in trouble. Comments that he believes are "off the record" have been known to end up in newspapers. He speaks his mind and, for a coach, that is not always a good thing.

* * *

The kitchen in the Friedgen family home is the center of the house, both literally and figuratively. Gloria Friedgen grew up in an Italian family where food, family, and church dominated life. It is in the kitchen on Friday afternoon that Gloria finds herself, wearing a white apron and stirring pots on the stove. Before every home game, she hosts a tailgate party outside the stadium for invited guests and walk-ups. The crowd can number in the hundreds. On Wednesday afternoons, she and her good friend and "tailgate coordinator" Debbie Bebee go out to the grocery store to stock up on ingredients. She cooks all day Friday, typically offering a menu of antipasto, sausage, and ziti. As she works, her mother and stepfather mingle about, having moved in with the Friedgens last year when Gloria's mother became ill. She talks, cooks, and answers the phone all at once. She is a multitasker, just like her husband.

The Friedgens live 18 miles from campus in Silver Spring, an upscale locale where home prices are high and the Washington elite head for privacy. A large turtle greets guests on their front porch. On the way downstairs to the basement, there is a framed needlepoint of the phrase, "You have to pay the price"—a philosophy Friedgen lives by. On the basement walls are framed newspaper and magazine clippings of his hiring at Maryland, Georgia Tech's 1990 upset win over then #1 Virginia, and a plaque engraved with Vince Lombardi's famed "What It Takes To Be #1." There is a large portrait of Friedgen given to him by the Atlanta Touchdown Club upon winning the National Coach of the Year honors in 2001. Along with a large-screen television, a VCR, and couches, there are signed pictures of the San Diego Chargers teams he coached in the mid-1990s.

Upstairs, in his first-floor office are plaques, trophies, and footballs, honoring many of his achievements along with his diplomas from the University of Maryland—a Bachelor's in Physical Education and a Master's in Psychology of Sport. There are shelves filled with the family's books, from John Grisham novels to a *Fathers Are Special* keepsake. A case holds the priceless rings and watches earned over a 30-year coaching career: ACC Champion rings won as an assistant at Maryland, the Georgia Tech national title ring, bowl rings, and watches. Below the case are cabinets filled with clippings, articles, and artifacts that Gloria has kept over the years. "I will get to them soon," she says. The family room has pictures dating back four decades, some with Friedgen sporting a mustache. His former boss and close friend, Bobby Ross, is pictured as well, as he is the godfather to one of the Friedgen's daughters. They have three: Kelley, Kristina, and Katharine.

They are a partnership, Ralph and Gloria, perfect for one another. She takes an active role in the program, advising players as a mother, tutoring players in the academic center, arranging the annual gala and auction. Each year, she has a sheet made up of the freshmen players' pictures and names so she can memorize them and greet them like family. Having been a Phys. Ed. and Biology teacher for 28 years, she understands the dynamics of education—and she understands teenagers. She has also learned what it means to be a coach's wife. "You have to be very independent. You cannot be the center of your husband's life."

Tomorrow, game day, Gloria will be in the stands, right where she has always been for her husband.

• • •

The coach tapes an interview with ABC on Friday afternoon, speaking with play-by-play man and Maryland alum Tim Brandt. At 3:30, he puts on his red Terps' jacket and walks downstairs onto the field for the team walk-through. It is cold, but the players and coaches ignore it. They stretch and walk through plays separately, as offense and defense. Then everyone moves to the sidelines and Friedgen calls out over 30 different plays and formations for the offense, defense, and special teams, and players sprint onto the field and begin their movements. It is all over by 4:15. The players are loose and joke with one another, and in his postpractice comments, the coach makes sure to remind them just how big a game it is. He knows that the outcome will decide which way his team goes this season and he fears the game will be tougher than his players think.

The team arrives at the Hilton in Silver Spring and sits down for dinner in a second-floor banquet room. Some players finish eating before others and, as has become tradition, players Wesley Jefferson and Russell Bonham sit down at a piano in the hallway and entertain their teammates. As the last scoops of ice cream are gulped down, Friedgen announces that Devotions will start in the adjacent meeting room. Forty of the players attend, all dressed in black Nike warm-ups. They sit in chairs and listen to Joe Daniels, a pastor in a local church and former basketball player at Maryland, read the detailed story of David versus Goliath. Perhaps Daniels doesn't realize that the teams are evenly matched, so the metaphor is a bit of stretch. But he goes on to talk about being champions in life and on the field, about doing the best with what you have.

After Devotions, Gary Blackney shows his players game film in the defensive meeting, as Friedgen looks on. Blackney asks for the proper calls for the alignments on the screen. "Left! Right! Vegas! Reno!" the players mumble. At one point, Friedgen interrupts and asks specific players why they are making that call. The offensive players join them 15 minutes later for the special teams meeting, which Friedgen runs, as assistant Ray Rychleski is on the road recruiting. He checks personnel by calling out punt and kick coverage and returns and having the players on those teams stand up to be counted. The entire team soon joins the meeting, and Friedgen shows them a highlight video of catches, runs, and hits from the Eastern Michigan game. It gets the players excited. When it is over, Friedgen stands up in front of the group.

"You guys are loose. It's the loosest I've seen you. I don't know if that is a good thing or a bad thing." He reads a quote, which comes from Clemson's Tommy Bowden, who has said his team is hungrier than Maryland. "What I think he is saying is that you guys don't want it. That you are not hungry." Friedgen calls on individual players, challenging them in a loud voice and removing his glasses. To receiver Latrez Harrison : "Are you going to get stuck on the line when they hold you? You complained when the scout guy team shut you down. Is that going to happen tomorrow?"

He calls out other players and challenges their heart, their toughness. He indicates that maybe this team isn't hungry, that maybe it is complacent. "The older guys in this room know. When we got here you guys would have given your right arm to play in a bowl or to wear a championship ring. Do you not care anymore? The seniors know what it was like. No respect. The students would tailgate in the parking lot and have no interest in coming into the stadium. No respect from the media. I thought a ring meant something to you."

He continues, "Tomorrow is a big game. I think it is going to dictate the rest of the season. Are you hungry? I know I am," he jokes, a reference to his girth that cracks up the players. "You are loose. I guess we'll see tomorrow. I don't know, but I guess if you're loose that's a good thing. I don't know."

• • •

Friedgen is well rested for breakfast on Saturday morning, and he and and the team have taken on a different mood. The laughs and smiles from Friday night have been replaced by silence and faces forged of stone. Dressed in a black sweater and black suit pants, Friedgen sits at a table with his coordinators and discusses aspects of the game plan. At nine, the team meets as offense and defense, but Friedgen stays behind in the breakfast room. He sits alone as the servers clear the tables and lays out the game plan charts in front of him. Using multicolored highlighters, he begins to detail the game plan.

By 9:30, the entire staff gathers in yet another meeting room for something most staffs do not do on game days. The seven assistant coaches who have been on the road on Thursday night and Friday give their reports on recruiting. Some met with high school coaches, some spoke with guidance counselors. Some flew as far south as

Tampa, some drove on the Beltway to local schools. They discuss the status of the recruitments and the academic standing of recruits. They talk about a few of their committed kids who are trying to finish up high school early and enroll at Maryland in January. Friedgen is astute in his memory and warns some of the assistants that "sure things" can always fall apart.

The coach asks the defensive staff questions about the game plan, then excuses them, and reviews the battle plan with the offensive coaches. He tells them he thinks that Clemson will play a lot of man coverage and that Maryland should run the option frequently. Though Friedgen actively involves himself in the offensive meetings during the week and helps construct the game plan, he does not make calls during the game, so he wants to be assured that Charlie Taaffe knows where he stands. He's made three calls in three years and two of them went bad.

With a full police escort, the team buses make their way to campus before 1:00 and Terp Alley is there to greet them upon their arrival. Initially, Terp Alley consisted of only a handful of onlookers. Today, there are more than a thousand, cheering, holding signs, and shaking hands as the team walks along a street, painted with large "M"s, to the Gossett Team House. Friedgen is the last to walk, 20 yards behind the team. His hip prevents him from moving fast, but the fans don't mind, as many shake his hand, give him hugs, and shout, "Go get 'em Fridge!"

After the team warms up, Friedgen spends six minutes walking around the locker room, shaking every single player's hand while looking them in the eye. Before heading upstairs to the coaching box, Taaffe walks to the offensive players in areas around the room and tells them the first play. Friedgen is done with the handshaking and the team takes a knee with him to say a pregame prayer. They rise to their feet and the coach has a few words. "The winner of this game is going to be the tougher team . . . You've got to be determined, you've got to persevere. You're tougher than this team, you've worked harder than this team. Are you going to let them take it from you?" As the team shoots out of the tunnel, the players slap a "Win" sign above the locker-room door and rub the bronze turtle just outside. A third straight sellout crowd awaits the game's start.

• • •

Clemson receives the opening kick and, right from the first play, the Tiger offense lines up at the line of scrimmage, prepares to get set, and then looks over to the sidelines for the play call. It is a rare version of the "no-huddle" offense, which at times seems to confuse even them.

Early in the game, the headsets for the Clemson coaches are not working. Per rules, the Maryland staff has to take off their headsets until the problem is fixed. The glitch is resolved in a few minutes.

Clemson quarterback Charlie Whitehurst impresses on the first drive. He completes a 20-yard pass to Derrick Hamilton for a first down and another one to Hamilton for 17 yards. The Terps' defense, led by Shawne Merriman, is able to stuff any rushing attempts by Clemson, and after Whitehurst misses Hamilton on a pass attempt, Clemson attempts a field goal from Maryland's 31. The kick is short.

Quarterback Scott McBrien takes the reigns and the Maryland offense mixes it up. Run, pass, run, run, pass, run, pass, run. McBrien is efficient and running back Josh Allen is sharp as he gains 26 yards on the ground. Maryland's 68-yard drive culminates in a 25-yard touchdown pass from McBrien to wide receiver Steve Suter. Byrd Stadium roars as a cannon explodes near one end zone.

After Whitehurst hits Hamilton again for a first down on Clemson's ensuing drive, the Terps defense steps up and Merriman sacks Whitehurst on third down for an eight-yard loss, forcing a punt. The punt from Cole Chason travels just 15 yards, giving the Terps great field position. As the defensive line returns to the bench, Dave Sollazzo taps each one on the head and says, "Good job!" before getting on his knee in front of them to answer their questions.

Starting at Clemson's 44, McBrien runs and passes Maryland down to the 12. On third and goal, McBrien hits Rich Parson on a 10-yard pass just 90 seconds into the second quarter to increase the Terp lead to 14-0. The offense is moving the ball well, the defense is thwarting Clemson's running game, and the kick coverage has been excellent. On their next two offensive possessions, however, Maryland is hampered by holding penalties and poor blocking. At one point, Maryland even faces a 3rd and 29 from inside their own territory. As the offensive line comes off the field, Friedgen makes his way to the bench and points directly at the line, saying, "You have got to stop that [holding]. That killed us. That killed the drive. Watch for it!"

Though the offense begins to sputter, the defense continues to step up and pressure Whitehurst, including sacks by Conrad Bolston and D'Qwell Jackson. With under three minutes to play in the half, Whitehurst throws a pass to the man of the hour, receiver Derrick Hamilton, who makes two tacklers miss and weaves his way to the end zone on a 70-yard touchdown. Though they still have the lead, the mood on the Maryland sideline changes dramatically. All teams like to have the momentum going into halftime, and Maryland just gave it away. On top of that, star receiver Latrez Harrison, instrumental to the Terps' offense, sits on the bench, woozy from a hit. He will not return. Will the Maryland offense return before it's too late?

• • •

In the locker room, as players get retaped and stretch out, the coaches huddle to make changes. Friedgen meets in the coaches' lounge area with his offensive staff and reviews diagrams on transparencies. The coaches from the box, including Taaffe, join them shortly. Friedgen takes suggestions from the assistants and adds, as he did earlier in the day, "we need to run the option." A few feet away, the defensive coaches meet in the shower. Taped to the wall are diagrams of Clemson's offense drawn up by the GAs. The coaches review the charts like doctors looking at X rays, defining the problem, and determining how to fix it. They have been shutting down the running game, limiting Clemson to negative yards rushing, but the Tigers are putting up big numbers passing the ball. As Friedgen passes by on his way to the team, he tells Blackney the "D" is playing well. "Let's stop those passes," he adds.

Position meetings are under way at various locations around the locker room. Before long, Friedgen blows his whistle three times and the players once again gather around him. "You are better than this football team when you play. When you don't play, you're not. You've got to decide. They were ready to fall, they were ready to go but we couldn't pull the trigger."

The second half is full of momentum swings—Maryland trying to hold on tight and Clemson attempting to find a spark. The Maryland offense goes three and out on its first possession. Clemson moves into Maryland territory on its first drive of the half, helped by Duane Coleman's 26 yards on the ground. Clemson has a fourth and two from Maryland's 31 but the Terps stop running back Chad Jasmin as he tries for the first down. The sideline erupts. On the fifth play of Maryland's next drive, McBrien is hit as he runs. He fumbles and Clemson's LeRoy Hill recovers at midfield. Clemson takes a chance when it gets the ball back, throwing deep on first down. Kevin Youngblood apparently scores on 48-yard pass from Whitehurst, but Youngblood is flagged for offensive pass interference, nullifying the score. Coach Tommy Bowden goes ballistic on the Clemson sideline.

The Terps try to go deep when they get the ball back and McBrien hits Derrick Fenner on a 69-yard pass play for a touchdown that energizes the crowd, as the game heads into the final quarter with Maryland ahead 21-7. As Fenner takes a seat on the bench, receivers coach James Franklin congratulates him, but says, "You scored but when the ball is over your other shoulder, you need to adjust." He demonstrates the proper way to do it. Coaches are never fully satisfied.

Late in the third quarter, Blackney gathers the secondary on the bench and makes a critical switch. He tells safety Madieu Williams to cover Derrick Hamilton, whose catches are keeping Clemson in the game, telling Williams to "be all over him."

On a fourth and one from Maryland's 25 early in the fourth quarter, Bowden elects to go for the first down instead of a field goal. Whitehurst's pass to Cliff Harrell is incomplete. The next time the Maryland defense takes the field, Williams, whom Blackney has switched to cover Harrison, picks off a Whitehurst pass intended for Harrison with seven minutes to go in the game. The maneuver has paid off. Maryland has the ball back but is forced to punt with four minutes left and a 21-7 point lead. Sollazzo stops the defense on their way onto the field, imploring them, "Don't let them out of this hole!" The Tigers engineer a 16-play, 64-yard drive to get to the Maryland 24. With a touchdown, an onsides kick recovery, and another touchdown, Clemson could force overtime. But it is not to be. On third and 10, Maryland's Leon Joe intercepts Whitehurst at the 15 and returns the ball to the 38. McBrien takes a knee. The Terps have won.

Maryland held Clemson to just 10 yards of rushing but gave up 320 yards through the air, including 175 yards on seven catches by Derrick Hamilton. The special teams that the Maryland staff was so focused on performed well. Hamilton had four punt returns for a total of just 32 yards. For Maryland, running back Josh Allen rushed for 65 yards on 16 carries and Bruce Perry had 33 yards on 17 carries. Merriman had six tackles, including two for losses totaling 20 yards, and two huge sacks, while Jackson led the defense with nine tackles.

Friedgen walks hurriedly to midfield where he greets Bowden with a handshake and best wishes. He immediately heads over to the far corner of the end zone to the student section, where he is handed a portable microphone. He calls the seniors up onto a small podium and the players and coach lead the students and the band in a rendition of Maryland's fight song. Friedgen can't sing half as well as he coaches, but no one seems to mind. He gets down from the platform at the conclusion and, as he walks off the field, his daughters and wife run up and give him hugs and kisses.

"It was a good win, a big win in your season," he says to the excited players in the locker room. "You're 4-2 right now, you're like a bullet." He warns them that they can't have a letdown against lowly rated Duke the following Saturday. He then gives the team a gift, removing curfew for the night, though not without a warning. Before the team breaks, the seniors step up onto a bench in front of a row of lockers, take off their helmets, and lead the team and coaches in the Maryland fight song and a ritual of counting wins.

• • •

It is a song that Ralph Friedgen knows well. He learned it 35 years ago as a player and sung it many times as an assistant coach but somehow, the lyrics make more sense, the melody is smoother when you are the head coach—and especially when your vision is taking Maryland football to the highest levels. No matter how long it took you to get the job.

The Maryland-Clemson game was huge for both teams, but the following weekend there was no bigger game in the country than Ohio State-Wisconsin, which was full of surprises.

CHAPTER 6

I'm In, I'm On

The University of Wisconsin

#23 Wisconsin vs. #3 Ohio State
Madison, Wisconsin
October 5-11

Most Badger fans have forgotten about the upset loss to UNLV a few weeks back. Wisconsin is now 5-1, atop the Big Ten, as it prepares to face unbeaten Ohio State (OSU). The defending national champions come to Madison riding a 19-game winning streak. A win for Barry Alvarez would rank among his all-time greats. But Wisconsin star Anthony Davis is nuturing an ankle injury and is questionable and Ohio State comes into town on a roll. It will take masterful coaching and an inspired effort by the Badgers to pull off the upset of the year.

• • •

Rubber bands. The topic of utmost concern at the Monday staff meeting is rubber bands. They have used them before, last season employing them four different times with separate meanings. The tradition began years earlier after a loss, when coaches suggested the players wear bands on their wrists to help the players "bounce back."

"What can we do to make this game special for the team?" Barry Alvarez asks. "I mean, they are smart, they know the rankings. The television and the media this week will certainly remind them. I don't think we need to point it out but I would like to do something special."

One suggestion is quickly dismissed by the coach without a pause: wearing red uniforms. The coaches decide on an "I'm In" campaign. The staff will have rubber bands with "I'm In" written on them, and when players believe they are fully ready to work hard and focus on Ohio State, they can tell any coach and they'll be given a rubber band to wear on their wrists. Not only does it add meaning to a practice week, but Alvarez points out that wearing the bands forces players to think about the game 24 hours a day. On a suggestion from assistant coach Brian Murphy, the words "I'm On" are added, emphasizing the significance of being totally committed. "The bands let you know that the coaches are pumped up," says star senior middle linebacker Jeff Mack. The players will also get T-shirts late in the week that read, "I'm In, I'm On."

For their part, the coaching staff has been in and on since 9:00 a.m. on Sunday, watching game film from Saturday's win at Penn State. It wasn't a pretty game, and the Badgers didn't play spectacularly, but it was a win. After grading the film, the coaches look forward to an awesome challenge: welcoming the #3 ranked Ohio State Buckeyes, the defending national champions who are riding a 19-game win streak, to Camp Randall on Saturday night. The staff spends time looking at Ohio State game film, Alvarez spends time in his office watching both sides of the ball, and during the day on Sunday many of the freshmen gather for the "Badger Huddle," a group led by a Madison psychologist where players can share their fears and concerns with one another.

By the time the staff assembles for the 7:00 a.m. "rubber band" staff meeting on Monday, they are consumed with Ohio State. Dressed in a blue shirt, a colorful tie, and dress pants, Alvarez comes in just after seven. The staff is dressed very professionally, in khakis and collared shirts. Only one of them wears red and sports a Wisconsin logo. The first order of business is Tuesday's practice. On the plane trip home from State College, Alvarez thought his team was tired and worn down entering the seventh week of the season. So, since Monday is already a light and short practice, the coach thinks changes to Tuesday's schedule might help alleviate his concerns. He brings it up with the staff. Most of them want to keep things as regular as possible—they do not want to deviate from the usual schedule even though they understand that fatigue is a factor. A compromise becomes a consensus, and the coaches decide that the number of individual periods on Tuesday will be reduced from four to two.

Alvarez concludes the meeting and some of the assistants go back to their offices. The coach stays with the special teams' coaches and reviews the kickoff coverage from the Penn State game. The group watches all of the Wisconsin kickoffs. When they are finished, Alvarez says, "We need to replace at least one or two guys." The staff throws out suggestions, looking at the personnel board in the staff meeting room, but ultimately Alvarez comes up with a simple idea: "Let's have the scout coverage go against the scout kick and see who runs down there with abandon. Somebody's got to step up."

The coach retreats to his office where he continues to watch film. Wayne Esser, the director of the Badger football booster organization, the Mendota Gridiron Club, stops in. He wants to get Alvarez's thoughts on how best to celebrate his 100th win. He is on 97. "I don't want to talk about it, Wayne. If it's not about Ohio State, I don't want to hear it," he says, nicely enough but with unmistakable force.

The offensive staff meets and watches clips of passes against the OSU defense. They begin to compile a list of potential offensive plays. Offensive coordinator Brian White keeps a list, as assistants Jim Hueber (offensive line), Jeff Horton (quarterbacks), Henry Mason (wide receivers), and Rob Ianello (tight ends) throw out suggestions. White is not your typical football coach—or at least that's what strangers think. "Because I went to Harvard, people initially have this impression until they meet me," he says. "I never say I graduated from Harvard. But my dad is a coach, both my parents teach. I never saw myself do anything but coach."

Just before 1:00, Alvarez heads over to the Kohl Center, the on-campus arena, to meet reporters for his weekly press conference. There are roughly 20 reporters in the room, along with some Wisconsin athletic department staff members and fellow coaches. Seated behind a microphone, Alvarez takes questions. He talks about the health of his players, the team routine when playing at night, the attitude of a team defending a national championship (he won one with Notre Dame), and the lessons learned from the loss to UNLV three weeks ago.

"I have a hard time with the lazy media or those with an agenda," the coach says. When it comes to the Internet, he is even more passionate. "Nothing is a secret any more," he says. "There is no accountability and no credibility."

Adds longtime voice of the Badgers, Matt Lepay, "He is slow to trust the media. At times, it is an adversarial relationship."

The entire press conference is over in less than 20 minutes and the coach gets back in his car to return to his office, where he meets with the senior athletic staff at 1:30.

• • •

All Barry Alvarez ever wanted to do was to be a head football coach; it didn't really matter where. After a successful playing career at Nebraska, where he lettered as a linebacker, Alvarez took a high school assistant coaching and teaching job in Lincoln. During his senior year of college, he had married his "best friend" Cindy, and soon became a young father. The family moved again to another town when Alavrez got a head coaching job at a high school in Lexington, Nebraska, and Alvarez's success there garnered the attention of the coaching community. When a high school in Iowa came calling, the coach made his move again. He took over a football power in Mason City and led the team to a state championship. University of Iowa head coach Hayden Fry asked Alvarez to come aboard as an assistant. Alvarez accepted. Under Fry, Alvarez learned much about the game and even more about coaching. In his eight years at Iowa, he coached in six bowl games.

His next stop was at the holy grail of college football—South Bend, Indiana. Under Lou Holtz at Notre Dame, Alvarez moved up the coaching ladder to become defensive coordinator, a position that brought him national attention and acclaim, especially after the Irish won the 1988 national championship. It was only a matter of time before he had his own program. That opportunity came in 1990 when he was hired to revive a stagnant Wisconsin program. "All I really ever wanted to do was to take over a program and build it into a winner." He did just that. By 1993, the Badgers had won the Big Ten conference and capped off a Cinderella season with a Rose Bowl victory in January 1994. Alvarez became a household name and the program flourished on that success. He again won Rose Bowls in 1999 and 2000, and Wisconsin became firmly established among the elite of college football.

"A lot of people didn't think the program could go to Rose Bowls," says longtime Madison resident and UW women's hockey coach Mark Johnson.

Matt Lepay has seen it all develop. "When they hired Barry, he had a reputation as a great recruiter who didn't shy away from high standards. When he came, he told everyone why they *could* win at Wisconsin, selling the campus, scenery." Lepay continues, "He has a presence about him. Some coaches have it, some don't."

His success along the way opened up other opportunities on the collegiate and professional levels, but he never moved. The program wasn't right, the city wasn't right, the contract wasn't right. Destiny seemed to keep him in Madison. Over time, he has learned to be a manager along with being a coach. He knows which invitations to accept and which to pass on. He knows that hiring the right staff brings a team a long way toward success. He has accepted and met the challenge of being a head football coach at the highest level. But there is more.

He always believed that he would enjoy athletic administration and in the mid-1990s he turned his eye toward becoming an athletic director. Wisconsin athletic director Pat Richter was contemplating retirement, and when Miami went after Alvarez hard in January 2001, the Wisconsin chancellor made it harder for Alvarez to leave by telling him that he would be a serious candidate for the AD job when Richter stepped down. When the time came in 2003, Alvarez called John Robinson, the head coach and AD at UNLV, as well as John Mackovic, who had done the same double-duty at Illinois. They both strongly encouraged him to accept the job if it was offered to him and if he was excited about it. He was. He also spoke with Wisconsin basketball coach Bo Ryan. "If he didn't want me to do it, I wouldn't have taken the job," Alvarez says matter-of-factly.

Many prominent boosters wanted him to be the new AD, predicting that his appointment would provide stability as fund-raising and stadium improvements continued. The other head varsity coaches at Wisconsin supported Alvarez as well. Mark Johnson, a member of the 1980 "Miracle on Ice" U.S. Olympic team, sees the fact that his new boss is also a coach as a positive. "I'm real comfortable with it and everyone else is, too. In today's environment with budget crunches, there is talk of bringing in a financial guy to be AD. But I like having an AD who has been a coach. He understands our needs. He has been in the trenches."

Officially, Alvarez will take over in April 2004, and oversee a budget of $51 million for the athletic department, including $9.8 million spent annually on football. Among the football program's costs are the $32,000 spent on subscriptions to recruiting services, the $75,000 dedicated to telephone charges, and the $900,000 that is set aside for guarantees—the money paid to nonconference schools that come to Madison to play. Surprisingly, football revenue comprises just 43 percent of the total take from athletics, a smaller percentage than is seen at comparable programs. (Of course, the percentage can change depending on how a department calculates revenue.)

On a daily basis, the department will be run by Deputy Athletic

Director Jamie Pollard, who has been at UW for the last five years, after four years at Maryland. The coach sits in on meetings, raises funds, and helps with decisions, but football still dominates his time. "On a day-to-day basis, I am a good number two person," Pollard says. "When Barry asked me to do this, I was really excited. We talked about how it would work. He knew what he was getting into and he knew he couldn't do everything. The day he thinks he is more valuable as an AD than as a coach, we've got a problem."

• • •

Camp Randall. The stadium that is home to the Wisconsin Badgers is named for a Civil War–era base that once stood on the same ground. It is one of the centerpieces of the UW campus, home not only to the football team and its offices, but to the athletic administration, and various other sports. In the fall of 2003, Camp Randall is getting an $84 million face-lift. An additional 3,000 seats are being added, in addition to luxury suites and new offices for the football staff and administrators. The people who work here deal daily with the cranes and jackhammers that come with construction. The inconvenience will soon pay dividends.

The current football offices sit just one story above the field. The atrium area outside the office suite has three simple displays. There are the Heisman Trophies of Alan Ameche (1954) and Ron Dayne (1999), along with portraits of the winners and there is a silver football trophy from the 2002 Alamo Bowl, the latest of the bowl hardware. Just inside the double-glass doors is the reception area, with black leather sofas and chairs. Here, in two large glass display cases, sit more awards, including Kevin Stemke's Ray Guy Award (Punter) and Jamar Fletcher's Thorpe Award (Defensive Back). There are Big Ten Championship trophies and Rose Bowl accolades from 1994, 1999, and 2000. Jerseys from all of the Wisconsin bowl victories hang in the hallways, as do team pictures and marketing posters with themes such as "Gladiators" or "High Voltage." Sitting on the reception desk is a holder for "Weekly Truth Statements," a questionnaire sheet that players must complete every week revealing their class attendance, their upcoming tests, their grades received, and their "positive actions for the week." The players sign and date it.

Adjacent to the reception area, to the left, is Barry Alvarez's office. It is a spacious office with plush carpet and a conference table, desk, and cabinet set. There are team pictures on the walls and family pictures on the shelves. The shelves also hold books on the Pittsburgh

Steelers, Hayden Fry, and Bobby Bowden. Behind his desk, Alvarez has a video computer system that is connected to the large flat-screen television mounted on the wall to his right. There is a high-tech stereo system and small speakers currently pumping out R & B. For a coach's office, it seems sparse and uncluttered.

The assistant coaches' office area looks more like the suites of a trendy advertising company loft in New York City than football offices in Madison. The individual offices surround an open space with black leather chairs and a black-and-white checkered sofa. The carpet is red and black. Protruding through into the middle of the open area is a red steel staircase that leads to the second floor, where there are workstations and black-and-white pictures of Wisconsin All-Americans. The offensive and defensive coaches' meeting rooms are just feet apart, each with a video screen, a wood table, leather chairs, and wipe boards. Hanging in the offensive meeting room are timelines for every day of the week. Hour by hour, day-by-day, meeting and practice times are detailed.

Down a few hallways and up a few stairs is the McClain Center, the home of football's indoor practice facility, weight room, locker room, and team and position meeting rooms. On the bottom floor, the expansive weight room is decked out in red and white. Inside the locker room, players are greeted by a large message board that carries opponent bios, team messages, and various posters. There are goal charts and Player of the Week award listings. The wooden lockers are spacious and modern but not arranged numerically or by position. Alvarez and his staff assign players' lockers to make sure that different kinds of players are together—young and old, black and white, offense and defense.

• • •

Wisconsin follows a unique routine on Monday afternoons. The special teams players meet, then the full team meets as Alvarez reviews the previous game. Next, the players break into offense and defense, where the coordinators get more specific. They then break down into position meetings, where the game film is reviewed. Afterward, the entire team reassembles in the team room for another round of meetings, this time looking ahead to the upcoming game. They are given a scouting report as a team, then meet by positions for a more detailed look at their opponent before hitting the field for a light practice.

The Wisconsin coaches and players know the routine—and they love it. Wide receivers coach Henry Mason has been coaching for

25 years, nine of them in Madison. "Things are stable here and it starts at the top. The thing I noticed when I got here was that Coach has a plan and he doesn't deviate from it. Everyone knows what's expected of them."

The staff and players follow this routine Monday as they look back at the Penn State game. In the first meeting, special teams coach Brian Murphy shows some of the kick coverage from the Penn State game, while some of the other coaches, including Alvarez, add their thoughts. They make a point of calling out two players who did little on kick coverage, the ones most likely to be replaced against Ohio State. Alvarez is not happy and the volume of his voice indicates it. As the film runs, four of the coaches talk at the same time and confusion ensues.

When the entire team joins the meeting, Alvarez congratulates them on "a good conference win on the road." There are mistakes, he points out, but a win is a win. Looking ahead to Ohio State, he tells them, "If we play our best, we are a better team than them and will win." He reviews some of the preseason goals that the team has set. Did they win all of their nonconference games? No, they lost to UNLV. Besides that failed goal, they have achieved the rest, including a pertinent one for this week. "We said we wanted to make the Ohio State game a big game—we've done that," the coach tells the players.

The defense stays in the room while the offense moves down the hall. Defensive coordinator Kevin Cosgrove, who sat in the special teams meeting, is already angry with the defense since some of his players also play on kick coverage. Looking at the defense against Penn State game, he tells them, "We had nine of 11 guys contributing to the game. That's not enough. We'll need all 11 on Saturday."

By the time the players regroup as a full team for the scout meeting, the Penn State game has been put to rest. Alvarez begins by telling the team about the "I'm In, I'm On" rubber bands and the meaning behind them. When the players are ready, they can tell their position coaches that they are in and on, and will be given a band. He tells the kids, "I'm in and you can bet your asses that I'll be on Saturday!" He reminds the team to be gracious and predictable with the media, not to guess at the outcome or otherwise add any fuel to Ohio State's fire.

Offensive coordinator Brian White is the assistant in charge of the Ohio State scouting report. During the summer, Alvarez assigns every assistant, including GAs, a team to scout. That assistant will then deliver a brief scouting report to the team and appear on Alvarez's radio show during the week to talk about the game. It's a way to give assistants valuable experience. After speaking briefly about Ohio State and reviewing their personnel, White plays on emotions. "We can beat them. This is a game you will remember for the rest of your lives—how you prepared that week and how you played."

The team congregates on the field in Camp Randall at 5:45 p.m. on Monday for an easy practice. Most of the early evening workout is used by the staff to introduce the Ohio State game plan to the players. By practice time, most of the game plan is set. Unlike many staffs, which focus on one aspect of the game plan a day, the Badger staff puts it all in on Monday and then adjusts it through the week. Each staff member is assigned an area, such as run, goal line, etc., and offers his thoughts on the subject to the offensive or defensive staffs as a whole, who then shape the game plan. The defense runs through plays against the scout team for almost an hour while the offense does 45 minutes worth of run-throughs. After practice, the staff watches the practice film, easily pointing out what works and what needs adjustments—a benefit of putting the whole game plan in early in the week. They continue to look at Ohio State game film and tweak the game plan before leaving the office at 9:45 p.m.

• • •

There is an extra bounce in the step of the coaches this week, for they, too, understand and enjoy the magnitude of this game. Alvarez has already gotten across to the players and, just as importantly, to the staff.

"I have to set the tone," says Alvarez. "I have to tell the guys [staff] what to say to their kids. They have to believe that they will win."

The coach himself relishes the chance to play in big games and recognizes he can always learn more about how best to prepare his teams. He talks with other coaches, including Frank Solich, Bob Stoops, and former boss Lou Holtz, about new methods of motivation, using them as sounding boards. He reads books on coaching to find out how others do it. And, of course, he learns from his own experiences.

After the unexpected loss to UNLV, the coach faced the tough task of getting the players to move past the loss. "I was worried. We had North Carolina the next week and they had had a week off to prepare. I was scared to death we wouldn't be ready." They won. To Alvarez, letting go of losses and letting go of big wins are the same. About big wins he says, "You enjoy it that night and you're a little high on Sundays but by Monday morning, you better forget about that game and be totally focused."

Focus is a crucial component to Alvarez's philosophy during practice weeks, particularly for big games. "You can't play till Saturday," he tells his team on more than one occassion, while acknowledging that coaches must be careful not to burn out the players. In other words, knowing when to say when. Players will not react if every week the staff is going full velocity. Coaches need to pick their spots. "Only three times a year I will get them jacked up and that started right after the Penn State game on Saturday. The kids knew I was stoked."

Just how big is the Ohio State game? Students have been lining up for *weeks* outside the Kohl Center to get the best seats. Students can buy season tickets at the beginning of the year but must turn those vouchers in the Wednesday before home games to actually get a seat assignment, so students camp outside Kohl. Sophomore Amber Wheney from Minnesota is one of the diehards. "This is a big game," she says. Wheney is part of a group of 12 students who coordinate a schedule for saving a place in line. On a computer printout, a daily schedule is created, based on class and work demands, so not all members of the group have to be in line at the same time. When Wednesday comes, each student in line gets tickets for up to 12 other students.

Alvarez is stoked early Tuesday morning but appears calmer toward lunchtime. He relaxes in a leather chair in offensive line coach Jim Hueber's office, feet hanging over the chair's arm. They talk a bit of baseball, discussing the surprising Red Sox win the night before in Game 5 of the American League Divisional Series against the Oakland A's, then talk about the Tampa Bay–Indianapolis Monday Night Football game.

Down the hall, Kevin Cosgrove looks at film with Ron Lee and John Palermo. Their stockinged feet rest on the conference table as they exchange ideas on personnel until Palermo leaves to draw up cards for practice. For much of the morning, the offensive and defensive staffs do not come together. In fact, many of the assistants leave meetings when areas of their concern are off the table. For example, if the offense is working on how to attack the secondary with receiving routes, Hueber retreats to his office to watch film and work on his own.

Alvarez does his weekly Big Ten media conference call a little before noon, and then works on some thoughts he wants to get across to his team at practice. Though he believes in discipline, order, and routines, he's almost always willing to be flexible when necessary. But this week is not a time for flexibility.

• • •

The players are in meetings Tuesday afternoon, gearing up for the week's longest and toughest practice. Special teams focus on punt and kick returns and coach Brian Murphy makes a few adjustments to the kick coverage units, moving two players to different spots on the line. In the quarterbacks meeting, quarterbacks coach Jeff Horton hands out a detailed note chart, including bullet points like "expect blitzes" and "must convert on third and medium and third and long." He gives the three quarterbacks, starter Jim Sorgi and backups Matt Schabert and John Stocco, play diagrams, both new and old, along with coaching points on what to look for in reads. They watch film of the Ohio State defense in the red zone this season, but there isn't much to watch. Most of the Buckeye opponents never got that far. Among the suggestions from Horton: Hold on to the ball or throw it away, watch for the blitz from defensive backs, and read the safety. Hopefully, all three quarterbacks are paying attention.

With the shortened practice agreed upon by the staff on Monday, Tuesday's practice will be only 18 five-minute periods, plus pre- and postpractice kicking. It is an unusually balmy day in Madison, the temperature in the high 70s. Wearing a white Adidas shirt, red shorts, and sunglasses, Alvarez kids with players and coaches before warm-ups. After field goals and punt kicks, the scout teams line up against each other for a kickoff—the drill many players and coaches have been eagerly awaiting as they want to see who will step up. There is enthusiasm and hustle during the four kicks, all live, full tackle. Teammates on the sideline cheer on friends, encouraging them with shouts. The coaches will have to watch the practice film to see who will join the starters. (Redshirt freshman Zach Hampton steps up and the coaches insert him onto kick coverage.)

Some of the players are already wearing their "I'm In, I'm On" rubber bands on Tuesday, having already told their position coaches they are ready. Alvarez stands at the 40-yard line, watching both sides of practice as the defense and offense work against scouts and, occasionally, each other. The offense wears red and the defense white, but the defensive starters wear black—an honor. When the first teams go against each other, the intensity picks up noticeably. All told, the offense runs over 100 scripted plays during the practice.

The offense is working on goal line plays and on one option play—

tailback Booker Stanley takes the pitch from Jim Sorgi in for a touchdown. But he does not cradle the ball properly, a tiny miscue that would escape the average fan—but not Brian White. The coach is all over the freshman. "Every detail counts. You've got to focus," he says.

At the end of practice, after announcements from the academic advisor and Sports Information Director Justin Doherty, Alvarez addresses the team. "That was a great practice today and a great tempo. This was a good start to the practice week. When you are in and on, committed to playing your best, get your bands from your coaches. Listen, you gotta believe you can win. You *have* to believe you can win."

· · ·

"It means a lot to me to be able to come back," says senior wide receiver and team captain Lee Evans about his recovery from a devastating knee injury in 2002. "The comeback journey is almost unpredictable. You go through peaks and valleys. Even in rehab, you have some good days and bad days. I dedicated myself to doing it." Evans's return to the field was part of the reason for Wisconsin's lofty expectations this season. In 2001, his last season on the field, Evans had 75 receptions for 1,545 yards and nine touchdowns. He *averaged* 20.6 yards per catch.

The Bedord, Ohio, native has spent five years in the program and knows the routine well. "Coach Alvarez is very much a players' coach. He is always connecting with the players, especially seniors and captains. You can go in and talk to him. He is very down-to-earth and expects you to work hard."

Evans understands the coach's motivations this week and gladly goes along. It has worked in the past. But he doesn't need a coach to tell him how important this game is. "It has been a big game since they won the national championship. How many times do you get to play the defending national champions?"

· · ·

The staff is jovial on Wednesday, with much of their work behind them. Though football obviously dominates their time, Alvarez and White do find time to take a 45-minute walk around campus at lunchtime, as they try to do each Tuesday, Wednesday, and Thursday. Sometimes they talk football, sometimes they talk life. As they make their way, well-wishers greet them. Alvarez used to run every day but a few years ago knee problems made him change his routine.

Back in his office, the coach wears his athletic director's hat as he reads e-mails on the status of potential buyers of the new stadium suites. A weekly update is e-mailed to him from his senior staff, letting him know who has toured the suites, who placed calls inquiring about them, and who may be a prospective buyer.

Meanwhile, White works on technique with the running backs during afternoon position meetings. Sophomore Dwayne Smith asks about practice today, and when their coach tells them it will only be 17 periods ("Like Club Med," he jokes), Smith remarks, "Boy, things have changed, man. When I was a freshman, we'd be out there for hours." Perhaps it's revisionist history. White shows them Tuesday's practice film and points out the basic fundamentals: tucking the ball away, hitting landmarks, getting hands up when blocking. "If you're making the mistakes now in practice, you're going to do it Saturday night." The star back, Anthony Davis, who currently is nursing a high-ankle sprain and is questionable for Saturday, munches on Guacamole-flavored chips while redshirt freshman Booker Stanley, who had a breakout game against Penn State, sits at attention.

For the second day in a row, kicker Mike Allen misses a field goal early in practice, prompting a not-so-subtle comment from Alvarez. "Same thing as yesterday. Missing them left. You got to make some kicks." On a very hot day in Wisconsin, with construction workers working high above the field, the staff keeps a lively pace. The 17 periods go quickly, and Alvarez once again paces at midfield wearing a whistle around his neck. The offense is not as sharp on Wednesday— the quarterbacks are throwing bad passes and the receivers are dropping balls, but at least the intensity is there. The coach reiterates that theme at the close of practice, staying positive and keeping it short. "Another good practice. I like the way you have gone about it this week and we need to finish up strong tomorrow. You can have no hesitation when you step on that field Saturday—none at all. They've had two weeks to prepare for us. Heck, they just started classes. So you've got to catch up and I think you have. Come in and watch film, study, and take care of all the ticket business and off-field stuff."

Alvarez knows from experience that off-the-field stuff can be the Badgers' downfall.

●   ●   ●

In the basement banquet room of Herreman's Supper Club in Sun Prairie, a town 10 miles north of Madison, anticipation and excitement are in the air as 150 fans await the arrival of their guest. All are dressed in bright red sweaters or shirts, proudly wearing their name tags. One fan wears an electronic badge that scrolls, "California here we come." The weekly meeting of the Mendota Gridiron Club is normally held in downtown Madison, but once a year it moves out of town to attract some new attendees. People arrive by 5:30 to enjoy cocktails—which in Wisconsin means beer—and the steak and potatoes dinner is served a bit after seven. Barry Alvarez arrives with friends in tow, including close friend and local businessman John Flesch and son-in-law Brad Ferguson. The faithful have come to be close to the coach and hear him talk. (The author is invited to talk for a few minutes about what he has learned during the season.)

Alvarez talks about how big the win over Penn State was and how running back Booker Stanley really stepped up, particularly in the second half. Looking ahead to Ohio State, the coach tells the crowd that the Buckeyes can be beaten but it will be a classic football battle, a running game against a tough ground defense. He speaks for seven minutes, making the crowd laugh a few times, before opening it up for questions.

"What is the status of Davis?" one attendee asks. "Is it a coaching or player's fault when we get so many delay of games?" another bravely inquires. "Do you like playing a night game?" To every question, Alvarez retorts humorously, and soon the coach has the place in stitches. These fans seem loyal enough that they'd laugh when he coughs or applaud when he hiccups, but Alvarez is truly funny, sometimes answering questions with a witty two-word answer and moving on. He answers every last question before picking raffle tickets for prizes and auctioning off two press box passes for the game, for which he raises $400.

The coach and "friends," who now number in the dozens, walk across Main Street to Toot's Tap, a neighborhood bar barely large enough to hold the crowd. Pictures of Alvarez hang above the bar and Wisconsin colors and paraphernalia cover the walls. The coach takes a seat at a small round table against the back wall and, one after another, the fans come up, asking him, "Coach, what are you drinking?" He signs some autographs, jokes with friends, and shows kindness even to the most intrusive fans. His group is the first to leave. There is a game to be won.

• • •

The names Mike Price and Larry Eustachy have become infamous among sports fans, not because of their accomplishments on the field, but because of their indiscretions off of it. Price was forced out at Alabama before ever coaching a game after a well-publicized visit to a strip club. Eustachy lost his job after attending parties with college students on an *opponent's* campus. Football and basketball coaches have taken note and, though some may not change their lifestyles, they certainly are aware of the pitfalls. For Alvarez, it means thinking twice about situations which once wouldn't have given him pause. A picture with fans at a cocktail party. A photo and autograph with two young coeds outside a store or restaurant. Where will the photos end up? What will be construed? "I can't live in a bubble," he says. "If I want to have a drink, I'll have a drink. But I think twice now."

Alvarez has close friends, both inside and outside the game, and he stresses that he doesn't intend to ignore his relationships just to avoid impropriety. "I like to be around people. I have to be or I'll go nuts. I get to meet interesting people in this job and people like to be around coaches. I think there is an overlap with business and sports. I have friends outside of football who are successful in their own business and they are interested in mine."

· · ·

The Thursday staff meeting gets under way late by Alvarez's standards—that is, nine o'clock. The coaches are well-dressed in suit pants, collared shirts, and dress shoes. For many seasons, Alvarez required everyone to wear a shirt and tie every day, but he eventually downgraded the requirement to Fridays only. Now he allows the coaches to dress casually every day. So, with staff swiped from GQ gathered around the table, the coach begins.

First things first: the academic counselors give an update. They talk about the test schedule for next week and the great support they have received from professors, and tell the coaches a little bit about the two university faculty members who will be "guest coaches" for the game. They will attend Thursday's practice and spend time with the team on Saturday. The next item on the agenda is the recruiting list for the game, a computerized printout detailing each recruit, his guests, his high school, the Wisconsin coach recruiting him, etc. There are 25 recruits on the list. Jeremy Sinz, the Director of Football Operations and Alvarez have decided to limit the unofficial visits to only the top guys, some of whom already have verbally committed to Wisconsin. Sinz takes the staff through each player, reminding them of who they are.

In a unique segment that follows, Alvarez calls on both coordina-

Sonny Lubick gets his Rams ready for kickoff.

Mark Richt handles the media.

Ex-Marine Tom O'Brien leads his Eagles into battle.

Phillip Fulmer makes a point to his Volunteers.

Ralph Friedgen leads his Terrapins in a spirited rendition of the Maryland fight song.

Barry Alvarez runs onto the field beside his Badgers.

Bobby Bowden keeps a
watchful eye from the
sideline.

Nick Saban gives credit to a loyal Tiger crowd.

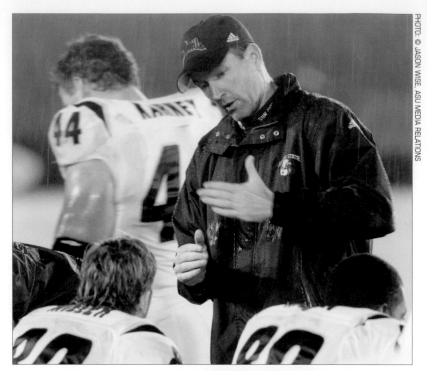

Dirk Koetter takes a moment away from the game to impart a lesson to a Sun Devil.

The author shadows
Nick Saban on the sidelines at the
Nokia Sugar Bowl in
New Orleans.

tors and, in fact, all of the coaches, to talk about their keys to the game. Brian White is up first, showing the staff a five-minute cutup of Ohio State defensive tendencies and how UW plans to counter them. When the film concludes, he gives his three keys to the game for the offense and for the running backs, the position he coaches. Alvarez calls on the other offensive assistants to present the keys for their positions. Kevin Cosgrove and his defensive staff follow the same routine. Alvarez takes detailed notes as the coaches speak. The process lets everyone on the staff know what everyone else must do for victory. Too often, staffs get so focused on their side of the ball that they have no idea what their counterparts are trying to do. Wrapping up the 45-minute meeting, Alvarez encourages his staff to be positive from here on in and to remind the kids they can win. "All we expect is their best shot on Saturday, that's all we can ask, and I think our best shot will win the game."

In the offensive meeting later that morning, each coach comes up with his own ideas for the first 15 plays or "openers." Then they debate the suggestions, which are written with blue and red marker on the wipe board, finally creating a list of 15 by consensus. Scripting openers has become popular among coaches, but these plays are not necessarily the first 15 of the game. Rather, they are the order of plays for normal down and distance, which are first and second down. So play #3 may actually be the fourth or fifth offensive play of the game for Wisconsin. The openers allow coaches to see how the defense will react to certain formations and motions so it helps them decide what to run throughout the game. Brian White copies down the list as Jeff Horton jumps up to erase it, lest anyone see it. In between each offensive series during the game, White will create a miniscript for the next series, adjusting it for field position. "My approach to coordinating is to be as collaborative as possible," he says. "Allow everyone to be decision-makers. We all feel inclusive, take ownership in the game plan. It is foolish to exclude anyone."

In the defensive line position meeting, coach John Palermo points out in his deep voice that Ohio State quarterback Craig Krenzel can run with the ball. "He's their second-leading rusher and he has missed two games." A few doors down, offensive line coach Jim Hueber reviews film with his players. He sits off to the side holding the remote control tight, enlivening the session with his wry wit. In the defensive staff room, coordinator and linebacker coach Kevin Cosgrove has his men going over a "Tip Sheet" for the game, reviewing play diagrams and coaching notes. He goes play-by-play, making sure everyone, particularly Jeff Mack, knows their responsibilities and calls. As middle linebacker and a senior, Mack is the leader of the defense.

At practice, it's a bit cooler today as crews spruce up the stadium for Saturday. The ESPN crew in town for the game takes notes on the sideline. After the relatively short practice, the players gather in the McClain Center meeting room alone with Alvarez, as he tries once more to set the tone. "I've told you this before, but Thursday is the most important night for rest." He then talks about Ohio State. "Let me tell you why they win." He bullet-points reasons behind Ohio State's success, and the most important reason is this: They know how to win. "They believe they are going to win. And on their opponents, one or two guys get doubts, thinking, 'We're not supposed to win,' so they don't break up a pass or make the catch. If you guys go out there and give it your best shot, we'll win."

• • •

Friday mornings before home games, Barry Alvarez indulges in a massage before heading into the office around 10:30. The staff does not meet until noon and the coach has open hours to fill. He hates waiting around for afternoon meetings.

Once in the office, he greets friends and former players who have arrived in town for the game and does some media interviews. He speaks with the ESPN crew, answering questions about the health of Anthony Davis and how Ohio State's offense and defense have changed from last year. He walks outside his office to the reception area where lunch is laid out—shrimp cocktail, scallops wrapped in bacon, chips, meatballs, chocolate brownies—and grabs a few bites. He strolls around the offices, popping his head in his assistants' offices, looking for someone to talk to. Finally, the special teams meeting gets under way and Alvarez sits in the back, contributing a few thoughts. During position meetings, he retreats to his office and makes notes. He keeps a journal of every season dating back to his days as a Notre Dame assistant. Quotes and techniques he learned from Lou Holtz in South Bend have become themes and drills he uses in Madison.

The coaches wear their dress clothes on the field for the afternoon walk-through, while the players wear helmets, jerseys, and shorts. When the players arrive in the locker room, they are given T-shirts emblazoned with red and black letters: "I'm In, I'm On."

After the walk-through, the players head by bus to a nearby Best Western and indulge in dinner. Alvarez joins them shortly thereafter and does a phone interview with ESPN's Chris Fowler and Kirk Herbstreit, who are hosting a Friday night radio show. He makes sure to remind Fowler of comments made years back, when Wisconsin played in the Rose Bowl and Fowler said Wisconsin was the worst passing team ever. He also takes a jab at Herbstreit, letting him know that when putting together a "hit" tape to show the players later in the night, he made sure that a hit made on the former Ohio State Buckeye was included. As soon as he finishes the phone call, a camera crew is ready to tape an interview with the ESPN studio crew back in Bristol, Connecticut. Alvarez gets hooked up with an earpiece and a microphone.

Friday night, the team goes to the movies. They arrive at The Point Cinema movie complex in Madison in time for the 7:15 showing of *The Rundown*, an action flick starring The Rock. Moviegoers in line getting popcorn begin to point at the players and coaches as they enter, and a few even say, "Good luck, tomorrow, Barry." The players seem to enjoy the movie but there are some tired faces as they re-board the buses. At the request of the coaches, one of the bus drivers tunes to an Ann Arbor, Michigan, radio station to listen to the second half of the Michigan-Minnesota game, which is of vital interest to Wisconsin.

In a rare move, Alvarez has the buses drive to the stadium around 9:15 p.m. The lights on the field have become an issue. On top of the fact that Wisconsin rarely plays night games, the coaches have gotten word that new temporary lighting—being used because of the construction—is too bright and will shine in the eyes of the players on the Badger sideline. Alvarez wants the team to test the nighttime lights by messing around on the field for a few minutes—it breaks the tension a bit. The coaches and players toss balls around and act as if the biggest game of the year is weeks away, not mere hours.

● ● ●

Because Barry Alvarez is the soon-to-be athletic director, he rises early on Saturday. He is joined by John Chadima and they head downtown for a presentation. An Alumni Advisory Board has been formed by the University, consisting mainly of wealthy donors. Alvarez is asked to speak to the group on Saturday to try and encourage further giving—no better time to hit them up than on the biggest game day of the year.

It is hot and windy as the team buses over to Camp Randall for a brief warm-up on Saturday morning. Alvarez wears a red short-sleeve shirt, gray slacks, his customary leather dress shoes, and no socks. Ohio State had just left the field from its warm-up, but the teams do not encounter one another. The 40-minute session consists of stretching, a few drills, and a run-through of plays on both sides of the ball. Then the coach gathers the players on the far side of the field.

"Get off of your legs today, give them a rest. If you watch the games on TV, don't get emotionally invested in the games, just watch as a fan. This is a tremendous opportunity for you tonight and you have to take advantage of that opportunity. There are guys that never get the chance to play in these games. When you step on the field, there can be no hesitation," the coach continues, his eyes and voice turning serious. "You can't be in awe of them. Yes, they are a good football team and you have to respect them but you can't be in awe of them."

As the group breaks up, Brian White pulls Anthony Davis aside as they walk across the field. Davis's health is of particular concern to the coaches. They thought he would be ready based on Friday's walk-through, but today White is noticing hesitation in Davis's cuts. "You have to prepare yourself not to play," the coach tells his player. "I can't justify putting you out there, I have to look out for you and the team. I'm not saying to lose all hope, but be ready not to play. Get your treatment and therapy and if in the next seven hours you can honestly convince me you can play, then we'll see."

As Davis walks away, Alvarez walks over to White and the coordinator relays the news to his boss. Alvarez concurs with the plan.

"I mean, he would have to do a hell of a job pleading for him to go," White adds.

"No, just sit him," Alvarez says.

• • •

As is the case at many other schools, the agenda handed out to the Wisconsin coaches and players is not exactly accurate. The closer to game time you get, the earlier the events begin. The coaches are already dressed and the assistants are seated quietly at three circular tables in a banquet room at the Best Western when the head man arrives at 3:30 for a 3:45 meeting.

Alvarez begins by asking for a weather report, as rain showers are predicted for game time. John Chadima reports that there are showers about two hours west of Madison and the rain might last for two hours. They all know that a wet field would help Wisconsin, as it might slow down Ohio State and affect their passing game.

Next, the coach says that if they win the coin toss, they will defer the ball until the second half. He asks special teams coach Brian Murphy to check the wind before kickoff to determine which end to defend. He asks each coach if there are any injuries or changes to the lineups that he should know about and confirms with White that Davis will sit out.

"This is a big game for us," Alvarez tells his staff. "Not just for the kids, but for the coaches as well. We love the big games, too. We need to be at our best tonight. This win can put us in the driver's seat."

• • •

On the cover of a recent *Sports Illustrated On Campus* magazine— a supplement of the sports weekly distributed in student papers nationwide—was a Wisconsin fan with a painted face with the headline, "The Best College Sports Town." There is no other major college sports teams in the state, so the state's passion is poured into the Green Bay Packers and Badger football. The state capital building is just blocks from the campus and the local streets are lined with hundreds of bars, restaurants, and stores. In bars on the famed State Street, like State Street Brats, the topic of conversation is always, it seems, Wisconsin football. And game day is like no other.

As a police escort leads the buses through Madison, red-and-white-clad fans raise their beer cups to the team. One young man comes running onto the street and pounds on the side of the first bus. The caravan makes its way through throngs of people on Regent Avenue, the masses dressed in red and white, both Wisconsin and Ohio State fans. As the team crosses over Randall Avenue and walks through the famous Arch en route to the locker rooms in the McClain Center, fans form lines on both sides of the sidewalk. As he leads the group, Alvarez is greeted by shouts of support. He takes the time to shake hands with fans, including a young man wearing a shirt that says, "F—k Ohio State."

Time passes slowly as kickoff approaches, and Alvarez checks in constantly with Chadima, who uses a stopwatch to monitor the approach of game time. Finally, with seven minutes to go, Chadima and the coach walk next door to the locker room. It is silent. At this point, there isn't much to be said. The coaches and players know what they must do, and Alvarez knows that the consistent message delivered many times throughout the week is much more important than the few words spat out right before kickoff.

"You are ready for this," he says. "You had a great week of practice and you are ready. No hesitation now." As he speaks, his voice grows louder, and the players begin to shout and hop around. They are raging by the time Alvarez shouts, "Let's go kick their asses!"

With that, the players make their way out of the locker room, each of them tapping a red horseshoe nailed above the door. They walk the hallway in McClain and then up a long artificial turf ramp. Above the exit, there is a sign: "The Road to the Rose Bowl Begins Here." They walk across thirty feet of blacktop connecting the McClain Center and the stadium. The moment they hit the stadium concourse, pandemonium erupts. The shouts echo in the enclosed space and fans hit players on their shoulder pads as they walk through. The team pauses at the tunnel entrance to the field and then explodes in a full sprint into Camp Randall. The crowd roars and the blast of tubas from the band mark the team's entrance. A rainstorm greets them.

The Badgers win the toss and elect to defend. On the first Ohio State possession, the Badger defense holds the Buckeyes to three downs and a punt. The Wisconsin offense takes over with Jim Sorgi at quarterback and a plan for Dwayne Smith and Booker Stanley to share the running back duties while Anthony Davis sits out. On the first series, Smith gets the carries as the Badgers move from Ohio State's 44 to the 36.

After Wisconsin is stopped on a third and six, the players and coaches wait for the call for a field goal or punt from Alvarez. He sends in the field goal unit. By the time backup quarterback and holder Matt Schabert calls for the snap, the play clock has expired, moving the ball back five yards and forcing Alvarez to call for a punt. He is not pleased. As Schabert and kicker Mike Allen jog off the field, he meets them a few yards into the playing area and wants to know why the delay. Schabert says he was set and ready; Allen says he was waiting on Schabert. Neither answer suffices. The coach tells Allen, "You have to be on top of it." By this point, Alvarez is soaked down to his underwear in the pouring rain. His fingers begin to wrinkle from the wet cold. The baseball cap on his head provides little protection.

Fighting through the heavy rain, the Wisconsin defense plays strong, stopping two runs and forcing an incomplete pass. The crowd noise at Camp Randall reaches fever pitch as the Buckeyes face a third down. After the defensive stand, the Badger secondary sits on the benches listening to Kevin Cosgrove and John Palermo. "It's your turn," Cosgrove says, cajoling an already invigorated squad.

On Wisconsin's second offensive series, Alvarez looks down the sideline and sees Stanley standing there. He immediately takes off his headset and hastily walks down the sideline, motioning with his arms, and yelling for Stanley to get in the game for Smith. Alvarez has a hunch that Stanley might be more effective. The Badger offense conducts a long drive that chews up much of the first quarter. The 0-0 tie is finally broken just six seconds into the second quarter when Stanley takes the ball two yards in for a touchdown, culminating a 13-play, 63-yard drive. The crowd is ecstatic. Before the ensuing kick-off, Alvarez pulls kicker Scott Campbell aside and tells him where to kick the ball. He follows instructions and gets a touchback. Alvarez is involved in all facets of the game, suggesting switches and plays to the coaches on the sideline and in the box, talking to players as they come off the field, working the officials continuously.

Momentum shifts away from Wisconsin halfway through the second quarter after usually reliable punt returner Jim Leonhard fumbles on his own 19-yard line and Ohio State's Jason Bond recovers, giving the Buckeyes a golden opportunity. Since Leonhard also plays on defense as a safety, he doesn't have time to think about the miscue. He helps rally the defense, which stops the Buckeyes inside the 10 and forces a Mike Nugent field goal, making the score 7-3. After the kick, Leonhard, a player and fan favorite, takes a seat on the bench and wipes his face with a towel. Cosgrove makes his way over and, after a rub on the head, tells him not to worry about the fumble.

After Badger penalties kill their own drive, Ohio State has the ball as the half comes to a close. It isn't pretty but it is Badger foot-ball: run, block, and hold on.

• • •

Wisconsin runs off the field but it takes close to three minutes to make their way through the crowds in the concourse and back to the locker rooms—an eternity for a halftime. Because of the weather, most of the coaches change into bright red full-body rain gear that equipment manager Mark Peeler has rolled into the room. It is a strange sight as coaches are in every stage of dress as they discuss making adjustments: some fully clothed, some without shirts, a few completely naked. After just a few minutes in their locker room, most of the assistants bolt next door and immediately begin to meet as offense and defense. White has made his way down from the coaching box and takes turns with Hueber talking to the offense. Cosgrove and Palermo do the same with the defense. Alvarez finally comes over, after putting on his rain gear, and stands in between the groups.

The equipment staff is frantic, drying clothes and fixing helmets and pads. The meetings last barely four minutes and it is time to head to the field. The team does not gather as a group and Alvarez does not talk. As the offense breaks, White implores them to play hard. "We need 30 more minutes. We have the ball first, so let's make it happen. It's our half."

Before the team walks out, Anthony Davis, he of the high-ankle sprain, becomes enraged. The offense huddles around him as he releases his energy in a 10-second pep talk that concludes with him slamming his helmet into the floor, so hard that pieces fly off. The team follows Alvarez through the path to the field again, and fans in line for the concessions or for the toilets form a cheering gauntlet.

The offense needs to set the tone in the second half and, after a solid 18-yard kick return by Brandon Williams, Sorgi takes the field. On the third play, the quarterback begins to scramble, then decides to throw the ball downfield at the last second. The Buckeyes' Dustin Fox picks off the ill-advised throw. The crowd lets out a groan. Alvarez shakes his head. But the defense continues to play well. OSU gets no further than their own 35 before punting but Wisconsin doesn't do any better, starting from their one and getting to the 10 before punting. But Buckeye All-American Chris Gamble fumbles the punt on his own 48. It is recovered by UW's Matt Katula on OSU's 38.

With just over five minutes left in the third quarter and the Badgers facing a third and long, Sorgi takes off running. The Buckeye defense stops him short of the first down. At the bottom of the pile, however, defensive tackle Robert Reynolds of Ohio State appears to choke or strangle Sorgi. The QB lays on the field and the training staff sprints out. Because his throat has been harmed, he can't yell for help from his teammates. Alvarez saw the play, as did players on and off the field, and a shouting and shoving match erupts around the fallen Sorgi. Alvarez runs onto the field, incensed at the action and at the fact that no penalty has yet been called. The referee, Dave Witvoet, calms him down and sends him back to the sideline. But he doesn't stop, asking the side judge standing near him, "How could you not see that?" The official responds that he was too far from the play, an excuse Alvarez doesn't buy. The official promises "to keep a close eye on things." When things calm down, Mike Allen kicks a field goal to increase the lead to seven, 10-3.

On the bench, the medical staff huddles around Sorgi, who still cannot speak, and the trainers and coaches decide to have him sit. Backup quarterback Matt Schabert warms up. After a few minutes,

Alvarez walks back to the doctors to get an update and just shakes his head, mystified at what has occurred. Suddenly, the Badgers' upset bid rests with a backup, who has thrown just a handful of passes in his career. In his first possession at the helm, he runs twelve yards outside for a first down, sparking some hope from the Camp Randall faithful that maybe things are not so bad.

As the quarter comes to a close, a remarkable in-stadium tradition takes place. The PA system blasts House of Pain's hip-hop song "Jump Around" and the sections go berzerk. Tens of thousands of people jump up and down in unison, including the band, which has moved into the end zone. Some of the Ohio State players look around in amazement. A few on the field join in, as if to spite the crowd.

A single quarter remains. OSU has at stake a winning streak, their national ranking, and national championship hopes. The Badgers have on the line the Big Ten lead and a possible Rose Bowl appearance. Wisconsin's drive is halted at their own 35. After receiving the punt, Ohio State returns the ball when, with 11:28 left in the game, Jim Leonhard intercepts a deep pass thrown by Krenzel, who is having a rough game in his first game back from injury. The interception further ignites the crowd but the Badger offense can do nothing and the Buckeyes get the ball back. Krenzel switches to a shotgun formation and begins to distribute the ball to his receivers, who are often isolated against the Wisconsin corners. After Krenzel throws for three first downs, Alvarez feels things slipping away. He tells Cosgrove, "They [corners] are not competing and can't get it done." The doubts that Alvarez warned his players about may be creeping into the heads on the sideline.

With 6:09 left, the Buckeye signal caller hits Michael Jenkins on a six-yard touchdown pass. The game is tied at 10 after the extra point. The stadium falls silent. The Badgers have been playing well, fighting on every play and the crowd is with them. But Wisconsin has come close in past seasons to beating Ohio State; perhaps the ghosts are out in this final quarter.

The offense, which has had trouble moving the ball, takes the field behind Schabert. On the second play, with 5:30 left on the clock, Schabert drops back, looks to his right, and throws a perfect pass to receiver Lee Evans, who catches the ball in stride and sprints to a 79-yard touchdown. There is bedlam. Players jump on each other on the sidelines, coaches high-five anybody near them. Schabert is so delirious he skips down the field but then quickly settles in to hold for the extra point. As he comes off the field he is mobbed by teammates.

On the bench, he has recovered his calm and acts like it was just another play.

The final minutes are gut wrenching. The Badger defense gives up a first down and panic begins to creep back in on the sidelines. Alvarez asks Cosgrove, "What are we doing?" after yet another OSU first down. Alvarez is 10 yards onto the field between plays and during time-outs, encouraging the defense. They respond. They force an OSU punt and Wisconsin has the ball with 3:27 remaining. Ohio State uses its final timeout with the Badgers facing a third and two from their own fourteen. After the time-out, Wisconsin lines up, but Schabert doesn't like what he sees on defense and calls a time-out. During the time-out, White and Alvarez discuss the play call and decide to run a naked bootleg with a fake handoff to Stanley. Sure enough, the defense buys it, going after Stanley, while out to the right, Schabert is alone as he scampers for six yards and a first down.

Stanley comes to the rescue again shortly thereafter, breaking a 24-yard run for another first down. There is nothing the Buckeyes can do to stop the clock. Alvarez finally lets out some emotion, embracing Sorgi, QB coach Jeff Horton, and outgoing athletic director Pat Richter. It is an emotional moment. As Schabert takes a knee and the clock winds down, Alvarez is drenched with a bucket of water. As if it matters.

He makes his way across the field with a policeman, searching for Ohio State coach Jim Tressel. The Wisconsin students begin to rush the field and the field quickly transforms into a sea of humanity as they attack the goalposts. The coach can't locate Tressel and makes his way toward the tunnel as fans pat him on the back. Back in the locker room, he hugs Evans for a few seconds. "Everybody was in and on, now weren't you?" he says to the team in the locker room. "You were focused all week and it shows you what you can do. But we can't lose focus, this was one game, we've got a very good Purdue team next week. Yes, I would be disappointed if you didn't celebrate tonight, but be careful."

With that, he greets more visitors and close friends with hugs, who seem to be enjoying the win as much as Alvarez. He is escorted into a hallway where he does his postgame radio interview, along with Evans, and then gets on an elevator to go upstairs for a press conference. The coach and player are greeted by 40 reporters. It is a big win for him personally, Alvarez admits, and he cuts Evans short when he starts to talk about the reaction to the choking of Sorgi. "Look at the film," Alvarez tells the reporters. (Ohio State's Reynolds was later suspended for one game for the incident.)

They head back downstairs where Cindy Alvarez waits outside the coaches' locker room, and husband and wife embrace. Alvarez goes inside and showers and redresses in his sport coat and tie. He and his wife walk over to the adjacent parking structure, where a traditional postgame tailgate for players and coaches is under way. His daughters and son are there, as are most of his assistants, but the coach and Cindy stay for just a few minutes. What they really want to do is go home and celebrate with their close friends.

It is time to be out and off.

• • •

Barry Alvarez trusts his staff and he trusts his players to work hard, to make progress, and to understand the importance of relying on one another. He makes the game fun for the players and his coaches, but he makes them play their best. After all, his understanding of the psychological components of the sport is perhaps more critical than his ability to X and O. With his eye on administration, he may not be on the sidelines much longer, but the skills that make a him a great coach will no doubt make him great at whatever he does.

Exactly a week later, on another rain-soaked field, LSU faces rival Auburn with the stakes just as high and the passion just as intense. Can the home team win again?

CHAPTER 7

Focused on the Future

Louisiana State University

#9 LSU vs. #17 Auburn
Baton Rouge, Louisiana
October 19-25

Each year when the schedules are announced, certain games automatically stand out. Great rivalries, match-ups between two top teams, late-season conference clinchers. The LSU-Auburn game has become one of these games, and this year it takes on more meaning because both teams had a shot at the national title. By the time they meet in Baton Rouge, LSU has lost just once while Auburn is struggling to prove that their preseason #1 ranking was no fluke. LSU's Nick Saban's intensity and discipline has apparently worn off on his players.

• • •

The 2003 LSU Football Media Guide is thick, coming in at 380 pages, held together by a black spiral spine. Within its covers, no aspect of the football program or the University is left untouched, from bowl records to media interview times, from the newly built academic center to the famous alumni of Baton Rouge. Images dominate, as it's easier to show a picture than to paint one with words. But what sets LSU's Media Guide apart from most others is its first five dozen pages. Player and coach bios don't even appear until page 68.

It's all about recruiting.

The inside of the front cover displays pictures of head coach Nick Saban and some of his players beside the slogan "Three Seasons, Three Bowls, One Title," along with emblems from the Peach, Sugar, and Cotton Bowls. The first page is the LSU fight song, the second and third the Table of Contents, spiced up with pictures and an offer to "relive LSU Football's finest moments" on page 50. Then comes the coach and player roster and the 2003 season preview, followed by a "Nick Saban Football" section, which includes his philosophies on work ethic and education and pictures of the coach with recent graduates. The academic staff is highlighted, as are players who have graduated under Saban. There is a full-page testament to the new Cox Communications Academic Center for Student Athletes. The Communications Lab has its own page; it features Tommy Karam, a professor who runs mock interviews and press conferences for players to instruct them how to handle the media. It is noted that this "also helps the LSU football players get prepared for the NFL combine."

There are four pages devoted to Campus Life, including a spread on the African-American Cultural Center and pictures of newly furnished apartments. Descriptions of the career development programs at LSU, profiles of Baton Rouge and Louisiana, and four pages of Tiger Stadium are included, as is a timeline of game day traditions. After a two-page highlight of the "National Spotlight," then come the facilities. The tour takes readers from the Charles McClendon Practice Facility to the renovated locker room and Captain's Lounge, the Lawton Room with auditorium seating for over 100, and the Hall of Champions. There are pages on strength and conditioning, athletic training, championship football, bowl games, and great moments in LSU history, as well as Tigers in the NFL. The next 10 pages are filled with shots of football greats, prominent LSU alums, and pictures of Tiger Pride members, those student volunteers—mostly women—who assist in recruiting. If you've made it through all of that, and a page devoted to the SEC, then you are free to meet the 2003 Tigers.

It is no accident that the media guide is arranged as it is. No detail is missing. After all, the media guide is not for the media. It's not for the players or the coaches or the campus bookstore. The media guide is put together for one group: the recruits. By the time a star running back gets to page 68, even if he's only looked at the pictures, he can't help but be impressed. And that's the point.

The media guide is just one of the tools that Saban and his staff have at their disposal, one of the tools that helped them secure 2001 and 2003 signing classes rated the best in the nation and a 2004 class rated a split-winner.

"How do we get recruits? It's Nick Saban," says assistant coach and recruiting coordinator Lance Thompson. "We sell the hell out of Nick Saban. The future is great. His philosophy, his system." Recruiting is a year-round job and the staff takes the cue from Saban. "This is the best recruiting staff I've ever been around," Thompson continues. "We have nine guys that can recruit. No school has 100 percent positives and you have to be honest and address the negatives. We do."

Talk to any staff member and he points a finger at the big man. Dr. Sam Nader, the Assistant Athletic Director for Football Operations, has been at LSU for decades, and has never been around a coach so focused on recruiting. "Why does Nick Saban have the top recruiting classes? He works at it year-round and not everybody does. He puts an emphasis on it."

Like most major football schools, LSU has the resources, the facilities, the bowl trophies, and the pro players to sway recruits. So there must be something that sets LSU apart. For Saban, it is the people. "I think we have success in recruiting because of the program. We do things to help players be successful as people . . . We care about them as people. We have a commitment to academics. Everybody wants to play in a successful program."

Recruiting is such a big part of LSU football that $595,000 was budgeted in 2002–2003 just for recruiting. That figure includes $450,000 for aircraft charters and $35,000 for recruiting publications, not including the $60,000 the program budgeted for all mailings. When Signing Day comes around in early February, the Bayou Bash is held by the football boosters. It is a 5,000-person party in Baton Rouge, with beer, gumbo, and jambalaya, which lasts from dawn till dusk. As letters of intent are faxed into the football office from recruits committing to LSU, they are relayed to the ballroom party and announced.

The coaches, including Saban, spend an enormous amount of time watching recruiting tapes in February and March, times when some staffs cut down on the work at the office. LSU reviews close to 1,400 tapes each spring according to Thompson, but only about 15 percent of the players on the tapes are able to play at the SEC level. The staff starts with a base of 5,000 or so potential recruits in February; after watching film, evaluating players during the month of May, and speaking with one another, they narrow that list to approximately 350 by summer. Then it becomes a battle. LSU inundates players with mail, faxes, and handwritten notes. "We err on the side of sending too much," says Nader. They keep after the kids through the process—something that doesn't go unnoticed.

Star receiver Michael Clayton, a Baton Rouge native, was at the top of everybody's list. Miami, Florida State, LSU—they all wanted him. He chose to stay home, not just because of the location, but because of Saban and the love that the LSU staff showed him. "I felt comfortable talking with Coach Saban. We would talk on the phone a lot. And he put in effort during the recruiting process. I knew that LSU wanted me."

There are two times when coaches can make an enormous impression on recruits: on the home visit and on official visits to campus. "Nick is a professional in the home. His lays out his philosophies, his goals, and how LSU can help launch a successful career," Nader points out. He's not one to cozy up with players and families; instead, he tells them his plan in a matter-of-fact way. By contrast, Thompson, who usually has made a home visit before joining Saban on his, takes a softer approach. "I'll feed the dog, do the dishes, play cards."

An official visit to LSU is much like one to any top school. It's about impressing the recruit and his parents with tours, meetings, and food. "In 48 hours, we want the kid to come away thinking, 'I can build a hell of a life for myself by going to LSU,' "Thompson says. The LSU coaches try to schedule official visits after the season, on weekends when the coaches can spend a lot of time with the recruits and their families. Occasionally, a recruit will make an official visit during the season, which is great in that it exposes him to the game day atmosphere, but coaches prefer a December or January visit when they have more time.

The highlight of the recruit's campus tour is the Cox Communication Academic Center. The $15 million center is a building on par with the world's finest museums. Consequently, the building, which opened in the fall of 2002, looks out of place on the Baton Rouge campus. With white marble floors, white walls, glass doors, and a lot of empty space, the center has become the centerpiece of the recruiting tour. A first-floor auditorium, which seats 1,000 and boasts wooden flooring, walls, and ceiling, is the largest on the LSU campus and is used for lecture classes. Each seat is equipped with computer hookups and Internet access. The second floor houses a library, 14 private computer rooms, a computer center with 75 flat-screen computers, and more rooms for private study, each equipped with a computer.

But again, it comes down to people.

"In recruiting, the head coach has to be very involved," says special teams and running backs coach Derek Dooley. "You have to sell everything. It takes a lot of work but you have to develop relationships. The players help tremendously and make kids feel wanted."

The evaluations and recruitment of players is never perfect but the system works for LSU. "We trust our system," Thompson points out. "Everybody makes mistakes. We'll evaluate anyone. But there's a saying, 'If they're recruiting you harder than you're recruiting them, then you probably don't want them.' "

Of course, recruiting is not the only thing Nick Saban and his coaches focus on every day. There is the small matter of preparing the team to play games. And to win them.

• • •

Monday morning brings a very early wake-up call—and not just for the staff. The players come to the meeting rooms in Tiger Stadium at 6:45 a.m. to meet with their position coaches. For the next 45 minutes, they review the game film from Saturday's win over South Carolina and discuss the positives and negatives. Saban's philosophy is to put the previous game behind them as soon as possible so when the team reconvenes for meetings and practice on Monday afternoon, the game has been laid to rest. The players are accustomed to the predawn meetings, even if they're not thrilled about them.

Later in the morning, Saban and his staff look ahead to #17 Auburn. The coaches watched Auburn film on their own on Sunday and into Monday, each responsible for a different aspect of the game plan: for example, red zone or blitz. The offensive and defensive staffs gather near noon to start putting it all together for the game plan. Saban himself is busy watching film alone in the staff conference room. He is a film nut. His assistants and players acknowledge that he has his hand in every facet of the game and that is largely due to the fact that he spends hours watching film.

For Nick Saban, there are not enough hours in the day and certainly not enough time to ever fully prepare.

• • •

Saban grew up outside the small mining town of Fairmont, West Virginia, the son of a service station and Dairy Queen owner who was also the proud coach of a midget football team. His childhood was tough by most people's standards, as he was under the stare of a perfectionist father. He excelled in sports at the high school level and continued his athletic career in college. Kent State University in Ohio is not known for producing football greats, but it is the alma mater of legendary coach Lou Holtz and Saban has now added his name to the list of distinguished alums. As a defensive back in the early 1970s for the Golden Flashes, Saban was not contemplating a career in professional football. He played shortstop on the baseball team and majored in Business. He really had no desire to coach until his college coach, Don James, hired him as a GA right out of school in 1973. He joined the staff full-time as a linebackers coach the following year, taking the opportunity to earn a Master's in Sports Administration. His father passed away unexpectedly during Saban's year as a GA and it proved to be a devastating blow. In his last conversation with his dad, Saban told him just how happy he was coaching.

After staying at Kent State for three seasons, the coach worked his way up the ladder—at Syracuse, West Virginia, Ohio State, and Navy. In 1983, Saban landed at Michigan State. He worked as a secondary coach and defensive coordinator under George Perles, but it was only a matter of time before the fast-rising coach would either become a college head coach or move on to the NFL. The pros came calling and, in 1988, Saban joined the Houston Oilers and Jerry Glanville as a secondary coach. The University of Toledo gave Saban his first head coaching job in 1990, and the coach led the team to a 9-2 season, enhancing his already growing national reputation. But again, he didn't stay long. After just one season at Toledo, he joined the Cleveland Browns and Bill Belichick as defensive coordinator, a job he would hold from 1991 to 1994.

When his former employer, Michigan State, came calling in 1995, Saban jumped at the chance to be a head coach at the elite level of college football. In his first season, the Spartans went 6-5-1. They followed that with a 6-6 season in 1996. Over the next two years, they hovered around the .500 mark, going 13-11. But in 1999, Saban and Michigan State exploded onto the national scene, going 10-2, finishing second in the Big Ten and #7 nationally. Saban, his wife, Terry, and their two kids, Nicholas and Kristen, were happy in Michigan. But then LSU fired Gerry DiNardo and was looking for someone to bring the Tigers back to glory. Saban, ever the journeyman, moved to Baton Rouge and became the 31st coach in school history. In his first season, the Tigers finished a respectable 8-4 and won the Peach Bowl. In 2001, they did even better, winning the SEC and the Sugar Bowl. Year 2002 was disappointing, as key injuries and tough losses conspired to keep them from reaching expectations. They finished 8-5 and lost to Texas, 35-20, in the Cotton Bowl.

Saban is not tall or physically imposing. He's of medium build and has brown hair peppered with a little gray. Expressive eyes and a stern smile make people think of the actor Tommy Lee Jones. He has earned a reputation for being intense. He starts early every day and the staff takes no lunch or dinner breaks, instead having food delivered, which allows them to get out of the office by ten on most nights.

"He's not one to pat you on the back when you do something good," says one assistant. "And he's not afraid to get on you in front of the players. It's just the way he is. But he is fair and successful and that's why guys want to work for him."

Saban acknowledges that there is a perception that he is difficult and distant, but doesn't agree with it. "A lot of people mistake my personality because I'm intense. The media makes a big deal out of it. I feel sometimes my image is way off the charts. People that know me say, 'That's not you.' "

He adds, "I was a GA for Don James. He had a systematic approach. [Here] we are out by ten and start at 7:30. I've always done it this way. I think you can't maintain focus unless you are rested. You can't run everybody down to nothing. We try to be as time-efficient as possible. It's not easy for anybody this way but we do it, evaluate it, and adjust."

"I think I failed to realize just how intense he is," says starting quarterback Matt Mauck, a former pro baseball player who resurfaced at LSU. "He is 100 percent all of the time. It is amazing how focused he can be." The star acknowledges that he and his teammates are not emotionally close with Saban but attributes that to Saban's position, not his personality. "You are much closer to your position coach than the head coach. The head coach can't be close to everyone because he has to be authoritative."

The guys who truly have their fingers on the pulses of the players are the medical and strength and conditioning staffs. They serve as a bridge between Saban and the team, often hearing things that players wouldn't tell a coach. "The players are around us with their hair down," says head trainer Jack Marucci. "This is like a sanctuary to them. Sometimes we'll pass things on to Coach Saban without using names and he listens." Tommy Moffitt, the strength coach, adds, "I think something that people don't realize is just how much Nick Saban cares for people."

Saban is active in every aspect of the program and is on the field during practice. Unlike many head coaches, who may survey practice from midfield, Saban is in the trenches with the defense. "When you're a head coach," he says, "you can get to be where you're not even coaching. I won't do that. I love being on the field. I would be bored to death if I just watched practice." Saban devotes "about

20 percent" of his time to the offense and tries to sit in with them every day to review film and talk about the opponent.

Working and playing for Saban is not easy. But he is fair, knowledgeable, and works harder than anyone else in the program, which earns him the respect of coaches and players alike. He is a football coach—and that's plenty.

· · ·

Upon entering the second floor of the LSU Athletic Administration Building, you are assaulted by purple. The carpet, the walls, the pictures hanging on those walls. A receptionist with a smile is there to greet you. On the wall to the right are framed portraits of each football coach, including the strength coach and equipment manager. Saban's picture is in the center of the top row, flanked by pictures of his two coordinators, Jimbo Fisher and Will Muschamp. On the opposite wall hang color photos of recent Tiger teams, as well as shots of players in action. The football office is split into two main wings—the defensive staff works on one side of the hall, while the offensive coaches fill the offices on the other side.

The defensive side also houses the recruiting suite, an offshoot from the hallway that is home to three offices, including those of Sam Nader and Lance Thompson. Directly across the hall is a student workroom. Further down the hall are the offices of defensive assistants Kirk Doll, Travis Jones, and Tim Walton, as well as the defensive meeting room. Muschamp has a spacious office connected to the meeting room. Next door is the video center for LSU football. It looks something like mission control at NASA. At the other end of the hallway are the offices of offensive coaches Stan Hixon, Derek Dooley, and Stacy Searels, as well as Fisher's spacious suite.

In the middle of the two wings is Nick Saban's office. The space is dominated by purple, accented by a large white rug with the LSU emblem embroidered on it. There is a sitting area underneath a purple wall where pictures and paintings hang, including one of a very large tiger. The office is sparsely decorated, quiet. There are game balls from memorable victories, a few pictures of Saban's family. But the inhabitor of the office is a bit more complex than the room would indicate.

· · ·

Saban spends Monday morning watching film in the conference room adjoining his office. A few minutes before noon, Sports Information

Director Michael Bonnette and Assistant Athletic Director for Television (yes, television!) Kevin Wagner arrive. Saban's weekly press conference is scheduled for noon, and he is jotting down notes for his opening statement. Dressed in a casual short-sleeve blue shirt, tan sport coat, and black slacks, the coach looks more ready for a night out in Los Angeles than a lunch in Louisiana. Saban, Bonnette, and Wagner take a private elevator up to the fifth floor where a crowd of 75 wait in the media room. Most are reporters but some are athletic department employees, including Athletic Director Skip Bertman. The crowd finishes up its lunch of gumbo and coleslaw and gets quiet as Saban takes the microphone.

He speaks briefly about the win over South Carolina, making sure to praise the play of his offensive line. He reviews the list of injuries and talks about how the Auburn game is important but no bigger than any other game, a message he will give his players during the week. When it comes time for questions, Saban's answers are short. Tension seems to exist between the media and Saban. He will never be a coach who makes friends with the media. He tries to avoid answering the silly questions, tries to avoid being manipulated into giving sound bites for reporters to use. But eventually, they get what they need and Saban can go back to work.

The reporters move on to the players, whom they meet in the media room inside Tiger Stadium. Typically, the players spend time with Professor Tommy Karam on Mondays before seeing the press. A 20-year Speech Communications professor with a Ph.D., Karam has been working with LSU athletes and coaches since he began working with Shaquille O'Neal in 1994. He conducts mock interviews and press conference sessions, tapes student-athletes' and coaches' deliveries, and breaks it all down like a football coach. "The visual delivery and tone in answering is key," the doctor says. "I want players and coaches to be comfortable in what they're doing." Many schools bring in media specialists for a two-hour seminar in preseason, but this kind of attention is unique. It is a seminar that continues throughout a player's years at LSU. "I think student-athletes deserve media training," says Karam. "The kids are fascinated by it."

The large media room is in the north end zone of Tiger Stadium, adjacent to the home of the LSU players. A new players-only lounge—Captain's Lounge—has a purple felt pool table, a Foosball table, leather chairs, and a large-screen television. Outside the lounge, in the chute leading into the locker room, there are colorful displays on the wall. One wall has a pyramid, labeled "Tiger Goals 2003." In the pyramid, opponents' logos are stacked atop one another. During a game week, that opponent's tile is removed and placed on display in the locker room or team meeting room. After a victory, the entire team signs the 18-inch tile and it is placed back into the pyramid. A loss means no signatures and a removal of the tile. Previous years' goals and signed tiles are displayed across the hallway.

The Florida tile is missing, LSU's only loss on the year, as is the Auburn tile which now rests on an easel in the team auditorium. Will it find its way back to the pyramid?

• • •

At 1:45, special teams and running backs coach Derek Dooley commands the attention of most of the team in the auditorium, the Bill Lawton Room, as he reviews special teams from the South Carolina game in preparation for Auburn. Dooley is the son of the legendary Georgia coach, Vince, and also is a former lawyer.

"Football has always been part of my life," he says. "I was accustomed to the routine. I had no intention of coaching and actually enjoyed law school but it seemed like something was missing. After reading Colin Powell's book, *My American Journey*, where his fondest memories are of being with his troops, both positive and negative—that's the part I was missing."

He speaks to the special teams' players in a voice booming with enthusiasm, rapidly moving from one clip to another, or one diagram of Auburn kickoff coverage to another. Saban enters just as Dooley begins and takes a seat, front and center. He contributes comments throughout, at one point telling the kickers they did a poor job against South Carolina and reminding them that kicking "is not rocket science." Pointing out poor technique on kick coverage, Saban tells one player, "God gave you hands, use them." In a very short full-team meeting that follows, the coach tries to keep the game in perspective, noting that the media will try to make this a "game of the century." But, he says, it's just another game.

When the meeting ends, the offense stays in the room while the defense and Saban head across the hall. Offensive coordinator Jimbo Fisher, dressed in suit pants and an LSU windbreaker, reviews the Auburn defensive personnel, player by player, as the team follows along in a massive scouting report. He goes over diagrams of Auburn defenses, blitzes, and tendencies, as the players begin to fade. "They're a good football team but they're not great," he tells them. In fact, the Auburn defense is ranked #8 nationally in total defense.

In the running backs meeting that follows, Dooley echoes that sentiment, telling his backs that the Tiger defense is solid but that LSU can run on them. Turning to the group—and his freshmen running backs in particular, who all had big games against South Carolina—the coach says, "You think this [South Carolina] week was tough. That wasn't tough. What have you been getting all week?" he asks. "Phone numbers," one of the players jokes. But the coach's point is made: The freshmen are no longer a secret and Auburn will be ready. "This week will be tough."

• • •

Afternoon meetings do not last long, as the players have to catch the bus at 3:35. The bus? The practice field and indoor facility are a half-mile walk from the locker room in Tiger Stadium down a busy street, so the players take converted school buses, painted white with purple stripes and a Tiger sign, to and from practice each day. There are four outdoor grass fields at the facility, one of which is shared by the University High School team for games. The coaches drive over and park next to the indoor facility. Saban arrives wearing purple shorts, a white shirt, sunglasses, and a large straw hat to protect himself from the sun on this unusually hot mid-October day.

Practice starts with kicks but quickly moves into the "Correction" period. For 10 minutes, the offense and defense split and their coaches walk the players through mistakes that they made against South Carolina. The defense makes sure the positioning is right, while the offense makes sure the proper routes and blocking schemes are run. Once practice gets going, the expected intensity isn't there—too many passes are dropped, too many poor routes are run. At one point, Fisher stops the work, paces in front of the offense, and screams, "I don't like the attitude today and I don't like the tempo today." Point taken. Saban works solely with the defense and, in individual periods, with the cornerbacks and safeties. He is active the entire practice, moving around, yelling, and making changes on defense. The team runs ten 40-yard sprints as part of conditioning.

After showering, the coaches meet up to review practice film before looking at more Auburn film. For Tuesday, they are focused on runs on first and 10 and second and long, as well as goal line situations. As is typical, the staff leaves by 10:00 p.m., though there are often later nights.

Just as there are often early mornings. Defensive coordinator Will

Muschamp is in the office at 5:30 a.m. on Tuesday, and the defensive assistants join him by 7:30. As Kirk Doll, Travis Jones, and Tim Walton look on, Muschamp stands at the wipe board, checking off plays that they ran in practice on Monday and those they will run Tuesday. Each practice day is assigned a colored marker, so by Thursday the staff knows which plays they ran in practice and how many times they did it. Instead of "21" or "11" personnel terminology used at many schools, the LSU staff uses colors to identify personnel groups: Silver, Green, Blue. On the table sit scouting notebooks filled with Auburn offensive plays diagrammed in previous weeks by the GAs.

Muschamp, Saban, and the defensive staff are most concerned with Auburn's rushing game. Led by Carnell "Cadillac" Williams, the three-time and reigning SEC Player of the Week, as well as Ronnie Brown and Brandon Jacobs, Auburn has averaged over 260 yards rushing over the past five games. But Muschamp knows that the LSU defense is playing well. Last week against South Carolina, they held the Gamecocks to officially *zero* yards rushing. The LSU defense is ranked #1 in the nation in scoring defense (9.9 points per game) and rushing defense (53.1 yards per game). The defense is anchored by tackle Chad Lavalais, ends Marquise Hill and Marcus Spears and corner Corey Webster.

There is a different feel to the start of Tuesday's practice. Saban and his assistants are animated while walking through plays and during individual drill work. Saban throws deep balls in a long ball position drill for his corners. As it turns out, the former high school QB has a good arm. When practice shifts to team versus scout work, his positive attitude begins to crumble, as he kicks a scout team player off the field for not putting in effort.

In 9 versus 7 drills things look better, but the offense still struggles to be sharp. Not only are receivers dropping balls, quarterbacks missing targets, running backs being lazy, and linemen lacking intensity, the scout team is bungling their assignments. Fisher loses it, screaming, "Get the right card! Get the right card!" as the GAs scramble for cover with no place to go. When the first-team offense and defense go against one another, the intensity picks up again. As each scripted play winds down, the coaches immediately jump into action, screaming and injecting themselves into players' faces.

Back in their offices at night, the offensive coaches realize practice looks even worse on film. "We had a bad practice," Fisher tells his assistants on more than one occasion. "Just no intensity." As the staff chows down food, they watch the various practice drills and take notes of what went wrong. At this point in the week, the LSU offense does not look ready. Maybe on Saturday night they'll pay the price.

• • •

On Wednesday morning, the mood in the offensive meeting room is grave. Fisher, Thompson, Hixon, Dooley, and Searels are shaping the game plan, erasing from the master board plays that didn't work in practice or won't work against a tough Auburn defense. Saban joins them at 10:15 and they rise to attention. They fill the coach in on what they are thinking of running in third and long and the coach agrees on most. The coaches are brisk and attentive, perhaps in part because of the large box of Krispy Kremes nearby.

But yawns abound during the quarterbacks' meeting with Fisher at 2:00 in the Bill Lawton Room. Even Fisher cannot help contain his yawns; the late nights and early mornings are finally catching up with him. He talks through some of the plays that worked in practice and those the coaches are planning to implement in the game plan. "Matt, did that feel comfortable?" he asks Matt Mauck on numerous occasions, making sure the signal caller is confident running certain plays. As Fisher points out after the meeting, "It's one thing if it looks good on paper or on film but if he [Matt] isn't comfortable, then we're not going to run it. He's the one out there doing it, not me."

Fisher tells the quarterbacks that Auburn blitzes close to 60 percent of the time when the offense faces a third and medium or long. Then, as if suddenly struck by a reminder, Fisher picks up his cell and calls equipment manager Greg Stringfellow to ask him to have wet footballs ready for practice. There is a chance of rain on Saturday night and the coach wants the quarterbacks and running backs ready.

As a surprise gift to the players, practice is moved inside into the indoor facility. Temperatures are in the 80s Wednesday afternoon, so it isn't due to the weather. Saban wants to mix things up, break the routine, create more intensity in practice. The players love it, as they get to practice in air conditioning for the first time in a long time.

Practice begins with the offense running game plays at full speed. A few of the assistant coaches play a mock defense against the team, and Derek Dooley uses a tubelike pad to whack approaching QBs or running backs who carry the ball. But soon, the full first teams are going up against one another from the 15-yard line. Saban is running around—standing in the secondary, then at the line of scrimmage. When the offense completes passes or makes huge gaps for the running backs, the coach lashes out at the defense. At one point, he bows his head into the defensive huddle and yells a single word: "Compete!"

As each period concludes with a blow from a horn, there is movement not only on the field but up on the skylifts as well. The video crew's coordination is impressive, involving ropes, bags, tapes, and runners. At most schools, the camera operators lower down tapes on rope pulleys to video crews who take them inside to begin the process of digitizing and editing so the coaches can review them right after practice. At most schools, that process happens once or twice during the practice. But at LSU, the camera crews lower tapes after *every* period or drill. Every drill is on a separate tape. Videography Director Doug Aucoin or one of his student assistants will move around the fields collecting the tapes, which are then given to a driver whose sole job is to drive the tapes back to the offices, drop them off with a waiting editing crew, and then return to the practice facility to repeat the process.

With Saban's reliance on film it is no surprise that the video staff takes their work to another level.

• • •

Early Wednesday evening, Saban pays a visit to Jeff Boss at his home. Boss has been with the LSU coaching staff for 24 years, most of them as equipment manager. Coaches and players come and go, but Boss is a constant, providing a listening ear, a favor, the latest joke. Before he came to LSU in 1980, he was a high school teacher and coach in Louisiana.

In recent months, Boss has not been there to welcome players to the locker room or to handle every request from the coaching staff or to be the loudest cheerleader on the sidelines. In January, he was diagnosed with brain cancer. It was blow not only to his family, but to the entire LSU family as well. The diagnosis hit Saban particularly hard, as he had grown quite close to Boss in his four years in Baton Rouge. After months of surgery, chemotheraphy, and treatment, the cancer could not be contained and by mid-October Boss was resting comfortably at his home, knowing his fate.

He was never out of the minds of the LSU players and staff, however, as they dedicated the season to him, wore patches with "JB" on their uniforms, helmets, and football apparel and named the team locker room after him. At this point, he is clinging to life, but still able to talk and receive visitors. Saban pays a private visit before his most public weekly outing.

• • •

The coach presents a different side of himself at the Superior Grill on Wednesday night. The restaurant in midcity Baton Rouge is packed by the time the coach arrives for his seven o'clock radio show. In fact, some patrons arrived at the restaurant at 2:30 just to make sure they got a seat. Approximately 800 people are jammed inside, most wearing LSU shirts. Those in the adjoining dining room do not miss any action as Saban and the host, Jim Hawthorne, are beamed via closed-circuit television all over the premises.

When Saban walks in, the restaurant erupts. The coach immediately begins to shake hands and sign autographs. The hour-long show is dominated by callers from all over Louisiana, but also from Texas, Alabama, and South Carolina. They want to know about injuries, trick plays, and practice. Between segments, Saban hops off his stool, takes off his headset, and immediately hits the crowd again, continuing to work the room where he has left off.

This coach, who buries himself in film and preparation and has a reputation for being hard-nosed, is just the opposite for 60 minutes every Wednesday. Perhaps he knows how far an hour of appreciation can go with the fans; perhaps he enjoys getting away from the game, if only for a short time. He makes a quick exit when it is over and heads home to make recruiting phone calls and to watch part of the Virginia Tech–West Virginia game.

Saban's good feeling from Wednesday night carries over into Thursday afternoon. The mood at practice is jovial. Players and coaches are joking with one another, Saban included. Terry Saban, Nick's wife, arrives just at the start of practice, an occurrence that's not unusual. But today she is there with a purpose, to meet Dorothy Faye McClendon, wife of the late and legendary LSU coach, Charles McClendon. As it turns out, in all of the years that her husband coached the Tigers, Dorothy Faye never came to a practice. After she told this to Terry Saban at the luncheon meeting of the Bengal Belles, another football booster group, Terry insisted that McClendon meet her at practice. At 4:00 p.m., she arrives with friends.

The players are not in full pads as they go through a rather long Thursday practice, working on the two-minute drill, two-point conversions, and the kicking game. Punt coverage takes place in the middle of practice, while field goals, PATs, and kickoffs are run at the end. Saban's good mood allows him to walk over to the sidelines at times during practice, to shake hands with Dorothy Faye and others, before quickly jumping back on the field to coach. He breaks momentarily, but never stops coaching. The second he's back on the field, he pulls aside some secondary players and instructs them on the side. When the final horn sounds at 5:30 p.m., practice is over but there is one more meeting. On Thursdays, the team regroups to watch film one more time.

• • •

"This is the best team we've had here," Nick Saban tells ESPN's Ron Franklin, Mike Gottfried, Adrian Karsten, and producer Bill Bonnell at their Friday morning sit-down in the coach's office. "We've got good kids with good character. No off-the-field problems." In the 35-minute meeting, the coach tells the crew that his team and staff "choked" against Florida; that Auburn can "do a multitude of things"; that LSU must play the blocks and tackle the runner; that the play of both schools' quarterbacks may determine the outcome of the game; that the progress of Matt Mauck is impressive and that statistics can be misleading. The coach wraps up quickly as he is scheduled to speak at the LSU Gridiron Club luncheon at noon.

Arriving just in time at Drusilla's Seafood, the coach attaches a clip-on microphone and stands up in the middle of the banquet room in front of 175 or so LSU supporters. "We reestablished our identity and we need the fans to find theirs." He implores them to cheer loud and long and reminds them that the crowd makes the home field an advantage. He takes questions about playing Mauck in the shotgun, the trio of freshmen running backs, and how he plans to use the tight ends. He is humorous and charming and the crowd eats it up.

(After leaving the event the author is confronted in the parking lot by two members of the Gridiron Club who noticed a stranger taking notes in the corner while Saban spoke. They believe the author is an Auburn spy. A simple explanation clears it up.)

• • •

By Friday night's dinner, silence engulfs the Tigers. The feast is held in the banquet room of the Lod Cook Alumni Center, which adjoins the Lod Cook Hotel on campus, where the team stays the nights before home games. (For team travel, lodging, and meals, the program spends approximately $735,000 a year.) Table by table, the players line up to fill their plates with steak, chicken, pasta, potatoes, and banana pudding. As they finish eating, they head back to their rooms and change into bright purple LSU sweat suits. At 7:15 the team boards two buses for a night at the movies. Starters on offense, defense, and special teams sit on the first bus and everyone else is assigned to the second. Escorted by four police vehicles with sirens and lights in action, the buses make the 10-minute trek to a local Cineplex. They enter the theater through the back door and are seated immediately.

Set in 1970s South Carolina, *Radio* is the inspirational true story of a young man with special needs who is befriended by a local high school football coach. Though there is some football in the film, it is primarily a character-based drama. A few of the players fall asleep, and keep others awake with their snoring. Saban himself seems restless, tapping his fingers on the armrest and shaking his leg.

When the players and coaches return, the team managers have the Lod Cook meeting room doors opened, awaiting the team's arrival, and the players separate into offense and defense. In the offensive meeting, Jimbo Fisher keeps it brief, showing an Auburn defensive formation from a previous game and pointing with a red laser to each offensive position, asking for a call. All 11 position players shout out their call, and all 11 are right. They are focused and ready, so much so that Fisher doesn't even go through all that he had planned.

Then comes the highlight of the night—the presentation video. It begins with a quote from Auburn coach Tommy Tuberville: "When you win three of four, it's not a rivalry." A three-minute montage of big plays set to hip-hop follows. The video concludes with brief clips from some of the memorable LSU-Auburn games. There is the famous Earthquake Game of 1988, when a last-second touchdown caused the seismograph on campus at LSU to register an earthquake. There is the Barn Burner of 1996, when a nearby structure erupted in flames during the game in Auburn. There is the infamous 1999 Auburn win, when Auburn players lit cigars and smoked them at midfield in Tiger Stadium. But can they stop it from happening again?

• • •

In the morning, Saban makes a stop at his daughter Kristen's soccer game, then joins the team for a breakfast of eggs, waffles, and grits. After a brief team walk outside, the team splits into offense and defense one more time. On the defensive side, Will Muschamp calls on

11 different players who each stand up and give a scouting report on their assigned area: regular personnel, trick plays, the quarterback, the fullback. Some use note cards, some recite by memory; safety Jack Hunt comes well prepared with a folder. At the conclusion of the 15-minute meeting, Muschamp addresses the team. "This is a battle. You have to knock your guy on his ass then get back in the huddle and knock him on his ass again. Then get back in the huddle and do it again. You need to do it for all 60 minutes. If everyone does their part, we'll win the battle."

The two-hour break before the pregame religious services and meal gives the coaches a chance to relax, watch games on television, and review the game plan. There are two pregame chapels: one is a shortened Catholic Mass, the other nondenominational. Local pastor Ken Ellis leads the general service, as he has been doing for the past seven years. There are 18 players and six coaches in attendance, and they sit silently, dressed in coats and ties, waiting for the 2:15 service to begin. "Today, I want to talk to you about the Secrets of Champions," Ellis informs the group. "Winners and losers are not separated by different skill, but rather different decisions." After relaying the adage, "Winners never quit, quitters never win," he tells them of the remarkable perseverance of Abraham Lincoln who lost eight elections, failed twice in business, and suffered a nervous breakdown, yet went on to become President of the United States in 1860. He talks about Joseph of the Old Testament and his ability to overcome obstacles after getting knocked down. As if required, he speaks of David versus Goliath.

The pregame meal is silent. Most of the players eat quickly and walk out, waiting to rejoin their team in meetings at 4:10. The offense does a walk-through in a banquet room at the appointed time, but it really is more of a sit-through. The offensive starters grab chairs upon entering the room, and align themselves in an 11-man formation. They sit in their chairs and stare straight ahead. Some of the backups take chairs and place themselves directly in front of the offensive line and receivers, as if playing defense. It looks like a game of musical chairs being played by some very large men. Jimbo Fisher calls out plays and the defense and some of the offense simply adjust their chairs, while sitting in them, to indicate new positioning. Each player on offense points out or calls out his responsibility on the play. This continues for 15 minutes. When he is done, Fisher takes the extra minutes before boarding the buses to reemphasize his, and Saban's, message from yesterday. "When they walk off the field at the end of the game, we want them saying, 'I don't ever want to play LSU again.' "

. . .

The two large buses that make the mile drive across campus have no LSU logos or any indication that the buses carry the home team. So as they make their way down Dalrymple Drive toward the stadium, the revved-up faithful have no idea that it is LSU, and not Auburn, on the buses. They make hand gestures and they shout obscenities. One endearing coed decides to show her bare breasts. The buses drop off the team before they get to the stadium for the Tiger Walk—a downhill walk flanked by thousands of fans. Some of the players stop and shake hands, some give hugs and kisses to relatives. As they approach the entrance to the locker room, the crowd breaks out into chants of, "LSU! LSU!"

The crowd slowly begins to make its way in from the parking lots as game time approaches. The student sections, however, are filled 90 minutes before kickoff, as their seating is on a first-come, first-serve basis. Many of the students wear gold T-shirts and hold gold pompoms. They pack themselves in, tight enough to make a fire marshall nervous. Inside the locker room, preparations continue for the players as some of the coaches gather to watch the end of the Alabama-Tennessee game on a mounted television in the equipment room. Groups are called onto the field by strength coach Tommy Moffitt and the team begins warm-ups. Saban joins them, not pacing at midfield but rather working with the defense.

At 6:00 p.m., the public address announcer relays the following: "There is lightning reported eight miles from the stadium." Warm-ups continue as drizzle begins. Then things come to a halt as a bolt of lightning, coupled with thunder, strikes nearby. At 6:10, both teams run off the field into the locker rooms. For most teams, there would be panic. But the same scenario unfolded for LSU before the season opener against Louisiana-Monroe, so the staff and players have experience with delays.

After the officials speak with Saban and Auburn coach Tommy Tuberville, it is decided, based on radar images, that the storm will pass and if there is no more lightning before 6:38, the teams can retake the field and have 25 minutes to warm up. Saban informs his staff of the plan. He meets the team, which is stretching out in the meeting room.

"There is nothing in pregame—the weather, Auburn talking, disrespect, whatever—that has any impact on the game," he tells the anxious group. "We've been through this before." He informs them they will do a stretch with Moffit, followed by drills, before heading back to the locker room. On their way to the field, Saban stops at the exit and is introduced to two Sugar Bowl officials who are in town for the game, taking refuge in the LSU chute before kickoff. The introductions are brief but meaningful, as Saban hopes they will meet again.

When the team is back in the locker room, Saban turns red and his eyes flare so they match the purple in his shirt. "If your ---- isn't hotter than it's ever been, then there's something wrong," he tells his team. After reciting the requisite "giving 100 percent" and "playing 60-minutes of football," he appeals to their pride. "This is personal," he shouts. The players are smiling, almost in disbelief, since most of them have never seen Saban so worked up before a game. But they understand.

Just as the lightning had struck unexpectedly, so does the LSU offense. On a third and five from LSU's 36-yard line just minutes into the game, quarterback Matt Mauck drops back and spots receiver Devery Henderson, who has broken free on the near sideline. Mauck lofts the ball over a fallen defender and Henderson pulls it in and runs the rest of the way along the LSU sideline for a touchdown, just 119 seconds into the game. Mauck makes his way up and down the benches, slapping his teammates' helmets, telling them, "This is OUR game! This is OUR game!" When Auburn elects to go for it on fourth and one on their first possession, LSU defensive tackle Chad Lavalais moves untouched into the backfield and slams Cadillac Williams in the backfield for a five-yard loss. The tone is set.

Though it is just minutes into the game, defensive coordinator Will Muschamp is soaked in sweat, wiping his forehead with a large white wristband which doubles as an eraser for the portable wipe board he uses on the sideline. The defense takes their seats on the bench as Muschamp goes to work, making adjustments, giving reminders, backing off for a moment as Saban comes over. Throughout the game, the coaches never stop coaching. The LSU staff, on both sides of the ball, spends almost every minute with the players.

Mauck leads an LSU charge as the offense moves the ball at will on a supposedly tough Auburn defense. With 7:43 left in the first quarter, Mauck hits Michael Clayton on a screen and watches as the star receiver dodges, cuts, and leaps his way into the end zone for an

18-yard touchdown. After another defensive stand and an impressive 44-yard punt return by Skyler Green to the Auburn 28, LSU's running back Alley Broussard takes the ball in from five yards out to increase the lead. Just twelve minutes into the game, it is LSU 21, Auburn 0. It marks the first time since 1985 that LSU scored 21 or more points in the first quarter against an SEC opponent; they did it then against Vanderbilt. Players hug each other and the offense encourages the defense, but the coaches remain serious. At one point, Saban looks about to burst but retains his game face.

The defense begins to buckle a bit, but does prevent Williams or any of the three vaunted backs from gaining huge yardage. Phillip Yost's field goal from LSU's 18 is wide left. But soon the LSU offense gets stymied as well. After one of the more remarkable quarters of the season, they seem to sputter in the second stanza. They get a break when Auburn punt returner Tre Smith fumbles a kick, giving LSU great field position deep inside Auburn territory. But they can't convert—kicker Ryan Gaudet misses the field goal attempt. On the sidelines, Mauck talks on the phone with Jimbo Fisher up in the booth. When he finishes, Michael Clayton waves Mauck over and tells him, "I can't hear you out there. You need to signal."

Saban paces up and down the sideline. He is actively involved in all aspects of the game, from jumping into sideline huddles to high-fiving players as they come off the field to making "suggestions" to Fisher and Muschamp. The Tigers get another gift when Smith fumbles yet another punt with just under one minute to go in the first half. But again, LSU cannot convert, as Mauck is intercepted on Auburn's 14. Saban's good humor is gone. They have had two great opportunities in the second quarter to put Auburn away, but couldn't do it.

• • •

"Guys, we should have buried them. We missed two great chances," Saban tells the entire staff crammed into his dressing room at halftime. "We need to stay positive with the kids but, crap, what are we doing out there on offense, guys?"

The defensive staff stays in the room and goes over their plan. The offensive staff moves next door into the Captain's Lounge and struggles to find answers. As they lay out papers and diagrams on the covered pool table, Fisher takes suggestions from his assistants. More option, more sweeps are suggested, but it seems every idea has a negative.

With the team gathered in front of him, Saban has some last words at halftime. "We played our guts out the first quarter and played like [word] in the second quarter." He reminds them that they must play 60-minutes of football and that Auburn will try to come out and put points on the board. It is as emotional as his pregame talk, the passion still there in his voice and eyes. He has coached long enough to know that no lead is ever safe.

The offense plays better in the third quarter, and a 33-yard field goal by Gaudet increases the lead to 24-0, but the mood stays glum when star LSU cornerback Corey Webster cramps up midway into the third quarter. A game of "Pass It Down the Line" results, as the news goes from trainer Jack Marucci to Saban to Muschamp to Randall Gay, who replaces Webster.

After Mauck appears to hit Henderson on a long bomb for another touchdown, the usually steady receiver drops the ball and a sure seven points. But just a few plays later, he does earn the seven, making a difficult leaping catch for a 16-yard touchdown pass and the rout is clearly on. The players on the sidelines are back into the game and many of them try to stir up the crowd when the Tigers are on defense.

Heading into the fourth quarter, as the players, coaches, and managers all raise four fingers, the result of the game is no longer in doubt. But will they get the shutout? The offense does not move the ball early in the fourth and as the offensive line takes a seat on the bench, line coach Stacy Searels is not happy. Rudy Niswanger, who is starting in place of injured Nate Livings, missed an assignment and Searels is letting him hear it. "Don't come off the field the next time unless you score a touchdown," he demands. The 6'6" former Auburn player and coach seems to have more to say but holds it in check as he paces in front of the bench.

Facing a fourth and four from LSU's six-yard line with just over six minutes left in the game, Auburn quarterback Jason Campbell hits Anthony Mix for a six-yard TD pass, finally putting Auburn on the board. The air is let out of the shutout hopes, but the defensive performance is still hugely impressive. The Auburn players do not celebrate much, nor do their sidelines. By this time, most of the Auburn fans and students have exited the stadium, as have some LSU fans, eager to beat the traffic or get an early start on postgame tailgating. In the final six minutes, the loudest cheer comes when the PA announcer proclaims that the Florida Marlins have just defeated the New York Yankees to win the World Series.

Saban never stops coaching, and as LSU runs the ball down the field in the closing minutes, he screams at Mauck for not letting the play clock run down further before calling for the snap. After tight end David Jones catches a Mauck pass and runs 15 yards for a first down, Mauck simply takes a knee and the game ends. Saban runs to midfield, where he has an awkward moment with Tuberville, wanting to be gracious in victory but knowing how badly he wanted the win. The coach sprints to the student section where he is greeted by a loud roar. He responds with clapping of his own, acknowledging their role in the victory. As he makes his way off the field, two Fiesta Bowl officials shake his hand and congratulate him.

It was a dominant offensive and defensive performance by the Tigers. Against the acclaimed Auburn defense, they piled up 157 rushing yards and 381 yards of total offense. Freshman Justin Vincent ran for 127 yards. On the other side of the ball, the defense held Cadillac Williams to just 61 yards on 20 carries, with his longest run being 10 yards. Ronnie Brown and Brandon Jacobs, the other star backs, combined for eight carries for just 33 yards. Part of that is due to the stellar play of the LSU defense, part is due to the fact that Auburn played from a hole the entire game and had to pass to get back in it. In postgame comments, Auburn coach Tommy Tuberville says, "We have no excuses. They lined up and whipped us on both sides of the ball."

• • •

The team is in the chute tunnel, as the crowd inside grows larger with friends, recruits, and officials standing in the back. The team counts by ones up to 31, the number of points they scored, and then breaks into the LSU fight song, led by Saban. They take a knee and fall silent. Saban tells them before they pray to say a special one for Jeff Boss, whom he had visited on Wednesday. "He is in a good place and he is comfortable," he tells them. "Keep him in your prayers." Saban lets the players know how proud he is of them and how they dominated on both sides of the ball. He then talks about the 24-hour rule—never celebrating a win or bemoaning a loss for more than 24 hours. They play Louisiana Tech next Saturday, a team not be overlooked.

With that, they huddle for a team break and go into the locker room. Saban follows, walking around the locker room, shaking hands with each player. He emerges and shakes hands with recruits and their families, knowing most of them by name. He greets the Fiesta Bowl officials one more time for formal introductions and one says, "I know we're your second choice [the national championship game will be the Sugar Bowl], but we would love to have you. It was a great atmosphere." Saban thanks them for the invite, but the Fiesta Bowl is far from his mind. He meets with more recruits in the Captain's Lounge next door before giving a brief press conference in the adjoining meeting room. On his way back to his dressing room, two Citrus Bowl officials offer their praises as well as an invite. Not bad for a day's work.

But the night is not over for the coach. He does his postgame radio show and spends yet more time with recruits and their families, as do his assistants. He shakes hands, accepts congratulations, and is in a good mood, but not overjoyed. His team had played well, yes, but there were errors, and failing to capitalize on opportunities eats at him. He is a competitor, and that's why he is never satisfied and why, close to midnight, he is celebrating not with friends and family, but with teenagers he hardly knows.

Late Sunday, Jeff Boss falls into a coma. He passes away on Monday.

• • •

In many ways, Nick Saban is a simple man. He is focused on football, all of the time. He strives for perfection, as he learned from his late father, and that drive keeps him working overtime. But his teams win, his players go to class, and move onto the NFL and his program has few off-the-field problems. Not bad for a man who never aspired to be a coach.

Though LSU won this rivalry game, Florida State lost one of theirs, setting up a winner-take-all showdown against North Carolina State.

CHAPTER 8

The Governor

Florida State University

#13 Florida State vs. North Carolina State
Tallahassee, Florida
November 9-15

After rising to as high as #3 in the national polls, Florida State seemed to be on track for yet another appearance in the national title game, but they were stopped by an unlikely foe—Clemson. In facing off against his son, Tommy, for the fifth time, Bobby Bowden watched his team come out flat and lose 26-10. The loss was devastating for Bowden and his staff and now it will take a win against North Carolina State to win the ACC title outright and a guaranteed BCS bowl. With quarterback Chris Rix, as well as Bowden and his offensive co-ordinator and son, Jeff, under criticism, it will not be an easy week in Tallahassee.

• • •

Losing stinks. There it is. It's said. Any competitor, player, or coach will tell you the same. And when the ramifications of losing are so big, it stinks even more. How big are these for ramifications? A crowd of 81,000 people watch you lose in person and millions more see you lose on television, some people's jobs are at stake while others' are made more difficult, the regional economy is affected, and you no longer have a shot at the national championship.

As coaching staffs will, the football staff at Florida State University hunkered down after the loss. They relied on no one but themselves. They got to work earlier and left later. They answered fewer questions and were more suspect of strangers. They watched more film, evaluated more plays, joked much less.

In Bowden Bowl V, the annual match-up between father Bobby and son Tommy, the offspring finally got the best of the old man. Clemson dominated the Seminoles in every facet of the game: offense, defense, and special teams. The final score was 26-10 and it wasn't even that close. Bobby Bowden took the loss particularly hard. "I've never seen him like this after a loss since I've been here," says Athletic Director Dave Hart, now in his ninth year at FSU. From assistants to secretaries to administrators, everyone recognized that Bowden was not the same person this week; the loss had changed him. After looking at the game film, it wasn't that his team did not play hard, it was that Clemson played harder. The previous week, FSU had dominated Notre Dame on the road while Clemson was demolished by Wake Forest. The Seminole players went into the game with the wrong mind-set and Bowden took the blame. But he wasn't the only one. Offensive coordinator Jeff Bowden was blasted in the press for poor play calling during the loss. The running backs gained only 11 yards and were ridiculed. Quarterback Chris Rix was booed by FSU fans and talk turned toward replacing him for this week's game.

"When you lose, it's not a very good feeling," says 27-year running backs coach Billy Sexton. "You have to get back in, and analyze why." Saturday's game against N.C. State in Tallahassee was supposed to be a regular conference game. The Seminoles could have won the ACC title outright by beating Clemson. For now, they are assured of at least a share of the title, but not the BCS bid. They could have gotten the automatic BCS bowl berth and, with only one loss to Miami, they still had a good shot at the national title game. But the Clemson loss has changed everything. There will be no national title this year. The Seminoles have to play the Wolfpack, who have beaten them two straight times, including two years ago in Tallahassee, just to win the ACC. The game will be one of the most meaningful in Bowden's 28-year tenure at FSU. Now, as long as he can make his players see that . . .

• • •

The questions about the quarterback are not unexpected. Against Clemson, Chris Rix threw two interceptions, fumbled once, and missed open receivers repeatedly. Rix was bad enough that Bowden replaced him with backup Fabian Walker with just over eight minutes left in the game. Walker was 11 for 21 with one long touchdown pass.

For his 4:00 p.m. Sunday teleconference with the media, Bowden prepares for the inevitable. When asked if he is "comfortable with where you are with Chris Rix," the coach responds, "No. I'm not happy with the way we played, but I'm not happy with either one of them. Chris definitely was not hot, but Fabian missed enough passes—he had four or five people open, and he bounced the ball to them. I can't see why I would make a change." A follow-up question presses the coach about Walker, and Bowden acknowledges that he might act sooner to insert Walker in the future.

The coach expects more quarterback questions from the Seminole Booster Club during Monday's lunch. Held in a fourth-floor banquet room in a building attached to Doak Campbell Stadium, 350 Seminole boosters take their seats before noon, eating a buffet lunch of chicken, rice, and vegetables. Just after twelve, the crowd rises to its feet and launches into an ovation as the man of the hour arrives. Dressed in a dark blue suit and red tie, Bowden makes his way up to the dais and takes a seat. The coach feasts on salad and lobster—an upgrade from the lunch enjoyed by his audience. His wife, Ann, a usual presence, is not here. After some brief remarks by Charlie Barnes, Executive Director of the booster club, Bowden is introduced and, again, a standing ovation is given. The afternoon is becoming a State of the Union speech. And all of this following a loss.

Bowden rises and stands comfortably behind the microphone. Acknowledging a former player-turned-urologist who is present, the coach opens with, "I would have called you after the game but called my proctologist instead." The room explodes with laughter. He says all the press wanted to talk about in his Sunday conference call was his quarterback and he says Rix played well despite some critical mistakes. He says nothing to indicate that Rix will not be the starter on Saturday against N.C. State. Then, referring to a quote from General Dwight Eisenhower, the coach explains the loss this way, paraphrasing: "In war, before the battle is joined, plans are everything. The minute the shooting starts, plans are worthless."

Though early reactions to FSU's loss indicate that the question and answer session will be tough (these boosters generally don't hold back, despite their loyalty to the coach), there are no difficult questions. They ask about the status of defensive tackle Darnell Dockett, the double tight end formation, Rix's injured thumb, recruiting. In response to a question about the job status of Tommy Bowden, he acknowledges, "Ann and I are worried." The only two questions that even hint at controversy are why star redshirt freshman running back Lorenzo Booker, who played well late in the game, did not play more early and whether or not fans can expect to see Walker. In both instances, the coach remains political, and he gives his support to the backs higher on the depth chart than Booker. His #1 QB, he concedes, may change.

"Remember, 50 percent of the teams lost this weekend," he offers, generating a roar from the audience.

• • •

When Bowden gathers the team late Monday in the locker room, it is a rare sight. Typically, he addresses the team on the practice field on Monday nights, as they don't get started until after seven. But today is different. The loss to Clemson has changed everything. "Our goal was to play for a national championship," the coach tells the team, as if they need a reminder. And the goal now? To play in a major BCS bowl and win the ACC outright. The players' mental attitude concerns Bowden the most. How will they respond to the loss? To the idea that a national title is no longer within reach?

The locker room is shaped like a half-moon. The carpet is dominated by an FSU logo and walking over it is forbidden. Each of the rows of lockers flow into this open space, like spokes in a bicycle wheel. At the end of each row are two glass lockers. Most of these remain empty, reserved for recognizing the best to come in Florida State football. Inside those that are filled hang game jerseys worn by great players in their final game, among them those of Deion Sanders and Charlie Ward.

When the meeting breaks just after 7:00, the players and coaches walk from the locker room underneath Doak Campbell Stadium, through the concourse, around the construction site and onto the practice fields. The three fields are in the shadow of both the football and baseball stadiums, and just yards from the FSU circus ring. Yes, the University boasts the rare distinction of having a circus ring, used by FSU students. Only one practice field is lit tonight, for a practice in which the players are not in full pads. Ten minutes into the stretching period, Bowden arrives in a golf cart, carrying three student trainers he has picked up along the way. The coach is dressed in a garnet FSU jacket, tan pants, and a pair of black sneakers that look more made for bowling than football. He drives his cart onto a small ridge between the fields and observes the warm-ups before walking among the players. Monday's practices are geared toward conditioning, not execution, so after warm-ups the team splits into position groups and their coaches put them through drills. Even the QBs get into the act, starting in a down position, sprinting in place, and backpedaling around a set of cones arranged in a square.

Practice moves into individual position drills, some blocking, some throwing and catching, some backpedaling. They work for a short time on kickoff coverage in the middle of practice, and then the offense runs through a few plays. Things move quickly. At the start of the final period, Bowden drives his cart to the closed-off entrance to the practice fields, the gates swing open, and he is swarmed by reporters. These days, Florida State practices are closed to the media, except for the first 20 mintues. The coach sits in the golf cart as a dozen reporters stick recorders into his face and begin to fire away. They ask about what he told the team, how impressive N.C. State quarterback Philip Rivers is, and, of course, about his own QB situation. He spends 10 minutes with the media as his players do field sprints behind him. Practice ends, and so does Bowden's stay. He drives the golf cart back to his car and heads home. As Bowden drives off, the music of Sugar Ray, in town as part of Homecoming Week, fills the otherwise silent night.

It's typical of Bowden not to go back to the office after practice. His assistants stay, though he encourages them to be home at a decent hour in order to spend time with their families. Bowden is partially involved in the game planning, watching tape on opponents at home in the morning or at night, then giving some suggestions to the offensive staff each morning when they meet. But he does little, if anything, with the defense, reyling instead on coordinator Mickey Andrews, line coaches Jody Allen and Odell Haggins and linebacker coach Kevin Steele. It wasn't always this way. Bowden used to put in late nights. But the man and the game have changed.

"Things are very complicated these days," he says. "In years past, teams would play one formation the whole game and I could see it from the sideline. But now they have so many darn sets." And it's not just the formations that have changed. "The players are faster, stronger."

The coach also points out that most of the kids on his team do not "have papas at home," which alters his role as the head coach, forcing him to spend more time as a father than as a coach.

In the summer of 2003, Bowden was widely criticized by the local media for his less hands-on approach, as his team faltered on the field in 2002, finishing 9-5 and struggling with off-the-field problems, though they did win the ACC title, again. It made the normally open Bowden draw back and be protective of himself and his team. Then things got even tougher as he faced questions about his age (74) and how long he'll continue to coach.

"I have always thought that there are two things that would keep me coaching. The two things are my health—can I coach and walk onto the field?—and second, are we winning? I don't set a time period for moving on, like one year, two years."

Bowden's close friend, and the man second behind him in all-time wins, Joe Paterno, is suffering a cruel season at Penn State. The legendary coach is 2-8 with a six-game losing streak in mid-November, and the calls for him to step down have become a roar. "He'll fight them off," Bowden says. "I am quite close to Joe, and he is a good man. He's a battler." The same has often been said about Bowden.

• • •

Three stories above the ground, with the sun setting over Tallahassee, the man in the middle of it all sits in his office. He stays above the fray, looking out for the best interests of everyone. He must be politically astute, knowing whose hands need to be shaken and whose need to be avoided. He understands the financial magnitude of it all, but doesn't see it as a hindrance. Less than a mile away from where he sits, another man in power does much the same, also three stories above the ground.

The irony is too great to ignore. Less than a mile separates the head coach of Florida State and the Governor of Florida. But the gap isn't even that wide. The two most powerful men in the state do their jobs within sight of one another. Lobbyists drink cocktails at Clyde's & Costello's on weekday afternoons, a bar two blocks from the capital, and the topic of conversation is politics. Seminole fans flock to the 4th Quarter sports bar, with its smiling waitresses, wooden tables, memorabilia-filled walls, and an after-midnight closing time. Here, of course, FSU football is the topic of conversation.

The two, the coach and the Governor, are really very similar. Except that the coach could do both jobs.

He is not as big in person as he looks on television but his presence is impressive. He has lost some hair, wrinkles have begun to accent his face, and he is weathered from many summers spent outdoors. His trademark glasses rest on his nose. When he speaks, the irresistible southern twang makes you feel comfortable. He calls most men under the age of 50 "Buddy." He is the all-time winningest coach in Division I football history, the man who took a small institution in the panhandle of Florida to national prominence. He has won two national championships and 10 ACC titles.

He is a devout Christian and can be found on a church pulpit somewhere every Sunday, spreading the messages of hope, caring, and faith. In the spring and summers, he is on the lecture circuit, speaking to religious groups, Seminole booster clubs, and charitable organizations. He is an avid reader, devouring books on war, history, and leadership. A World War II fanatic, the coach has an encyclopedic knowledge of the great battles.

"Bobby will treat the janitor like the president of the university," Associate Director of Athletics for Football Operations Andy Urbanic points out, a sentiment echoed by coaches and players alike. He is such a popular and approachable figure, in the state and around the country, that fans reach out to him through the mail, at games, or in person. He has always been accessible and at ease, willing to sign autographs until there are no more requests. Those requests have grown so numerous that Florida State now employs a memorabilia director who, every three days or so, collects footballs, pictures, hats and such items that are mailed in or dropped off by fans. She puts them in a laundry bin and places them on a table in Bowden's office for him to sign.

A native of Birmingham, Alabama, Bowden began his love affair with college football as a player—he was a quarterback at Alabama before enrolling at Howard University (now Samford). When his playing days were over, the young Bowden got his graduate degree at Peabody College and then returned to Howard as an assistant coach, before leaving for South Georgia College to be the head coach. South Georgia had, quite simply, written him a letter offering the job. He stayed at South Georgia from 1955 to 1958, serving as the athletic director, football coach, basketball coach, and baseball coach. He headed back to Howard, this time with a promise of scholarships to award as the new head coach in 1959. In his four years as the head coach, he lost just six games out of 37, an indication of the bright future. In 1963, Bowden got an offer to come to Florida State to be an assistant coach to Bill Peterson, and Bowden and Ann began their first stay in Tallahassee. By then, Bowden had his eyes set on the prize.

"The job I wanted was to be the coach at Alabama whenever Bear [Bryant] stepped down. I figured that would be like a homecoming for me." But, as it is wont to do, life did not work out as planned. After three years at FSU, which was not the university it is today, Bowden accepted an assistant coaching position at West Virginia, where he served as an assistant from 1966 to 1969. When head coach Jim Carlen decided to go to Texas Tech in 1970, he recommended Bowden for the head job and he got it. In Morgantown, as an eager 41-year-old coach in 1970, he had his first act on a big stage. Aside from a disappointing 4-7 campaign in 1974, Bowden enjoyed five winning seasons and two Peach Bowl trips. His reputation was solidified, the West Virginia fans finally embraced him, and he was happy. But the Bowdens wanted to return to the South.

In 1976, his former employer was looking for a head football coach. He answered the call. They had little talent and even less history. During Bowden's first season at FSU, the Seminoles struggled to a 5-6 record. They would not have another losing season in the next 26 years. In his second year, Bowden led Florida State to a 10-2 record and the Tangerine Bowl. After an 11-1 record and Orange Bowl year in 1979, it was clear that as long as Bowden stayed put, FSU would be a player on the national scene. Before they made their first national championship game appearance in 1993, the Seminoles had defeated a who's who of traditional powers in postseason bowls, including Nebraska, Auburn, Penn State, and West Virginia. Beginning in 1987, FSU lost no more than two games in any season until 2001, and in 1993 they defeated Nebraska 18-16 in the Orange Bowl to win their first national title. Of course, FSU had come close before, and in the following years, would come close again. Remember Wide Right I & Wide Right II?

Over the next few years, the Seminoles made four more trips to the national championship game, coming away with one more title after crushing Virginia Tech in the 1999 Sugar Bowl. In the middle of the 2003 season, Bowden officially became the winningest coach in Division I history when Florida State defeated Wake Forest. He supplanted his good buddy, Penn State's Joe Paterno, whose team was floundering.

"You know, I never applied for a job in my life," the coach says proudly. And it's true. South Georgia, Howard, Florida State, West Virginia, Florida State—they all came after him. "We've really been blessed."

He has also been blessed with six and twenty-one—that's the number of children and grandchildren who make up the Bowden clan—and his wife, Ann, is a true partner. They met in Birmingham in the mid-1940s and their bond was so tight that Bowden left the University of Alabama to play at Howard University to be closer to her. They were married in 1949 and have been beside each other since.

The year that FSU won its second national title game in 1999, Bobby and Ann celebrated 50 years of marriage. But Ann is not the only Bowden to grab some of Bobby's attention. They have six children—Robyn, Steve, Tommy, Terry, Ginger, and Jeff. Tommy has gone on to fame as the head coach at Clemson. Terry is the former head coach at Auburn and now is an analyst for ABC Sports. Jeff is also a coach, serving as the offensive coordinator under his father at Florida State. And, as if they don't have enough coaches in the family, Robyn married Jack Hines, currently the linebacker coach at Clemson. Then there are the 21 grandchildren, from the very young to the young adults.

His players at Florida State are like family, too, and intensely loyal, as he is to them. "He is a grandfather-type figure," star senior linebacker Michael Boulware says. "One-on-one, he will give you advice and do everything to help the athlete." Boulware continues, "He knows more about what's going on than people think."

Under Bowden, FSU has become what is arguably the premiere program in the nation. Athletic Director Dave Hart points out that FSU football is big business, bringing in over $22 million a year in revenue while costing just $10 million. "Football and men's basketball bring in 98 percent of the athletic revenue," he says.

"He put this place on the map," says longtime sports medicine director Randy Oravetz. "Everywhere we go, people know Florida State. But with that has come expectations. We need to win 10 games every season."

Andy Urbanic has seen the change up close. "People who are successful are held to a different standard. Successful people are in a glass bowl. We are a premiere program and have a higher accountability." Hart agrees: "There is a misperception that there is a discipline problem in the program. But the athletic department has a Code of Conduct. If you get arrested, you are suspended. We also graduate our players." Over the last decade, the Seminoles have had their share of negative press, from the "Foot Locker" scandal, where FSU players went on shopping sprees paid for by an agent, to criminal arrests to the recent Adrian McPherson affair, where the quarterback was charged with gambling on his games and others.

"Bobby had been the darling of Joe Fan," says Urbanic. "We were the Cinderella program but when we won the National Championship in 1993, the glass slipper came off. We have to live with the adverse publicity and the off-the-field problems are magnified."

Until last year, the criticism and negative press were directed at the players and the program. But after the 9-5 season in 2002, the media turned on Bowden. "Bobby has been hurt by some of the stories," says Hart. "Especially the ones dragging his son in. His whole career he has been the most accessible coach ever, but then there were personal attacks.

"Perhaps Florida State has not gotten worse, but other teams have gotten better," Hart insists. "Just look at the upsets this year. Teams are catching up with us. Back in 1995, we could show up with the helmet with the spear on it and assume we'd win." Not anymore. And not after the loss to Clemson. "We were living a dynasty and perhaps the experience was taken for granted. The level of expectations became unrealistic."

· · ·

On the third floor of the Moore Center, which is connected to Doak Campbell Stadium, sits the Florida State football office. Though new administrative facilities are being built adjacent to the present offices, the football suite will remain as is. And "as is" is nice. Directly past the bronze elevator doors is a sizable display entitled "The Heisman." There are two identical glass cases, each containing the jerseys, helmets, and Heisman Trophies of FSU's two winners, Charlie Ward and Chris Weinke. Between the glass displays rests an unusual wooden sculpture of an alligator and a Native American. It is called the Makala Trophy. Apparently, the sculpture was found intact near Big Cypress Swamp in Jerome, Florida. It is given annually to the winner of the Florida State–Florida game, and the FSU victories, including 2002, are engraved on a bronze plaque underneath the wooden piece.

In the reception area are sketches of famous Seminole chiefs, including Chittee-Yoholo, Nea-Math-La, and Micanopy. There is a reception desk, behind which are black-and-white photographs of Native Americans, as well as real arrows. Down a long hallway to the right are the recruiting suite, the office of recruiting coordinator and tight ends coach John Lilly, and workspace for GAs and students. The carpet is, of course, FSU garnet.

Straight past the Heisman display, the lobby area resembles a shrine. There are trophies on display including the 1992 Lombardi Trophy given to Marvin Jones, Deion Sanders's 1988 Jim Thorpe Award, bowl trophies and, in a separate glass case, the crystal national championship trophies, from '93 and '99. On the walls are painted portraits of former greats, including Sanders, Weinke, Warrick Dunn, and Fred Biletnikoff. On the back wall are pictures of the championship teams and the 10 ACC Championship trophies. In the middle of the room, among the trophy cases, is the "Rings of Champions" case, which holds more than 22 rings from bowls and ACC and national championships.

Bowden's office is a space dominated simultaneously by war and peace. Hundreds of military books and pieces of WWII memorabilia sit beside numerous pictures of friends and family. On the floor, on either side of a guest chair, are his two national Coach of the Year awards from 1993 and 1999, as well as a two-foot-high Seminole statue of Osceola. On a coffee table in the corner is a small Bible. Above the bookcase on the floor, there is a large color photo of the Bowden clan at the beach, one of Bowden and his boys, and one with Ann. There is a picture of the coach with Arnold Palmer, one of former Seminole players after an NFL game between Green Bay and Atlanta, and one of Bowden with Ward, Weinke, and the Heisman Trophy.

There are books all over the office, most of them having to do with the military, golf, and, yes, football. There is a three-volume set of Shelby Foote's *Civil War* series, *Ghost Soldiers* by Hampton Sides, Frank Oppel's *The Photographic History of the Civil War, Instant Golf Lessons* from *Golf Digest*, and *Life and Times of Bobby Jones* by Sidney Matthew.

Beneath the glass on his desk, Bowden keeps meaningful pictures, including snapshots of his family and a signed photo of Y.A. Tittle. Donald Phillips' *Lincoln on Leadership* sits on his desk, as does a row of books including *My American Journey* by Colin Powell. Behind the desk, the coach has a picture of his childhood home and high school, memorabilia from the Masters golf tournament, and footballs—one signed by Ward, one signed by former assistant and current Georgia head coach Mark Richt. A small canister of sand from Omaha Beach rests nearby.

• • •

Bowden is holed up in his office on Tuesday until his assistant, Staci Wilkshire, interrupts him with lunch and a few questions. (Bowden takes a nap most days from 1:30–2:00 before heading to the fields, where he walks up and down the lines for almost an hour before most practices.) His staff meets through the morning, adding to the growing list of plays for the game plan. They started to put some plays in during Monday's practice, but today's practice will be far more critical.

Because it is Veteran's Day and there are no classes, the player meetings start earlier than usual. At 1:00, the punt return team meets and, at 1:15, the entire offense and defense meet. To start, the offense sits in position meetings while the defense does a walk-through in the second-floor Mat Room. The room, used for conditioning, has turf. The 60-yard by 30-yard field is surrounded by padded tan walls. After half an hour, the two sides of the ball switch and the defense meets with their position coaches while the offense walks through plays.

Out on the practice fields, the coach sits under a tree in the shade on the far side of the practice facility, perched on his golf cart with one leg up on the dashboard, before the players arrive. He has finished his daily walk and is preparing his notes on what to say to the team. Practice on Tuesday is 21 periods. Interestingly, Bowden has the team go through the first half of practice in half-pads and the second half with no pads in an attempt to keep them healthy and fresh. Linebackers Michael Boulware and Allen Augustin sit out, nursing injuries. Much of the second half is devoted to running scripted plays. Darkness falls and the air grows colder as practice comes to an end.

• • •

Chris Rix is 6'4", 205 pounds, with good looks. He's intelligent, pleasant, and self-possessed. Oh, and he is the starting quarterback at Florida State University. Does life get any better? After his redshirt year in 2000, Rix exploded into the Seminole world in 2001, being named the ACC Freshman of the Year and leading the conference in passing categories. Year 2002 was tougher—his numbers were not as strong as the previous season's and, in fact, Rix even lost his starting position. The 2003 season has been up and down, and as Rix went so did the Seminoles. The loss to Clemson was the low point.

"We know we can make up for it this week," he says. "N.C. State has beaten us before. But we are playing for so much, the next best thing after a national title. It would be easy for us to get down." Indeed it would be understandable if Rix got down, considering the criticism and abuse that have been heaped on him in recent weeks. "Freshman and sophomore year, I would read the papers. On the way to church on Sunday mornings, I would pick up a paper. I would hear what people have to say. But as I got older, I realized, *Who cares what people think?* People criticize me even when we win. You can't control opinions."

Perhaps one reason Rix is able to withstand the onslaught is the support that he receives from the man whom he admires so much. "I came to Florida State for a reason. That was to play for Coach Bowden. He was 90 percent of the reason I came here." Rix continues, "He is a man of character, a guy who I wanted to play for. There is more to life than football. We have the same outlook on life." Part of that similarity comes from both men's devotion to faith.

Being a handsome starting quarterback at a major college program may seem great, but it has its pitfalls. If fans could understand what Rix and his teammates go through, they might appreciate them more. "The time commitment. We just don't practice two hours a day, play on national television. It's not all fun and games. It's not Pop Warner. So much of it is mental. We don't have an off-season." He continues, "Some of the fans, especially the older ones, forget that we are just kids. We are still trying to figure out life."

And speaking of life, Rix might need the game of his life on Saturday.

• • •

Bowden is back at it on Wednesday morning, arriving before the 8:30 a.m. staff meeting to prepare for the day. As he did on Tuesday, he spends most of the morning in his office with the door closed, watching film and reading mail. His assistants are hard at work in their conference rooms until meetings at 2:15, notwithstanding a brief lunch and a quick jog. The defensive staff led by Mickey Andrews spends most of the morning together in meeting rooms. In fact, even when the coaches work individually, they tend to stay together in the rooms. The FSU coaches are most worried about N.C. State quarterback Philip Rivers, a veteran signal-caller who has set all kinds of Wolfpack records. There is also the speed of receivers Jerricho Cotchery and Tramain Hall and running back T.A. McLendon.

At 11:20, it is time for Bowden's weekly ACC conference call, and he spends 10 minutes answering reporters' questions with shorter-than-usual answers. He is asked about Rix, and he is asked if there are similarities and differences between the FSU and N.C. State defenses, since NCSU head coach Chuck Amato worked at FSU as an assistant for many years. At 12:30, Bowden is joined in his office by longtime Florida State and Tampa Bay Buccaneer play-by-play man Gene Deckerhoff. He has been doing FSU games for 25 years and counts Bowden among his closest friends. As he does every Wednesday, Deckerhoff tapes short interview segments with the coach for air on

Thursday and Friday, as well as a lengthier interview for the Saturday pregame radio show. As Deckerhoff asks questions, Bowden is relaxed. The coach wears a short-sleeve FSU shirt, along with tan pants with an FSU logo on one hip, and a pair of 1980s era Docksiders in Seminole colors. He chews on the end of a big cigar.

A little after 2:00, it is hectic on the second floor as players and coaches head to their meeting rooms around the Mat Room. Though the room is central to the team's activities, it took on a tragic connotation in the winter of 2001. Devaughn Darling's name is spoken in quiet tones around campus, as if maybe he is nearby listening. He would have been 23 this season and, most likely, a senior starting on defense. But Darling died in 2001. During off-season conditioning drills in the Mat Room, Darling fell faint and was immediately taken to the training room, where his condition worsened. Within an hour, he was pronounced dead at the hospital. Darling's death was a shock to everyone and left a lasting impression on the FSU program.

But there's no avoiding the Mat Room for the football players and the seniors especially are reminded of their fallen teammate. In fact, he is more on their minds this week than usual as this would have been his final home game. His family will be in town to recognize the occasion.

•   •   •

Since special teams' duties are split among the coaches at Florida State, John Lilly is first up on Wednesday, reviewing kickoff returns to a packed meeting room. The offensive and defensive coaches divide up the special teams units: kickoff, punt returns, field goals, etc. Lilly explains that the N.C. State and Clemson kick coverages are very similar. The players—some standing, some eating sandwiches—stare at the screen as Lilly spends 10 minutes going over film. In the room are Mickey Andrews, who occasionally chimes in, running backs coach Billy Sexton, and linebackers coach Kevin Steele. After Lilly finishes, GA Kirby Smart talks about kickoff coverage. It is unusual for a GA to be given such responsibilities, but Smart is a former coordinator at Valdosta State. Steele is in charge of the kickoff coverage, but he trusts Smart to do it.

The special teams meeting breaks and the position meetings begin, while a group of two dozen scout team players joke around in the Mat Room, waiting for the walk-throughs. In the defensive tackle meeting, coach Odell Haggins has a crowd of just five, including Darnell Dockett. Though Dockett looks disinterested, he's actually engaged in a discussion of the play calling, questioning the plan to have an end trail a man in motion.

Out on the practice fields, Bowden sits in his golf cart with junior Travis Johnson, a standout noseguard from the Los Angeles area. The two sit under a tree as the special teams' work before practice officially gets under way, talking as if they are lifelong friends. When the kicking period ends, Bowden blows his whistle and the team runs to him. The coach rises from the cart and stands among his men. "We need a good practice today," he tells them. "Remember, we're playing for the ACC championship and a BCS bowl."

The offense and defense split and for the early part of practice, the first and second teams go against scout teams, as the coaches review plays. Bowden stands on the side of the far field where the defense works, taking in all the action. After a few periods, he drives to the observation tower and walks up three stories. He has a bench on the top platform facing the offensive field with railings all around and this is where Bowden spends the remainder of practice, save for the last period. Aloft, he alternates between pacing and sitting, and he removes his straw hat midway through practice.

"Always been that way," says Billy Sexton. But after last season's 9-5 debacle, it's noted that Bowden does spend a bit more time on the ground.

Down below, practice continues with full-team scripted plays until late in the 19-period practice, when the defense moves over to the offensive field and they go first team versus first team. But with no real hitting, intensity is noticeably lacking, even as Jeff Bowden and Mickey Andrews do their best to fire up the troops.

• • •

Bowden arrives promptly at 8:30 a.m. for the Thursday morning staff meeting, chewing on a cigar. After Devotion delivered by video coordinator Billy Vizzini, the coach reads excerpts from a newspaper story about a young man in Georgia who plays for his high school football team despite the fact that he has no legs. The young man uses his arms and upper body strength to play defense and in a recent game was credited with three tackles. Bowden is so impressed with the story that he shares it with his staff and tells them he is going to share it with the players Friday night at the hotel. Bowden is quite inclusive of the staff during these meetings, which focus on most things not

X and O. (Every summer, the staff heads for a weeklong "hideaway," where they plan out every detail of the upcoming season.)

When the 10-minute meeting concludes, Bowden stays in the conference room, which is home to the offensive staff, and the coach joins the offensive assistants in going over the plan one more time. He stays in the meeting for more than 30 minutes; the staff stays much longer.

The atmosphere in the afternoon meetings is much lighter, for both players and coaches. Not that there isn't work to be done. Quarterbacks coach Daryl Dickey sits at the end of a large conference table, joined by Chris Rix, Fabian Walker, and Wyatt Sexton, the son of running backs coach Billy Sexton. Dickey spends time going over formations and plays. None of the three players are dressed for practice yet—Rix wears a T-shirt and jeans, Walker sports an Iverson basketball jersey, and Sexton has on a warm-up suit. Dickey makes eye contact with all three and rotates questions among them, making sure they all understand the points. Throughout the discussion, Rix's left leg shakes constantly. The big game is just 48 hours away.

Beneath them, on the second floor, Lilly talks to the tight ends, kickers, and specialists. He reads to the group the story of Al Simmons, a former professional baseball player, who came close to having 3,000 hits in his major-league career, but narrowly missed the achievement and later regretted not staying in shape and playing in more games. The message: Take advantage of opportunities.

One door down, the elder Sexton and the running backs review plays drawn up in a packet. Sexton sits in a chair off to the side, quizzing backup fullback James Coleman early and often, since it looks like he will be called upon to step in for an injured B.J. Dean. Sexton ingrains in his players' heads that they need to be able to run the ball effectively. "A physical attitude, not only as blockers, but as runners," he says. "Getting yourself in a physical frame of mind." The backs have a lot to prove on Saturday, as they rushed for just 11 yards against Clemson.

Upstairs, offensive coordinator and wide receivers coach Jeff Bowden sits and watches film with the receivers group. The players rest in large leather chairs as Bowden plays clip after clip. There are long periods of silence, as Bowden lets the players watch. One player points out a defense they saw used by Clemson; another one asks about a missed block in practice on Wednesday.

All of the players are on the field by 3:30, as both sides of the ball do walk-throughs of plays. When Jeff Bowden arrives, he joins his father in the golf cart and the two sit under a tree on the far side of the practice fields. It is a chilly day and the older Bowden has on a heavy FSU coat. When the team begins its warm-ups, he heads upstairs into the observation tower, where he will remain for the duration of practice. The team does not do a Friday walk-through, so this will be the last time on grass before the game.

Thursday night after practice, Bowden drives to the Channel 40 television studios, where he does his weekly live radio show. Yes, a radio show at the television station. FSU football has such status that even the radio shows are on the tube. He answers questions from callers, including one from a lady named Amy, who almost breaks down in hysterics because she is talking to the coach.

As for Bowden, the listless, downtrodden coach from earlier in the week shows no signs of returning. Unless, of course, he has reason to do so after the game Saturday night.

• • •

The "Iffy" meeting lasts about an hour on Friday morning. Iffy? It has become a Friday morning ritual for the offensive staff at Florida State—the last chance for Bowden and his assistants to review the game plan and to anticipate what they will call in specific situations. In other words, the "what ifs." The coach is out of the meeting before 11:00 and is in his office when he is summoned down the hall for a sit-down with Tim Brandt from ABC Sports. Like every other reporter this week, Brandt asks Bowden about Chris Rix, the loss to Clemson, and how it feels to be going up against a former assistant. The coach is relaxed, looking every bit the legendary Coach Bowden, a different man from earlier in the week.

By noon, the office is buzzing, with visitors and former players stopping by, cell phones ringing with calls for tickets and even a high school team on an office tour passing through. Bowden leaves the office in the early afternoon and goes home. Like on most weekends, he has family in town for the game—cousins from Chicago, close friends from the East Coast, and, of course, kids and grandkids. It is always a busy time at the Bowden house on game weekends.

The player meetings get under way at 2:15 in the position rooms. In between meetings, players make cellphone calls, lay on the turf, and mess around like they have no worries in the world. Two hours later, in the special teams meetings, the coaches rotate in for their various responsibilities. They each have just 10 minutes, and Jody

Allen flies through, showing the team practice footage from the week and from earlier games. "And I tell you what. That #21 [Tramain Hall] is better than I thought. He's got some moves so we got to get down the field and get some helmets on him."

Unlike most teams, FSU does no walk-through on the field, and when players are done with their meetings, they have free time until the bus leaves for the hotel, typically at nine. It allows the players three or four hours to hang with family and friends, or to catch up on sleep. This Friday night is different because it is Homecoming and the annual PowWow is taking place at the Civic Center arena, the home of FSU basketball. Thousands of students and locals jam the place by eight to hear bands, watch the cheerleaders, listen to Bowden and some players, and to catch the headliner, Cedric The Entertainer.

The coach has driven over in his maroon Cadillac Escalade and parked near the service tunnel. He relaxes in a dressing room near the stage until it is time. He walks into a side tunnel, just off the stage, and leans against a wall while waiting to be introduced. Three players—Michael Boulware, Greg Jones, and Brian Sawyer—join him. The MC for the night, play-by-play man Gene Deckerhoff, takes the stage and introduces "the winningest coach in major college football" to a rowdy crowd.

"We need the home field advantage," the coach tells the arena. He speaks about the importance of the game and brings his captains on-stage. Only Sawyer speaks—he fires up the crowd with a Tomahawk chop—and then the foursome is off. Bowden drives back to the stadium to meet the team and the bus.

The team stays at a hotel in Thomasville, Georgia, before home games, a 50-minute drive from campus. After getting their room keys, they settle into a banquet room to watch a highlight tape of the big plays from the previous week's game. It is a difficult loss, but there are some positives. After the video, alone with the team, it is time for Bowden to try one more time to get his message across. He tells the inspiring story of the high schooler with no legs, and reminds his men what they are playing for.

. . .

"There is no question that every week is important," Dave Hart says. "College football is a week-to-week proposition. In one week we went from being #3 in the country, on the cusp of the Sugar Bowl, to #13 and have to win on Saturday to win the ACC title."

This game means so much to so many. Will the players respond?

"The previous teams, we might not be able to come back," says Michael Boulware, "but this team is different. We know what's at stake."

Bobby Bowden certainly knows. You can find him on Saturday morning at 10:30, where you could find him most of the week—in his office, door closed. He welcomes recruits and their families. One by one, the assistant coaches who are hot on the trail of a top player, knock on Bowden's door and ask him to meet with a player, reminding him of who the prospect is, where he is from, and if they've met before. Not every prospect on campus gets the one-on-one visit, but the "money" guys do. Bowden is still active in recruiting, spending much of January on the road with home visits, meeting with recruits on campus, and, occasionally, speaking with them on the phone at the request of an assistant.

In between meetings with prospects, an assistant equipment manager brings up Bowden's game day wardrobe: FSU windbreaker, tan pants, white mock turtleneck, and garnet and white Nike sneakers. The coach talks with a few friends, makes notes on a small piece of paper and gets prepared to emerge. At 1:15, Bowden heads through the stadium concourse on a golf cart to Miller Hall. Here, in a third-floor banquet room, the coach has been summoned to speak to the families, coaches, and recruits on unofficial visits.

John Lilly introduces Dr. Kent "T.K." Wetherell, former FSU player and graduate, former Florida Speaker of the House, and current university president. Wetherell begins his remarks by saying that he, too, once sat in this room and listened to this pitch. At that time, a young assistant named Bobby Bowden stood in the back of the room. The president played three seasons with Bowden on staff before the coach left, and Wetherell jokes that he is now the boss. It is unusual for a school president to speak with such a large group of recruits; typically he is reserved for private meetings with the best of the best. But Wetherell seems at ease speaking to the group, as he was with the star prospects beforehand.

Next up is the head coach and Bowden is in his element. The room's heavy silence indicates that Bowden commands attention.

"You know, this is a big game for us today. This is for the ACC championship and BCS bowl. And we've only lost six games in the conference, and three of them to N.C. State."

The coach talks about why Florida State joined the ACC, not the SEC, two decades ago, pointing to the academic superiority of the league. But he quickly gets to what recruits want to hear. "And now with the fellas from Miami coming in, and Virginia Tech, and, of course, Boston College [see the Epilogue], that covers the television market from way down in Miami all of the way up to Boston." After imploring the high schoolers to keep their grades up, stay out of trouble, and make good choices, the coach exits through a back door.

By the time he gets back to the office, the team bus has arrived and the players are getting dressed and taped for the game. At 2:15, a voluntary pregame chapel, led by team chaplain Clint Purvis, begins in the weight room. The message from Purvis today is about finishing what you start. There are 18 seniors playing their final home game and a team battling back from the Clemson loss. Boys become men by finishing challenges.

Purvis tells the story of a runner in the 1968 Olympics held in Mexico City. The man, John Stephen Akhwari, hailed from Tanzania and was his country's lone representative in the marathon. Akhwari was not a top runner and, in fact, finished an hour after the winner had crossed the line. Many of the officials and fans had already left, but Akhwari continued on. After he finished, he was asked by a reporter why he didn't just quit when he was so far behind. "My country didn't send me to Mexico City to start the race. They sent me here to finish."

• • •

Less than an hour before kickoff, two close friends and former coworkers meet at midfield and talk. Bobby Bowden and Chuck Amato are face-to-face in front of more than 83,000 fans and dozens of cameras. There is a strong mutual respect between the two and it shows.

As it is Senior Day, the pregame routine is a bit different. Each senior is introduced and walks onto the field with his parents or close family members and heads to midfield, where Bowden stands, and they shake hands or embrace. But the sentimental moment quickly passes. It's game time.

Florida State loses the coin toss and receives the opening kick. On their first possession, they don't muster much—two incomplete passes and a QB sack—and there are some early boos for Chris Rix. The teams trade punts and FSU gets the ball back midway through the first quarter. On the sidelines, defensive line coach Odell Haggins talks to his players about two-point stances. For his part, Mickey Andrews talks to various players seated in rows of folding chairs. Just feet away, linebackers coach Kevin Steele kneels in front of his unit, drawing on a board—a teaching tool he will use throughout the day.

Just minutes after kickoff, Bowden replaces his straw hat with an

FSU baseball hat; he signs the cap under the brim before putting it on. There is a manager who is assigned to the coach, and he trails Bowden like his shadow. He wears the headset throughout the game, and Bowden only puts it on when he has a comment or suggestion. The coach first gets on the headset seven minutes into the game during an FSU offensive possession.

It is during that possession that the running game comes alive. With a stable of top backs, including Greg Jones, Leon Washington, and Lorenzo Booker, running backs coach Billy Sexton has a lot of options and decides on a series rotation. Washington carries most of the load in this mid-period drive and Jones caps it off with a six-yard touchdown run with 6:47 left in the first quarter. The Seminoles lead 7-0, which drives the crowd into a full Seminole war chant. On the sidelines, Sexton gathers the backs, tight ends, and linemen around him as he draws a diagram. "They're running a lot of Tiger," the coach says, referring to a particular defense.

The euphoria on the Seminole sideline does not last long, as Wolfpack quarterback Philip Rivers goes to work, picking apart the FSU secondary for 32- and 23-yard completions. With a full blitz coming at him on second and four from FSU's 17, Rivers dumps the ball off to Jerricho Cotchery for a 17-yard touchdown pass, evening the score at 7. The crowd gets quieter when, just under two minutes later, Rix is picked off by Alan Halloway, who runs the ball back 43 yards for a score, making it 14-7, N.C. State. The boos are now coming down heavy on Rix. As he takes a spot on the sidelines, numerous teammates come up, hit him on the shoulder pads, tell him to stay with it. Quarterbacks coach Daryl Dickey is also among them.

In the second quarter, the Florida State defense comes alive, forcing the Wolfpack to attempt a punt from their own eight. The call on the Seminole sideline is for "punt block," meaning they will attack the kick full force. They do but punter Austin Herbert gets the kick away. The defense heads to the benches, listening to coach after coach bark instructions. Linebacker and team captain Michael Boulware is in conversation with his backer mates, telling them he is having a hard time hearing the calls on the field, so they will need to use hand signals. On the field, the offense is starting to move the ball, and kicker Xavier Beitia kicks his first field goal of the day to cut the lead to 14-10 with 8:28 left in the half.

As time winds down, Rivers continues his impressive mastery of the passing game, leading the Pack down the field. He hits Cotchery again on a slant pass, who appears to score as he is hit crossing the goal line, but the Seminole defense knocks the ball loose. Is it a touchdown or fumble? After what seems like minutes, the lineman signals touchdown. Boos rain down from the stands after a replay is shown on the stadium video board. Andrews, whose defense has just allowed the score, is all over the officials. Bowden steps in and gets in the face of the side judge who made the call, but walks away after a brief exchange. N.C. State misses the extra point, and the lead stays at 20-10.

But the officials stay involved. On N.C. State's next possession, facing a third and long deep in their own territory with 51 seconds left, the FSU defense appears to stop them on the play. However, the officials rule that Florida State had actually called time-out before the play, thereby giving the Wolfpack another chance. On the very next play, N.C. State running back T.A. McLendon is hit and fumbles the ball. FSU recovers on N.C. State's three-yard line. After Rix is stopped for no gain and Florida State is called for a false start, Rix comes through, connecting with receiver Craphonso Thorpe on an eight-yard TD pass with 23 seconds to go in the half. The gap is now three, the score 20-17.

Halftime comes and Bowden is stopped by ABC's Sam Ryan as he walks off the field. She asks him about the possibility of replacing Rix. Bowden says he'll have to go inside and talk with the coaches and decide. He does point out that Rix had a touchdown pass late in the half, but Bowden's response is not exactly a ringing endorsement for Rix.

Inside the locker room, Bowden brings together the offensive coaches and tells them he thinks they should make a switch. But his assistants, led by son Jeff, convince him otherwise. Sticking with Rix is better than putting Fabian Walker in the game and then perhaps having to send Rix back in. Rix will stay in—for now.

For the defense, the halftime quandary is simple: How do you stop Phillip Rivers? Andrews is fired up as he addresses the issue. The Seminoles look like a team that is down, which they are, and lost, which they aren't. The fans seem to be yearning for a big play, for someone to make something happen. The longer N.C. State stays in the game, the worse it looks for the home team.

· · ·

The visitors take the second half kick and begin another impressive drive. But then comes the big play. FSU's A.J. Nicholson forces T.J. Williams to fumble the ball and the Seminoles' Rufus Brown picks it up and makes it to the N.C. State 33. The offense has great field position to reclaim the lead. For some reason, the Seminoles safety, Pat Watkins, is angry when the defense comes off the field. His coaches and teammates are not happy with him, either. Andrews is in his face the moment he steps on the sideline, and Watkins is so distraught that when a coach in the box upstairs wants to talk with him via headsets, Watkins shoves them away. Things get worse when Darnell Dockett comes over to intercede; Watkins does not take it well and he stands up as if to challenge Dockett. Andrews and Steele pull them apart. Boulware notices a television camera capturing the incident and immediately moves in to squelch the view. Finally, Andrews comes back over, stands in front of Watkins, and finds a way to calm him down.

Despite the excellent field position, the Seminoles have to settle for a field goal to tie the game at 20 with 9:22 left in the third. The decision to go for three is greeted by jeers from the home faithful. After the field goal, Bowden walks back to the bench area for the first time, pacing up and down, lending encouragement. It seems to help, because the defense holds the Wolfpack when they have a first and goal from the four, forcing them to settle for a field goal. N.C. State retakes the lead, 23-20.

Lorenzo Booker, who has seen limited playing time during the season, takes a second down handoff at his 29 on FSU's next offensive possession and makes an amazing 71-yard touchdown run that includes jukes, cuts, changes of directions, and a few tenacious blocks from his teammates. Now the joint is jumping as FSU leads 27-23. Running backs coach Billy Sexton is so excited for his player that he pulls his hamstring running and jumping his way down the sidelines. The trainers attach ice packs and give him a crutch. They know well what to do as line coach Jimmy Heggins pulled his hamstring running down the sidelines during the Notre Dame game.

Bowden goes for an unexpected onside kick, which the Seminoles do not recover. N.C. State has good field position. Rivers has been doing his damage through the air, connecting on short passes and long ones, on first down and third and long. As the third quarter comes to a close, he does the damage with his feet, running six yards for a score to put N.C. State ahead 30-27. Through it all, Bowden remains stoic. His eyes are hidden behind sunglasses and shaded by his cap, and his body language reveals little. Perhaps because he has been through so many of these games over the years, he doesn't move much on the emotional scale. Or perhaps inside, his heart is about to give way and he is doing his best to conceal it.

With N.C. State up 30-27, Seminole kick returner Antonio Cromartie takes the kickoff back toward midfield and a personal foul face-mask penalty on the Wolfpack adds 15 yards. Again, FSU has great field position. This drive ends with a touchdown, on a 15-yard pass from Rix to P. K. Sam to put the Seminoles ahead 34-30 late in the third quarter.

Before the defense takes the field, Andrews gathers them on the benches, appealing to their hearts and minds. "Are you gonna just lay down like dogs?" he asks them. "What's it gonna be?"

Sexton limps over to Booker, who is seated at the other end of the sideline and gives him a hug and smile, telling him he didn't have a chance to come over after the amazing run. It is a special moment for player and coach.

The clock runs out on the third quarter, and the players, coaches, and fans all raise four fingers in the air. Florida State has 15 minutes left to prove themselves, to clinch the ACC and a BCS berth, to render the Clemson loss an aberration. Daryl Dickey huddles the offense. A normally reserved man, Dickey is excited as he reminds them what is at stake. "This is for a championship!" he yells. "You have to finish," he says, referring back to the message from Clint Purvis in the pregame chapel.

The fourth quarter brings more drama and momentum swings. The Wolfpack's Adam Kiker misses a field goal early in the fourth, but Florida State makes one of their own, settling for a field goal after having a first and goal. The kick makes the score, 37-30. N.C. State has to score a touchdown to tie it up. In response, the amazing Rivers strikes again. He passes and runs the Wolfpack down field before getting the ball to Tramain Hall, who runs 44 yards for a score. The game is knotted at 37. On the FSU sideline, there are heads hanging down, players sitting in silence.

There is still time for a game winning score from either side, but Florida State cannot score on its possession. The Wolfpack begins to drive with just over two minutes remaining and it looks like their game to win. But on yet another memorable play, N.C. State's Brian Clark fumbles the ball after a catch on his own 42-yard line and FSU recovers. They have two minutes to set up a chip shot for star kicker Xavier Beitia. After a few impressive runs and first downs, Beitia comes on to the field. The game and the championship hang in the balance. No one on his team speaks with him—not through the time-out FSU calls to stop the clock and not through the two time-outs N.C. State calls to ice him. Finally, it is time. Beitia has been proficient on the season and this is not his most difficult attempt, but there are certainly flashbacks in the fans' and coaches' minds of famous FSU field goals that weren't. Just after the snap, N.C. State's Derek Morris comes through the middle of the line and gets a piece of the ball, causing it to fall short of the goalposts.

Missing a kick is never easy for a kicker, particularly one as steadfast and well liked as Beitia. He walks off the field with his head down and when he hits the sideline, he receives taps on his helmet from his teammates. He immediately goes to the back of the benches and begins to kick into netting. Bowden finds him and asks him what went wrong on the kick. "Move on," the coach tells him, emphasizing the point with a tap on his left shoulder pad.

So here we stand. The game is tied at 37 and the outright ACC Championship is on the line. Florida State has played only one overtime game in its history and is so new to the concept that Bowden and Sexton meet with two officials before the coin toss to clarify all of the rules. N.C. State wins the toss and elects to take the ball second, a typical move in overtime, so they know whether they need a field goal or touchdown to win or tie the game. Florida State gets to choose which end zone the overtime will be in, and Brian Sawyer chooses the one with the most Seminole fans, away from the sizable N.C. State contingent at the opposite end.

Chris Rix has had a difficult week leading up to the game, but his performance during the game is not at all shameful. Bottom line, his offense has put up 37 points and his only big mistake was the first-half interception. Though Fabian Walker has been waiting in the wings, Rix takes the overtime to put the past behind him. On Florida State's possession, he throws a four-yard pass to Craphonso Thorpe, who catches his second TD of the game. The extra point is good. FSU has the momentum back, and the bench is animated, cheering on the defense. Rix receives high fives from his teammates and a hug from Dickey.

It is now up to the Seminole defense that has given up 30 of N.C. State's 37 points. They know what the Wolfpack is going to do, but can they stop it? No. Rivers passes the 400-yard passing mark when he hits Hall again on a screen and Hall takes care of the rest, running in on a seven-yard touchdown. The critical point-after is good and the game is headed into a second overtime.

On the sideline, Greg Jones stands near Rix. Jones says, "Hey." He looks at Rix, and his eyes say, "We will not lose."

This time, N.C. State starts with the ball. The Florida State defense is up to the challenge, stopping the Wolfpack on three plays.

Facing a fourth down and one, N.C. State coach Chuck Amato has a huge decision to make. Go for the first down and hope to get seven points on a touchdown or settle for a field goal try. Having had problems with his kicking game on the night, the coach is not sure he wants to go that route. So on fourth and one, Rivers, in shotgun formation, drops back and throws a pass to Cotchery across the middle that looks like a sure first down. But the Seminoles' Allen Augustin, who has been injured most of the week and was not expected to play, sticks his hand in at the last second and breaks up the pass. Before the ball even hits the ground, the Seminole sideline celebrates. All FSU needs is a field goal to win it. Of course, Beitia's miss in regulation still hovers in the air.

The calls from Jeff Bowden in the second overtime are all run. There is no game clock, and at worst, they'll take a field goal if they don't get a first down. But after a superb first-down run by Leon Washington, a touchdown seems more likely. As fans and players celebrate the first down, some of the players on the field turn their attention to the near sideline. Craphonso Thorpe, who had been blocking on the run by Washington, lays writhing in pain. The Seminole trainers are immediately at his side and it is clear this is a serious injury. Rix kneels on the field and says a prayer; other players walk over to Thorpe and hold his hand as the medical staff looks at his leg. The early diagnosis is a broken right leg. As Thorpe is lifted onto a cart and wheeled off the field to a waiting ambulance, the crowd chants his name. The player winces through the pain and lifts his fist and then index finger as he is carted off. P. K. Sam comes over and promises Thorpe they'll win it.

The injury to Thorpe not only dampens the spirit of the players and coaches, it puts at risk the momentum. On the next play, Washington scampers into the end zone virtually untouched from 12 yards out to give Florida State the double overtime victory. The players rush the field. Many go over to the ambulance and talk with Thorpe. Some exchange hugs with their opponents. Some gather at midfield for a postgame prayer. Bowden remains expressionless as he calmly walks across the field with a police officer, searching out Amato. The two embrace. Amato is all smiles. He knows how hard his team has played and how close the game was. His first words to Bowden are about the fourth and one in the second overtime. "I was going for the win," he tells his mentor.

There is jubilation in the locker room. The critics said that Jeff Bowden couldn't call a decent offensive game—they were wrong. A maligned running backs corps, which had amassed just 11 yards against Clemson, finished with 272. Chris Rix, who was the target of so much criticism and so many boos, led his team to victory. He is speechless and in tears in the locker room. Perhaps they are tears of joy, perhaps tears of relief.

Bowden gathers the players around the FSU logo on the floor. The first to speak is Assistant ACC Commissioner Mike Finn, who, on behalf of the ACC and commissioner John Swofford, congratulates them on the championship. Dave Hart congratulates them on the victory and thanks them for making the community proud. Travis Johnson asks Bowden if he can say a few words. "I know we're excited but let's not forget Devaughn [Darling]. His family was here tonight and he was a big part of this."

In his postgame press conference, Bowden opens up by asking, "Everybody in favor of taking Chris Rix out in the first quarter, raise your hand. Mine was up." He explains how the decision came to pass that Rix would stay in the game. When asked if he would have gone for it on the fourth and one as Amato did, the coach evades a specific answer, but acknowledges that Amato's decision "takes some (guts)."

Bowden is at ease as he sips on a Diet Coke and answers questions. Charming, folksy, wise, funny. Bobby Bowden is back.

• • •

Sometimes, all it takes is a single win to change the face of a season. Instead of a two-game losing streak and a collapse of immense proportions, the Florida State coaching staff was able to refocus the team on a new goal, after their aspirations for a national title were lost. Through it all, Bobby Bowden presides as a patriarch over the program he built. His name and face are synonomous with Florida State. While some head coaches rely on their football knowledge or their skill for public relations or their ability to sway recruits, Bowden has a distinct advantage. He is Bobby Bowden.

But what if Florida State had been 4-7 headed into the game? What if the only thing they had to play for was pride? Arizona State faced that very scenario in the last week of the season.

CHAPTER 9

Redemption

Arizona State University

Arizona State vs. Arizona
Tempe, Arizona
November 23-28

It is a rivalry game, for sure, but it doesn't pack the anticipation and drawing power of the previous ones. Both Arizona State (ASU) and Arizona have had disappointing seasons, and there will be no bowl games for either team. But that doesn't mean the game won't be a battle. Previous seasons' games between the two have seen a brawl, personal fouls, and certainly no love lost. It may not be for everything, but it is for something.

* * *

Dirk Koetter takes a seat in a meeting room at the Sheraton Gateway Hotel, blocks from Los Angeles International Airport. It is July 30, PAC-10 Media Day, and Koetter is there with quarterback Andrew Walter. Before taking his turn at the podium for a press conference, Koetter, like all of the other attending coaches, is escorted into a hallway of rooms filled with various news organizations: Fox Sports Net, ESPN, *Sports Illustrated*.

A Fox Sports Net producer asks about the expectations for this year. Koetter has his answer ready: "Nobody has higher expectations for what we're trying to do than we do." His team came close in 2002 to having a remarkable season; a few caught passes here and there, a few less fumbles, and Arizona State would have been playing on New Year's Day. The taste is still fresh in the coach's mouth.

The producer presses Koetter further about his team's chances in 2003. In preseason rankings, ASU is ranked as high as #8 in one poll and is predicted to finish behind USC in the PAC-10. Walter is a Heisman hopeful. "Now that we are being talked about as one of the better teams in the conference, are we hungry enough to take the next step?" Koetter asks. He would get his answer soon enough.

Fast forward four months. After opening the season with wins against Northern Arizona and Utah State, ASU traveled to Iowa for their first real test of the 2003 season. They failed. Losing 21-2 was bad enough, but failing to score an offensive point hurt Koetter the most, since he is the offensive coordinator. Things did not get much better after Iowa. They lost on the road to Oregon State and, despite playing their best game of the season, fell at home to highly ranked USC. Maybe the Sun Devils weren't so hungry after all.

The coaches lacked good answers as to why the team was struggling. Perhaps it was the loss of superstar defensive end Terrell Suggs to the NFL, or the departure of receiver Shaun McDonald, the recipient of many of Walter's passes last season. Maybe the team chemistry wasn't right. Though the problems persisted, the team beat Oregon and then eked out a win on the road at North Carolina. There was still time to turn things around and get to a bowl game. But in the first half of the team's loss to UCLA, Walter injured his ankle. Neither he nor the team would fully recover. In fact, things would get worse. Losses to California, Stanford, and Washington State followed, leaving ASU at 4-7, tied for last in the PAC-10 with one game remaining: rival Arizona.

The good news? If things were bad for Arizona State, they were worse for their brethren down in Tucson. They had managed to win only one game all season and their unpopular coach, John Mackovic, was fired after five games.

What once seemed like a huge game in the PAC-10, and perhaps even in the national title picture, has turned out to be nothing more than a neighborhood scrap. It has been dubbed the "Basement Bowl," as the loser will finish last in the conference. Still, the game means a great deal to Dirk Koetter and his staff, a chance for redemption for a disappointing season.

• • •

Sunday is Tuesday. Monday is Monday. Tuesday is Wednesday. Wednesday is Thursday. Thursday is Friday. Friday is Saturday. Blame the confusion on a bye week. It is, indeed, rivalry week in Tempe and that's not the only reason it is a different kind of week for the Arizona State coaching staff. They are coming off a bye week, which has a profound impact on the game preparation. Dirk Koetter decided that the staff would prepare for Arizona the first week, leaving the second week for tweaking and review. Add to that the fact that the Arizona game will be on Friday, not Saturday, and you can see where the confusion comes from.

Last Sunday, after a loss to Washington State on the road, ASU began its typical game week schedule. That meant Sunday afternoon practice (the players traditionally get Mondays off) followed by staff sessions late Sunday night, all day meetings Monday, and then more planning and practice on Tuesday, Wednesday, and Thursday. There was no pregame routine on Friday, so many of the assistant coaches hit the road to use two days for evaluating recruits. For his part, Koetter got to do something he hadn't done all fall—watch soccer. Koetter spent Saturday driving to soccer parks around the Phoenix area, enjoying his chance to cheer on his kids.

As a result of the bye week, and his decision to plan for Arizona during the off-week, Koetter is refreshed as the staff gathers before Sunday's practice. There is still work to be done, for sure, but the bulk of the preparation is finished. The players and coaches meet outside Sun Devil Stadium and the attached Carson Center, where they board a yellow tram for the short ride to the practice fields. There is a good deal of pedestrian and vehicle traffic today, as the Arizona Cardinals and St. Louis Rams are playing an NFL game inside the stadium. Koetter wears black wind pants, a gray sweatshirt, a baseball hat, and sunglasses on the unusually cold day in the desert. The "prepractice" is a brief period when the offense walks through plays on one field and the defense does the same on another. As the team begins its stretching in "A" shape formation, the coach spends a few minutes with the media—in this case, the beat writer from the *Arizona Republic*. Unlike most coaches, Koetter has the media interview him and players before practice, so the distractions are out of the way.

Players wear four different colors: maroon, white, blue, and gold. The maroon are the offensive players, the white the defense, the blue the defensive scouts, and the gold the offensive scouts. Koetter is a detail man and leaves nothing to chance in practice. Every minute is planned and the practice moves quickly from period to period. After a brief kicking period, the offense and defense split and work against the scout teams. Koetter is not only the head coach but also the offensive coordinator, so he spends his time with the offense, getting involved in starting and stopping plays.

In just a few minutes, the entire team is back on the defensive field working on kickoffs. Special teams coach Tom Osborne (not the former Nebraska legend), wears a wireless microphone attached to his shirt and barks instructions as his fellow assistants help out. The assistants are involved because they each are responsible for a segment of the kickoffs and punts. The idea of having all of the assistants involved in special teams allows coaches to interact and coach some players they normally would not. For example, a defensive line coach may work with receivers in kickoff coverage.

The highlight of the two-hour practice comes when the first teams go against one another. There is some real hitting going on with the players in full pads. Even the quarterbacks are not immune— though they are not hit hard, they do not wear different colored jerseys to protect them from contact. They hate wearing different jerseys unless they are hurt.

Practice is interrupted numerous times by what sounds like gunshots, but are actually fireworks shot off a hill outside the stadium each time the Cardinals score. At the end of the 23-period practice, the field goal kicker, Jesse Ainsworth, gets a chance to kick. Koetter has the players who are not involved in the field goal attempts stand just feet away from Ainsworth and scream and distract him as he kicks. The freshman kicker has done okay on the season, hitting 10 of 14 attempts, including a 47-yarder against Washington State. He misses three in a row in practice. It isn't the noise, he explains to the coaches, but his holder. His normal holder is backup quarterback Chad Christensen, but he underwent shoulder surgery last week. The replacement, Kellen Bradley, is not positioning the ball correctly, causing Ainsworth to miss. During most practices, when kickers are off by themselves, Tim Parker, the punter, holds for Ainsworth and that's who the kicker wants handling the duties full-time.

"This is national television, a rivalry," Koetter tells the team at the end of practice. "This is important for our seniors." He pulls out a list and reminds players what specific classes have assignments due or upcoming tests. He wants them to know that he knows. He announces the list of players for CT, or Commitment Time, meaning four hours of study hall on Monday night as punishment for missing a class or not working in an earlier study hall. When the coach concludes, the players hop onto the yellow tram and ride back while the coach decides to walk. The Cardinals-Rams game is in the fourth quarter and, as some fans pass Koetter on their way out, they either wish him luck or wish him the worst, depending on their loyalties.

On a regular Sunday, the staff would work more on the game

plan. But tonight most head home shortly after practice, though Koetter and a few others stay and make calls, watch film, and think about Monday. The truth about Koetter is he never stops thinking about football, which helps explain his meteoric rise to the top levels of college football.

• • •

He is forty-four years old but looks younger, though there is a touch of gray hair near his hairline. He is tall and thin, with a strong jaw and crystal blue eyes. His wife, Kim, is a strikingly beautiful blonde, and the couple's four children, Kaylee (11), Derek (10), Kendra (7), and Davis (5), share their parents' good looks. They live in the desert, far from where they grew up, but they couldn't be happier.

Koetter's journey began in the small town of Pocatello, Idaho. He is the son of a high school football coach and grew up watching practices and playing ball with older boys. He drew up plays at the dinner table in his early years. When it was his turn, he was the star quarterback at Highland High School in Pocatello and accepted a scholarship to Idaho State, where he played from 1978 to 1981. Along the way, he earned a B.S. in physical education and an M.A. in athletic administration. When his playing days ended in the spring of 1981, Koetter served as a GA at his alma mater. Coaching was in his blood and in his heart.

He ventured into the high school ranks as an assistant coach at Highland and, in 1983—in just his second season with the staff—he was named the head coach. He moved to college ball in 1985 when he became the offensive coordinator at San Francisco State. He spent one season there before heading south to El Paso to become the quarterbacks coach and then offensive coordinator at the University of Texas at El Paso, where he coached in the 1988 Independence Bowl. His name became well known in the coaching world and he joined the big time when he was chosen to be the offensive coordinator and QB coach at the University of Missouri, where he stayed from 1989 to 1993. When the staff at Missouri was fired in 1993, Koetter was hired by Dan Henning at Boston College to be his quarterbacks coach, before being named coordinator. But the moves didn't stop. He packed up the family and moved across the country to the University of Oregon and joined Mike Bellotti as offensive coordinator for two seasons. By then, it was only a matter of time before Koetter became a Division I head coach. But where?

In 1998, Boise State was looking for a head coach to replace

Houston Nutt, who had moved on to Arkansas. It was only fitting that Koetter returned to his home state after a 13-year absence. In his first season at Boise, the team went 6-5 and finished fourth in the Big West conference. The following year, they went 10-3, won the conference, and played in the hometown Humanitarian Bowl. His third year was another successful one, and the Broncos went 10-2, undefeated in the Big West, again, winning the Humanitarian Bowl. In both seasons, Koetter was named the Big West Coach of the Year. He created an offense at Boise that ranked among the Top 5 nationally. As the 2000 season ended, a time of opportunity began.

ASU's head coach Bruce Snyder was fired by Athletic Director Gene Smith. Oklahoma State had an opening as well and both schools went after Koetter. Koetter actually verbally committed to OSU but changed his mind in a matter of hours. He became the 21st head coach in Arizona State history on December 2, 2000, although he would still coach Boise State weeks later in the Humanitarian Bowl.

"With a new coach, it was like a culture shock," says ASU senior receiver Skyler Fulton. "We heard it was going to be Dennis Erickson. Then the next thing we knew, Coach Koetter called a team meeting. It was over Christmas Break, so there were only 30 or 40 guys here. We met in the [Arizona] Cardinals locker room." Three years later, Fulton has a better perspective on what Koetter brought to ASU. "At first, it was a tough time adjusting. But it was better for the team, better people. We don't question our coaches. They tell it like it is, even though it's not always what you want to hear."

Similar to his tough first season in Boise, Koetter's Sun Devils went 4-7 overall and 1-7 in the PAC-10 in his first season in Tempe. But the second year, again, appeared to be the breakthrough. Koetter's team improved to 8-6 and played in the Holiday Bowl.

So the table was set for 2003. Despite the losses of Suggs and McDonald, the team had plenty of depth and a Heisman-contender at quarterback. Things looked rosy. Before the season, the man who brought Koetter to ASU, Gene Smith, met with the staff. "I told the football staff before the season that you may hit some bumps, but whatever you read or hear, you only have to worry about me and Dirk." But there would be more bumps than he expected. In early November, he met with the coaches again. "I told them, 'The AD did not come down here to clean house.' It is never hard for me to give them my full support. I am confident in my hires and in the plan."

Koetter does not need to worry about job security, despite what some fans, alumni, or radio show hosts think. Smith puts it simply. "Dirk's my head football coach and he'll be here as long as I'm here. Dirk is learning, growing. It takes five to six years to build a program. By the end of this year, the culture has changed."

The AD also likes the fact that Koetter has actually *decreased* the operational budget for ASU football since his arrival. The budget is $9.1 million and the program brings in over $20 million annually. For his work, the coach receives a total compensation package of nearly $800,000.

"Dirk works hard, is an excellent recruiter, and he understands the social, academic, and athletic development of kids," says former longtime Sun Devils coach Frank Kush, the man for whom the stadium field is named.

It has been a year of soul-searching for Koetter, easily his most difficult as a coach. The staff prepared for games as they always had, the talent level was decent, and the schedule was not overwhelming. But dropped passes, turnovers, and injuries have thrown everything off. Fortunately for Koetter and his staff, the most important game of the year happens to be the last one, and one which ASU can win. Of course, they said that about all the other games, too.

* * *

Koetter's office looks down on the field of Sun Devil Stadium. The windows rise six feet along the south end zone, giving him an impressive view. There are two leather chairs beneath the windows, a large coffee table in between. Resting on the table are trophies, including the 2002 Hendricks and Nagurski Awards—both for Terrell Suggs. There are also the silver Territorial Cup Trophy and the Saguaro Trophy, which are presented to the winning coach of the annual Arizona–Arizona State game. (The actual Territorial Cup was lost for decades until someone found it eight years ago in a local church. The original stays in the archives while the replica sits on Koetter's table.) On the walls of the office are a picture of the Grand Canyon and the signed and framed jerseys of former ASU greats John Jefferson and Mike Haynes. There is a stack of unopened golf ball boxes on the floor in a corner, and a Baltimore Ravens helmet that Suggs signed, "To Coach: Thanks 4 Everything."

On the wall behind Koetter's desk, an aquarium sits above a credenza covered with pictures of his family. There is one of his wife, Kim, leaning against a stone wall and another of his four children dressed to impress. His desk is clean, except for a few papers. On bookshelves there are footballs with painted lettering, including one from his first ASU win in 2001 and his first PAC-10 win the same year, as well as a football signed by every ASU player.

Koetter has an assortment of books in his office, arranged neatly on the cabinet shelves. Included in his literary collection: Jack Canfield's *Chicken Soup for the Sports Fan's Soul*, *Leadership Secrets of Attila the Hun* by Wess Roberts, Mike McDaniels' *The Pro-T Offense*, *Run and Shoot Football: Offense of the Future* (1965), Jim Dent's *The Junction Boys*, *When Pride Still Mattered* by David Maraniss, and Spencer Johnson's best-selling motivational book, *Who Moved My Cheese?*

The lower level of the Carson Student Athlete Center is home to the players. The locker room, weight room, and sports medicine clinic are all here. The wall outside the locker room is filled with charts and displays honoring ASU players. There is a "Special Teams Soldier Player of the Week" display, with a picture of one player from each game this season under the motto, "For warriors who fight the fight with all thy might; to thee our heads are bowed."

On the door of the locker room, there is not a team slogan or a piece of an old stadium, but a poster that asks, "Are You Ballin' or Fallin'?" The concept was created by Assistant Athletic Director for Student-Athlete Development Jean Boyd, a former ASU player, to get the student-athletes to understand that they must succeed in whatever they do, school work as well as football. The staff gives out awards (including Adidas sweat suits with "Scholar Baller" on them, as allowed by NCAA rules) to those who achieve in the classroom. "Dirk is very involved and lets me do my job," Boyd says. "I meet with the coaches regularly. In fact, three weeks ago Dirk asked me to put together a list of extra credit assignments so the coaches knew what was due." On the same poster on the door, there are set goals for the team, including every player maintaining a minimum 2.0 GPA and the team maintaining a minimum collective GPA of 2.60.

Just down the hall is the two-story weight room, recognized by *Sports Illustrated* in 2002 as a paradigm of the new millennium weight facilities. Within its 16,000 square feet, it is the most expensively outfitted weight room in the nation, with over $650,000 worth of weights alone. There are many lifting stations, each one with color-coded weights and a $24,000 price tag. There is a 40-yard sprint track along one wall and two large game day murals of the stadium on another. The phrase "Building Champions" is painted in large letters.

Along with a nutrition and juice bar on the bottom floor, there are treadmills and cardio machines overlooking the weight room on the second floor, stationed in front of televisions.

• • •

The coach is in early on Monday—real early. He makes a stop at Einstein Bagels on his way in and arrives a little after 6:00. He is at his desk working at seven, when the offensive and defensive staffs begin their work in adjoining meeting rooms. The offensive meeting room, which doubles as the full-staff meeting room and the quarterback position room, was endowed by a $250,000 gift from former Sun Devil great Jake Plummer. One wall is all windows and looks out onto an entrance to the stadium. A wipe board holds the tentative game plan for Arizona, another displays the depth chart, while a third bears diagrams and the practice schedule. On the back wall is a mural that shows off a list of ASU goals: 1) win the turnover battle, 2) win the game in the fourth quarter, and 3) win the third down battle.

The offensive staff begins by reviewing the practice tape from Sunday, and Koetter runs the video back and forth. In particular, the coaches look at some of the trick plays they had run in Sunday's practice, including flea flickers and reverses. "It's plays like these," Koetter says, after watching one trick play fall apart on film, "that go from the game plan to the floor." One of the advantages of the bye week is that the staff has extra time to tweak the game plan, including observing which plays work in practice and which ones hit the floor. Koetter is in charge but routinely asks for feedback and suggestions from tight ends coach Tom Osborne, offensive line coach Jeff Grimes, quarterbacks coach Mark Helfrich, wide receivers coach Darryl Jackson, and running backs coach Tom Nordquist. The staff takes 90 minutes to watch practice, as the assistants eat bagels smothered with peanut butter and sip coffee. The sun begins to creep through the blinds.

The offensive game plan against Arizona is simple. Run the ball with Loren Wade and Randy Hill, pass with Andrew Walter, throw in a few trick plays to keep the Wildcat defense guessing, and, most importantly, limit the turnovers. Wade is returning from a concussion and a bout with the flu. Walter needs just 237 yards to break the 3,000-yard mark for the second straight season. The Arizona defense has allowed more points on the season than any other Wildcat team in history, giving up an average of 36.5 points per game.

After the offense, defense, and staff meetings end, it is media time for Koetter. First up is a one-on-one interview with Fox Sports Arizona in a third-floor meeting room. Reporter Jody Jackson asks about the bye week and how it affects preparation, about injuries and, of course, about the meaning of the ASU-UA rivalry. When she finishes, the coach walks across the hallway to a large theater, where he is greeted by a gaggle of writers and flashing cameras. The coach's relationship with the media has been somewhat awkward since his arrival. The basic feeling is that they don't really know him. And with the disappointing season coming to a close, there is reason for tension. He is asked what, if anything, he would change from the season, and he immediately points to Andrew Walter's first half injury against UCLA. When asked if this game is important because the loser will finish in last place in the PAC-10, Koetter responds, "I think that there's a lot more at stake and a lot more positive things to come out of this than you'll hear a coach talk about undoubtedly other than, 'Let's win this game to stay out of last place in the conference.' " In response to another question about the anticipation, the coach candidly admits, "I could throw up right now."

With no Monday practice, the afternoon is spent by the coaches on individual work. Some watch game film, some review high school prospect tapes, some return phone calls. Koetter works on the call sheet and game plan. It takes him an hour and a half to write it out, before giving it to assistant Lora Borup to type up, color code, and laminate. Changes might still be made, as developments in practice warrant, but for the most part the plan is set. Typically, Koetter does not finalize the game plan until Thursday—but this is not a typical week.

In addition to his offensive coordinator duties, his media obligations, and staff management, Koetter finds time each week to read e-mail. On the Arizona State football website, fans can e-mail questions and comments to Koetter and, every week, he reads them and responds, assuming the critique or comment is logical. Even if it is just a one- or two-sentence response, Koetter points out that almost always, the sender will e-mail the coach again, this time with praise and encouragement. The little things go a long way.

One by one, his assistants turn off their lights, close their doors, and head home. Koetter stays. He sits behind his desk, talking on the phone to recruits, watching high school tapes on one television and taking peaks at the Monday Night Football game between Tampa Bay and New York on another. By 8:30, he is the only one left in the office.

. . .

The staff meeting on Tuesday morning is all about recruiting. The coaches talk about some of the tapes they watched the previous night and discuss junior college players. Because they are limited to the number of juco players they can bring in, each segment of the staff argues for guys who play the position they coach. Recruiting takes on more importance because on Sunday the official contact period begins; in that time, coaches can visit recruits in their homes. Coaches fan out around the nation and spend weeks on the road until a dead period around Christmas. It begins again after the New Year and culminates before Signing Day in early February.

On the walls of the defensive meeting room, diagrams are hung like Christmas stockings. Each one is of Arizona personnel groupings and formations. Interestingly, each piece of paper is attached to the board by a colored pin, each color representing a different Arizona opponent. For example, a blue pin may signify those diagrams that show how the Wildcats lined up against UCLA, a red pin for the USC game, etc. Why is that important? For defensive coordinator Brent Guy, he wants to see patterns and know what blocking schemes opponents ran against certain formations. Specific to Arizona, Guy knows that Wildcat coach John Mackovic was fired after the TCU game. By looking at the film and the diagrams, he notices a complete change in what Arizona did offensively within two weeks of Mike Hankwitz taking over. If the diagrams were not labeled, the staff may not have a clear idea of what had changed.

Guy and Ted Monachino, Kevin Ramsey, and Dan Fidler have a few concerns heading into Friday's showdown. They have to find a way to slow down back Michael Bell, the centerpiece of the Wildcat offense, and they know that the UA quarterbacks—particularly Nic Costa—can take off running. ASU employs a 4-2-5 defense, with four guys always over the line of scrimmage. With the extra secondary man, they do not need to sub regularly for a nickel package on passing downs.

The defensive staff stops their work just before 9:00 a.m. and walks downstairs, out the door, and into a six-person golf cart. In their hands are the class schedules of every player. All schools have class checkers, but usually it is a GA or a team manager who checks up on the athletes. But at ASU, one random day a week, the defensive staff hops into the cart and scrambles around campus, checking up on their charges. The offensive staff does the same on a different day. It's bad to miss a class, but it's much worse if your coach comes looking for you. The check takes 30 minutes with the coaches splitting up the classes and taking record of who was absent. The absentees are put on the CT list. There are more names than there should be.

• • •

Late Tuesday morning, the offensive meeting room is empty except for Koetter, sitting in a chair near one end, working on the scripted plays for Tuesday's practice. Since he serves as the offensive coordinator, it's part of his duties. He even draws the scout cards twice a week. "It takes time but it gives me a chance to really picture the play and make sure the cards are done right. It is very helpful to me." When he's done, he gets on the phone in his office to do a radio interview for the Arizona pregame show, then changes clothes and leaves for his daily run. He is an exercise fanatic, making sure he gets in a workout every day around lunchtime. He encourages his assistants to do the same, and most do some sort of exercise each day during their 90-minute lunch break. "When I don't get a chance to run," Koetter says, "I can be an SOB in practice. I just don't feel right."

After the run and a light lunch, he is back at it, meeting with the offensive staff at 1:30 for their daily prepractice meeting. Koetter goes over the scripted plays for practice and points out areas of emphasis. "We've got Sudden Breaks today," he reminds his crew, alluding to the surprise situations including field goals, two-point conversions, and long yardage third downs that are interspersed throughout practice. "It's a way to break practice up," he says. "We try to do different competitive drills throughout the week." These special situations in a game, including field goals and two-point conversions, may very well be the difference on Friday.

• • •

There is quite a crowd at practice on Tuesday. A throng of media awaits the players and Koetter as the team stretches. Also present are players' parents, former players, kids, and die-hard fans. The practices are open to the public but interested parties must call the football office and be "cleared," so as to avoid opponent spies. Before practice, Koetter tells the team about the Sudden Breaks but doesn't tell them what will be called—or when it will come. Immediately after he finishes, the first Sudden Break occurs, as indicated by a double-horn blast. It is a two-point try in the far end zone of the defensive practice field. The first teams face off. Andrew Walter throws a crisp pass to Terry Richardson and the offensive players and coaches celebrate with raised hands. The horn quickly sounds and the players move into specialty work.

Practice on Tuesday is physical. Offensive GA Eddy Zubey has encouraged his scout team to play with intensity and, at times, with fearless abandon. This even includes smack talk. It is an effort to replicate what the ASU offense can expect against the Wildcat defense. But the scout team takes it a bit too far and a few scuffles break out during drills, including one involving starting fullback Mike Karney. Walter is quick to jump in and separate the players. (Of course, with the media present, the incidents become known and before practice on Wednesday, the coach acknowledges the scuffles: "They [scout team] crossed the line and [upset] some of those guys, and that's not a good thing to do.") But it might get them ready for what's coming, if Arizona player comments are any indication.

On Wednesday, a letter from the commissioner of the PAC-10, Tom Hansen, to Arizona athletic director Jim Livengood, with Koetter, Gene Smith, and UA coach Mike Hankwitz cc'd, is faxed to the ASU offices. In an *Arizona Daily Star* article on Tuesday, Wildcat junior center Keoki Fraser was quoted as saying the following: "I think it will be dirty—physical—with a lot of pushing and fighting after the play. Neither team's going to a bowl game, so nobody has to be worried about being suspended for the next game." It was poster board material for ASU but Koetter largely ignored the comment, more concerned with his team than Arizona's. Apparently, Hansen did not think the same way. In the letter to Livengood, Hansen reminded the Arizona AD that players would be suspended from the first game of next season for infractions and that he expects a hard-fought but clean game between the rivals.

● ● ●

Many of the assistants go to lunch together at a local hangout on Wednesday while a few stay behind, working on reminder sheets for their players. As on Tuesday, position meetings last an hour starting at 2:15. Defensive coordinator Brent Guy also coaches the linebackers, and due to numerous injuries, he has only four sitting in the meeting room on Wednesday. He spends the hour rolling video of Tuesday's practice and Arizona's game against Washington, their only win of the season. The players are attentive and active in discussion, even pointing out options to the coach in certain formations. He lets the UA-UW game film roll, pausing before snaps to ask what defense the players will call.

Dressed in a long-sleeve maroon shirt with matching shorts, Koetter hits the practice fields before four and speaks with the media as the prepractice walk-throughs get under way. Practice will be in shells and shorts, a review day more than anything else. The first teams will not face off as they have during the week, and the coaches and players are less serious than they've been. Near the conclusion of practice, the first-team offense runs the clutch drill, a version of the two-minute offense. They start on their own 35, they have one time-out left, there is one minute left to go, and they need a field goal. Andrew Walter connects on every pass as the offense easily works its way into field goal position, and the kick by freshman Jesse Ainsworth, working with new holder Tim Parker, sails through the uprights.

"We are going to do our talking after the game," Koetter tells the team after practice. "We will be classy and handle ourselves well." He clearly is referring to the comments by Fraser. He informs the team that the PAC-10 is concerned about fair play. When he finishes, Jeff Copp, a three-year GA and a former player for Koetter at Boise State, takes the floor. Like for the seniors, it is his last practice at ASU, and Koetter gives him a chance to speak to the team. Copp talks about what it takes to play and win as a team, about players' responsibilities to one another, and about what rivalry games really mean.

The underclassmen head for the practice field exits and line up in single file, forming a line to the exit. The seniors, having finished their final practice, walk one by one, giving hugs and handshakes to players as they pass, thus continuing an Arizona State tradition.

• • •

Thursday is, for all intents and purposes, a Friday, except for the fact that it's Thanksgiving. After breakfast on the fifth floor of the Carson Center at 8:45, the players go to their position meeting rooms where they take tests, created by their position coaches, to ascertain their knowledge of the game plan. The tests take 20 minutes and by 9:50, the whole team is on the stadium field for a walk-through. Koetter, who has been in the office since seven working on his call sheet again, is in a carefree mood, and it catches on with the players. Before the walk-through gets under way, the offensive linemen play catch and simulate pass plays.

"What we have here is a castle," the coach explains to the team when it's time to get serious. "Castles are permanent and have tradition. They make their people feel protected." He is conveying a thought brought to him by an ASU grad, now a professor of medieval history at the University of California—Berkeley. "It is their job to protect their home, something permanent from the past and for the future."

Moving on to another metaphor, he compares Kamikazes and Spartans. "Kamikazes are unorganized and have no long-term plan after initial effort to scare the opponent. Initial violent action that cannot be sustained. But Spartans, Spartans are brave and disciplined for the duration. They establish superiority," the coach continues, and it is clear he's saying that his Sun Devils are indeed Spartans. "This doesn't have to be close," he concludes.

With that, he wishes them all a nice Thanksgiving and reminds them to be on the bus by 6:35. All of the players have someplace to go for the holiday, as many out-of-staters go home with the locals for dinner. The staff has gone to great lengths during the week to ensure that everyone has an invitation. The coach looks forward to an afternoon at home, something he hasn't experienced in a very long time.

• • •

The Koetters' home on the north side of Scottsdale is in a gated community, approximately 25 minutes from campus. On an unassuming cul-de-sac, their light-colored home is filled with the noise of children. The four kids are full of energy and gusto as the family sits down for Thanksgiving dinner in the kitchen. With the muted Dallas-Miami NFL game on a large-screen television nearby, the family feasts on turkey, sweet potatoes, green beans, and bread. Kim's parents are visiting from Santa Barbara, California, and after the plates are clean, the youngsters and their grandparents head out to the pavement of the cul-de-sac to play some soccer and volleyball. Koetter and his wife relax on a sofa in the family room. It is a rare day when the coach can be home for seven hours.

But sure enough, before long it is back to work. The coach is at the Scottsdale Hilton by 7:00, where he waits for the team buses to arrive. He has checked into a suite and will spend the night. At 7:30, the offense and defense meet separately in banquet rooms at the rear of the hotel. Koetter leads the 45-minute offensive meeting ("probably my favorite time of the week," he says), having prepared a cut-up video that shows an Arizona defense in a previous game, and then cuts to the ASU offense running a play in practice against that defense. It's a method that helps him show the players exactly what he means. Next door, Brent Guy does the same for the defense.

Traditionally, the captains of the various special teams units speak to the full team on the night before a game, followed by a few motivational words from Koetter. But since tomorrow will be the last time the Sun Devil seniors will be suiting up, Koetter asks the 10 seniors on the travel squad to speak to the team. One by one, Koetter calls out a name, and the players—some shy, some certainly not—stand in front of their teammates.

"I shouldn't have to pump you up for this game," begins Brett Hudson. Others speak about Sun Devil pride, how much they've enjoyed being part of this team, and how badly they want their teammates to succeed long after their last game. The final senior is Skyler Fulton, a well-spoken student-athlete, who actually left the program briefly to play baseball before returning. He insists everyone in the room, players and coaches, join him up front in singing the ASU fight song, complete with hand movements and clapping. It is an emotional half hour for the seniors and their teammates, but also for the coaches, who have watched the departing seniors mature over the past three years.

• • •

"We are a better team than they are in almost every area of the game," Koetter says on Friday morning after the team breakfast. He goes on to list the ways in which ASU is statistically better than Arizona, from passing yards to defensive turnovers to field goals. After hearing such a list, no gambler would bet on Arizona.

The bus ride over to the stadium is quiet except for a little music emanating from headsets. As the two buses near the stadium just before 11:00, the tailgating is already under way.

The coaches' meeting rooms on the lower level of the Carson Center, just outside the locker room, double as the men's and women's coaches locker rooms for all sports during the week. The football staff has their private dressing room and lounge on the third floor, but that is too far away. As the team gets dressed and taped across the hall, Koetter nervously paces while reviewing his call sheet. "I got a huge pit in my stomach," the coach comments. He is dressed in a short-sleeve, white collared shirt with an ASU logo, tan pants, and black-striped Adidas shoes.

The game referee David Cutaia and umpire Tim Morris knock on the door. As all officials do before games, they meet with each coach, write down the numbers of the captains, and ask if there is anything that they should be ready for.

"Well, there's one thing," Koetter says, as he makes his way over to a wipe board. "It's a punt we may run."

He proceeds to diagram a punt formation that could allow for a fake punt, with a throw to an outside blocker, after two men cross behind the line and get set. Cutaia picks up the pen himself and points to a circle, representing a player, and asks, "Is he eligible?" The officials thank Koetter for the heads up.

But there is one more thing. "I don't know if you have heard about all of the talk this week or what's gone on in the past," he says. "If any of my kids are involved, you let me know and I'll get them out. I know there may be a lot of talking and hitting after the play, so let me know if you sense something coming." The officials nod and wish Koetter luck.

There is little to say before kickoff and Koetter keeps it short. In fact, he spends most of the time reminding the players how they will be introduced. Because this is Senior Day, the underclassmen run onto the field first and then assemble in two lines to form a human tunnel. Each senior is introduced and runs onto the field, through his teammates, and greets his parents at midfield.

• • •

Minutes later, ASU receives the opening kickoff and the battle is under way. If the first drive of the game is any indication of what is to come, Koetter will be able to rest easy. Starting from their own 20, the Sun Devils march down the field. There are runs by Loren Wade and passes from Andrew Walter to Derek Hagan, who is closing in on 1,000 yards receiving for the season. After each play, Koetter checks off the play on the call sheet or makes a note of something that went right or wrong. Facing a first and 10 from Arizona's 28, Walter throws an end zone fade pass that Skyler Fulton hauls down for the first score. The usually reserved Koetter thrusts his hands up in the air and heads onto the field to greet his offense. The drive went 80 yards in just seven plays and two and a half minutes.

Arizona comes right back, moving the ball down the field, and gets to the ASU 29 after a 12-yard catch for a first down by the Wildcats' Steve Fleming. But Fleming decides to rub it in and gets caught by an official. It is the first personal foul of the game and moves UA back to the 44. A few plays later, facing third and long, the Wildcats are called first for illegal formation and then, on the next play, for an illegal block. They are not helping themselves. But they regroup and quarterback Kris Heavner finds open receivers, including a wide-open Mike Jefferson, who catches a 16-yard touchdown pass to tie the score at seven with 5:03 left in the first quarter.

As the ASU defense takes their seats on the bench after the series, Koetter makes his way back to the benches and tells them, "Keep your heads up. It's a long game." Perhaps, but the secondary was picked apart on the series and the Arizona receivers were wide open. Defensive backs coach Kevin Ramsey comes back and pulls off his headset. "They're wide open!" he yells.

Toward the end of the first quarter, after the teams exchange punts, ASU faces a fourth and one from Arizona's 42-yard line. The crowd cheers for Koetter to go for it and, after a long pause, he does, successfully converting as Wade runs for a three-yard gain. ASU is on the move again. Two plays later, Walter fumbles the snap and Arizona's Carl Tuitavuki recovers on ASU's 45. Arizona's Michael Bell, the biggest worry for Brent Guy and the defensive coaches all week, breaks multiple tackles en route to a 36-yard run that sets Arizona up with a first and goal from the nine as play moves into the second quarter. Bell is stuffed on first down and on second and goal, Heavner's fade pass is picked off by R.J. Oliver in the end zone for a touchback. The defense holds. After every series by the Sun Devil offense or defense, Koetter walks back to the benches and gives encouragement, regardless of what has just transpired on the field.

Remember back on Monday, after watching the video from Sunday's practice, Koetter and his staff eliminated some of the "trick" plays that they had tried in practice. It seems he hasn't gotten rid of them all. Facing a second and two from their own 42, Koetter calls for a flea flicker. Walter laterals to Wade, who starts to run and then stops and laterals back to Walter, who heaves it downfield to an open receiver. The play fails as Walter's pass is too far for a sprinting Matt Miller. But Koetter isn't done. On the very next play, Koetter calls for a reverse and Terry Richardson takes the ball outside for an 18-yard gain, setting up a first and 10 inside UA territory. A few plays later, Wade takes the ball on third and three from Arizona's 33, and it looks like he is headed for a first down. That is, until Paul Philipp knocks the ball out of Wade's hands and Arizona's Gary Love recovers it. Another blown chance.

The defense again steps up, forcing another Arizona punt. As he comes off the field after stopping Bell for no gain, linebacker Jamar

Williams celebrates the stop. "Nobody blocked you," line coach Jeff Grimes shouts out. "You should have made the play." ASU begins its fifth drive of the game from its own five. With running back Randy Hill now in and Walter completing big passes to Fulton and Jamaal Lewis, the offense looks like it did in the opening minutes of the game. Koetter is active as usual, moving up and down the sideline but hovering near the line of scrimmage. With just over three minutes left in the half, Walter completes a nine-yard touchdown pass to Lewis to make the score 14-7. It is an impressive 12-play, 95-yard drive that chews up five minutes. Koetter is pumped. He takes off his headset, hands it to the manager trailing him, and says out loud to no one in particular, "Ninety-five-yard drive! Ninety-five-yard drive!"

But the Sun Devils are not done for the half. With great field position at midfield after forcing an Arizona punt, it takes ASU just three plays to score another TD. Wade takes a handoff from Walter, breaks a tackle, and finds the end zone, increasing the lead to 14 with 1:34 left in the half. Unbelievably, ASU gets the ball again before time expires, after a strong defensive stand and wise time-outs. They are on their own 19 with just 46 seconds to go. Koetter wants another score but it isn't to be; the clock runs out with ASU still in their own territory. They are up 21-7, but many players and coaches do not sprint off the field with enthusiasm. On the last play of the half, a five-yard run by fullback Mike Karney, center Drew Hodgdon was injured, and he lays on the field. Koetter runs over to the fallen player with the medical staff. After a few minutes, Hodgdon sits up.

• • •

Over the next five minutes in their cramped meeting room, Koetter leads the offensive staff in what is best described as a review session. They go over plays that worked and circle them on their sheets, and cross off ones that didn't. Koetter writes the plays he intends to call in the second half on a yellow legal pad, each play going into a square labeled "Run," "Pass," or "Red Zone." "All right, go get 'em," is Koetter's indication that the meeting is over. The assistants head across the hall to meet with their players.

By that time, the entire defense is sitting on folding chairs in between rows of lockers, listening to Guy. "This team, right now, has two quarters left in it, ever. How do you want to go out?"

When it is his turn to address the team, Koetter reminds them that they are playing for anyone who has ever played at ASU. As he finishes speaking, Hodgdon enters the room in a wheelchair, ice wrapped around his ankle. The players swarm around him and they head out.

Things don't go well out of the gate. Arizona takes the kickoff and Heavner continues where he left off, finding wide-open receivers across the field. A 12-yard pass to Syndric Steptoe; five yards to Jefferson; a 14-yarder to Jefferson; a 20-yarder to Ricky Williams. All of a sudden, Arizona has third and two on ASU's 21. But the normally reliable Michael Bell coughs up the football and ASU's Ishmael Thrower recovers. The Devils have escaped again. When ASU faces a third and one on this drive, Koetter calls for a run play, but Wade is stopped for a loss of two. When Walter reaches the sideline, Koetter says into the ear hole in his helmet, "I should have called something else." Even a general can be humble in battle. Later in the third, with the score still 21-7, ASU moves the ball into scoring position, but after Walter is sacked, the Sun Devils face a fourth and 13 from the Wildcats' 26. Koetter calls on freshman kicker Jesse Ainsworth. The rookie has not been kicking well in practice this week, but they've made his requested change in the holder. The snap is bad and Ainsworth hooks the kick.

Koetter continues to coach, encouraging his players, making corrections. At one point, the coach grabs a small wipe board, kneels in front of Walter sitting on the bench, and draws a pass play, pointing out that the Arizona safeties are closing in fast. "But don't give up on your postplay just because it's closing."

Arizona returns the missed field goal early in the fourth quarter when kicker Nicholas Folk misses a chip shot from 23 yards out. It is not unexpected—he was 0 for 2 on the season after replacing a kicker who was 2 for 8. The quick strike ASU offense wastes no time. On first down from their own 20, Walter throws deep to Derek Hagan, who catches the ball over the corner and makes his way down the sideline, outrunning his pursuers for an 80-yard touchdown. The game is now 28-7 and the crowd, coaches, and ASU players sense victory. As Arizona drives on the ensuing possession, Koetter puts on his headset and listens in to the defensive calls for the first time all game. Perhaps he wants to keep the score 28-7. The defense holds and before the ASU offense takes the field with 12:56 to go in the game, Koetter huddles them near the sideline. He reminds them that there are still 15 minutes left.

The ASU drive does not last long. After Randy Hill runs for 11, six, and then three yards to set up a third and one at midfield, Koetter calls for a deep pass play. The pass is incomplete. The coach tells the offensive line on the bench that they are playing outstanding and then he seeks out Walter and again takes the blame, saying, "My fault. That was stupid of me."

The remainder of the fourth quarter sees the teams trading possessions. With the outcome no longer in doubt, a good portion of the Sun Devil Stadium crowd departs, wanting to beat the traffic. With Arizona facing a third and 14 with just minutes remaining, Koetter tries to get the crowd up by waving his hands up and down. It doesn't work.

By the time the clock is under two minutes, the head coach is more concerned about what happens after the game than what is left of it. He seeks out any assistant he can find, telling them to remind the players to act with class after the final whistle. Koetter keeps many of the senior offensive players in the game until the next-to-last snap, when he sends in the subs so the seniors and Walter can get an ovation. Koetter shares a laugh with senior fullback Mike Karney on the bench, the player's face filled with black eye paint, sweat, and a few tears.

After the final whistle, the coach walks to midfield and shakes hands with Mike Hankwitz, then goes up to a few Wildcat players, including Michael Bell, and wishes them luck. He is pulled aside by athletic department personnel for a trophy presentation on the field. Loren Wade and Andrew Walter share the MVP award while Koetter takes the "Victory in Bronze" trophy and the Territorial Cup and holds them high.

The final statistics for the game are misleading. Arizona had more first downs, more passing yards, and more offensive plays, and had possession of the ball almost 10 minutes more than Arizona State. On the other hand, ASU did manage to hold Bell to 95 yards rushing and Heavner and backup Nic Costa to a combined 28 of 48 passing. Receiver Mike Jefferson amassed 115 yards receiving on nine catches and had the only UA touchdown. The big surprise for the Sun Devils was Wade's 120 yards on the ground and Randy Hill's 67. Walter finished 16 for 26 for 281 yards and three touchdowns, 155 of those yards to Derek Hagan and 106 to Skyler Fulton.

Inside the locker room, there are happy faces and some tears from the seniors who have played their final game. Tony Aguilar leads the team in a postgame prayer and Koetter addresses them for the last time. "You did what you wanted out there. You did exactly what you planned to do." He tells them to have fun tonight, but to remember that they wear ASU on their chest—a message to stay out of trouble.

The coach walks across the hall for a few minutes of solitude. He wipes his forehead, packs up his papers, and, at last, exhales. Sports Information Director Mark Brand comes in and congratulates Koetter and leads the coach back out into the crazy world for his press conference. Sitting halfway back in the media room are Kim, their four children, and friends.

It seems a fitting end for the week.

• • •

The games are played on the field, not on paper. No one knows that better than Dirk Koetter now. It turns out that his squad still had an appetite for winning, even after the disappointing season. But every day, Koetter learns something new about strategy or leadership. Expectations will be high again for 2004. And that's not a bad thing.

Arizona State's season is over, but for our other eight teams, there is more football to be played. Some are playing for a shot at the national title while others will be happy just to get to a bowl. The outcome of the SEC title game between Georgia and LSU will have ramifications for numerous teams around the nation and help determine who will play in the Sugar Bowl for the BCS national championship.

CHAPTER 10

Second Chances

SEC Championship Game

#5 Georgia vs. #3 LSU
Atlanta, Georgia
December 4-6

It is a dream match-up for the SEC title game—a rematch between Georgia
and LSU. The consequences are huge for both teams: LSU is fighting for a shot
at the national title game and Georgia is fighting to win the SEC for a second
year in a row and capture a berth in the BCS. LSU won the regular season
showdown in Baton Rouge. Both sides come into the game with injuries, but
with a sold-out Georgia Dome, the game promises to be a classic.

• • •

"Rarely in life do you get a second chance," says Mark Richt to begin
his talk. It is Friday night and the coach is speaking to 70 Georgia
players in a meeting room at the Renaissance Concourse Hotel in Atlanta. "I mean, what do they say? You never get a second chance to
make a first impression. It is even rarer in college football to get a second chance. But that's what you got.

"We played LSU and we lost. Now we get a second chance. Three
times we were in the red zone and scored three points. But we get a
second chance. We missed three field goals. But we get a second
chance. Passes were dropped. But we get a second chance. Tackles
were missed. But we get a second chance. Coverages were blown. But
we get a second chance. We fumbled in the garnet zone. But we get a
second chance." Richt asks everyone to make two fists. "There is
power in there," he remarks. "Now, grab the guy's hand next to you
and press." There are some moans and laughs in the room but the

players do as told. "But there is so much more power when you are together, as a team."

The Bulldogs have made it through a difficult regular season with a 10-2 record, losing only to Florida and LSU. In the game in Baton Rouge, Georgia had every opportunity to win but could not "Finish the Drill"—as the players' T-shirts proclaim. In that late September showdown, the Bulldogs played without injured receiver Fred Gibson and tight end Ben Watson, but still could have won the game had they not given up a 34-yard touchdown pass from Matt Mauck to Skyler Green with just over three minutes remaining. Kicker Billy Bennett's three missed field goals didn't help, nor did David Greene's two interceptions and one costly fumble.

But now they have a second chance.

The game week preparation is no different this week than the previous 12, with the exception that the Georgia staff is preparing for an opponent they already played this season. Of course, the coaches watched, ad nauseum, the first game between the two, trying to figure out what worked and what didn't. "But they [the LSU staff] are doing the same thing," Richt points out. "So do you do what worked in the first game knowing that they know that it worked, or do you try something new or something that didn't work?"

In addition to watching their game against LSU, the staff watched four other LSU games from the season, but not the last four, as is commonplace. Instead, the offensive staff picked out four LSU games where their opponents ran offenses similar to Georgia's, including the game against Ole Miss, who lost to LSU in Oxford just weeks ago. The defensive staff did the same, finding four LSU opponents who played a similar defense.

It becomes clear to Richt and offensive coordinator Neil Callaway that Nick Saban's defense will blitz early and often, regardless of the down and distance. The Georgia offensive line struggled in the first game, allowing Greene to be sacked four times. But with the return of Watson and Gibson, the Bulldog staff thinks they have a better chance of beating the blitz.

The prep and practice schedule remains the same: Monday night, practice; Tuesday, Wednesday, and Thursday afternoon, practice; game planning for the coaches late on Sunday, Monday, and Tuesday nights. Richt keeps everything the same, not wanting to tinker with what has been working.

But will it produce the same result against LSU?

• • •

The SEC title will be decided 70 miles west of Athens in the Georgia Dome in downtown Atlanta, so the Bulldogs figure to have a home crowd advantage. And they have been here before. In December 2002, Georgia pummeled Arkansas to win the SEC title in front of 75,000 seriously partisan fans. But LSU is sure to bring a large contingent, and they always come with spirit.

By travel time on Friday morning, the head coach, like his assistants, is exhausted. Coinciding with the monstrous task at hand, Georgia, like all schools, is fully immersed in the recruiting period, making home and school visits and criss-crossing the state and nation in pursuit of players who will help you get back to these games in the future. Most of the assistants left Athens on Thursday and either drove to nearby towns or took private planes out of state. Depending on the location of the visits, coaches can do two or three in a day.

Richt is tired as he sits in the back of Steve Rushton's Georgia Highway Patrol car, headed for Atlanta on Friday morning. (Rushton and David Herring serve as Richt's protectors through the weekend.) They leave just after 9:00 a.m. and Richt takes a much needed nap before the chaos begins. They head directly to the Hyatt Regency in downtown Atlanta, where media, fans, and boosters await. The highlight of Friday is the annual Coaches Luncheon, where over one thousand fans pay to hear from the two head coaches and, hopefully, get autographs from them as they move about the hotel. Rushton makes good time and they arrive by 11:00. The coach is met by Georgia Senior Associate Athletic Director Claude Felton and heads down an escalator to a meeting room. It will serve as a holding area for Richt before the noon luncheon.

The coach yawns as he attaches SEC and Georgia pins onto his lapels. Dressed in a gray suit, white shirt, and red and white tie, he looks relaxed. A few SEC officials pop in, including Associate Commissioner Charles Bloom. Richt and Bloom engage in a 20-minute discussion of the bowl situation, of who might end up where, and what the process will be on Sunday, when the BCS and bowl representatives will conduct a conference call to determine the lineup. With a win, Georgia will most likely head to the Rose Bowl to face Michigan; a loss could send them to the Outback Bowl or to the Peach Bowl.

Richt and Felton make their way across the banquet floor lobby and into the main ballroom, with Richt stopping every few steps to graciously sign memorabilia for Georgia and LSU fans. The ballroom in the Hyatt Regency is decorated with the banners of the 12 SEC member schools and one side of the room has an enormous stage that holds a talk show stage setup, with three leather chairs, a glass coffee table bearing Georgia and LSU helmets, and large video screens. The main events of the luncheon are the interviews with the coaches conducted by Jefferson-Pilot television personality Dave Neal.

After a brief video highlight reel of Georgia's season, Richt is introduced and receives a standing ovation from part of the audience. When asked what was the "defining moment" for his football team this season, he responds, "It happened on November 29"—the day they secured their berth in the title game. When asked about the vaunted LSU defense, he responds "there's a lot to worry about." When asked for his keys for the game, Richt lists three: hold on to the football, do a better job protecting the quarterback, and find a running game. When the interview concludes, the LSU video is played and head coach Nick Saban takes the stage.

After lunch, Richt walks through the kitchen and down one floor for his press conference. "Preparation has been good, morale is outstanding, we're looking forward to a good game," he says in an opening statement. One of the 20 or so reporters asks about what will be different this time around. "Ben Watson and Fred Gibson are different for us offensively." Before he leaves, the coach poses for photographers with the SEC Championship trophy and when Saban arrives, the two men shake hands up on the podium with the SEC Championship trophy in the foreground. They don't say much as the bulbs flash away.

• • •

The Georgia Dome has been host to Super Bowls, the Olympics, the games of the Atlanta Falcons, and major college bowl games. The arena has been fitted with new FieldTurf® and the majority of the seats are turquoise-green. There is little signage throughout, save for the huge banners of SEC corporate sponsors. The temperature inside is cool, though it's a lot warmer than the 30 degrees outside.

The Georgia team arrives just after 3:00, changes into T-shirts, shorts, and helmets, and walks onto the field. As soon as Richt hits the field, still dressed in the gray suit, he is surrounded by a press horde who pepper him with questions. Practice is open to the media but photo and video crews can tape only the first 15 minutes. The practice is not heavy, and the focus is on the special teams. Richt wants the kickers and returners to get accustomed to the field, the lights, and the roof. The QBs and receivers do some passing drills on one end, as Richt stands behind them watching. On the other side of the field, the defense does drills under the guidance of Brian VanGorder.

At 4:30, the team buses to the Renaissance Hotel, a 20-minute drive, while Richt rides in the back of Rushton's patrol car. Having ridden in from Athens with the players, Richt's father is now on one of the team buses. The team arrives at the Renaissance and is greeted by the hotel staff, and the players have an hour of free time before dinner. After dinner, the entire team moves across the hall to a smaller meeting room, where the head coach waits behind the lectern for his "Second Chance" speech.

When Richt finishes, the players break for the special teams meeting, where coach Jon Fabris takes them through kicks, punts, and everything else. As position meetings get under way, Richt sits with his quarterbacks and receivers in a nearby boardroom and gives them notes on the changes they have gone over during the week. Richt shows them video clips and asks both the QBs and WRs about plays, including backup quarterback Joe Tereshinski, who moved into the #2 spot behind Greene after an injury sidelined D. J. Shockley. At 8:10, Richt finishes, telling them, "I don't want to blow your minds with too much."

The coach packs up the portable computer and gets onto the elevator, his work with the team finished for the night. He reaches the 10th floor and walks to his suite. He looks tired. He stays up and watches more tape of LSU's defense on the computer and works on his call sheet, something he usually has completed by this time of the week. Tomorrow morning, game day, he'll script the first 15 or so plays.

* * *

Downstairs, chapel gets started late as Brian VanGorder keeps the defense meeting in the room. The team chaplain, Kevin Hynes, does not say much tonight but introduces his friend—author, speaker, and military veteran Lt. Clebe McClary. McClary wears a black patch over his left eye, and his left arm is missing. He tells the group of about 30 that he was wounded seven times in Vietnam and has undergone 39 operations. A former player and coach, McClary volunteered for duty and on one devastating night, as his platoon came under attack, an explosive changed his life forever.

"We need to have character in today's world," he says passionately. "We need to read a book a week. We need to open the doors for ladies. Treat people with respect." He lets them in on some of his favorite acronyms, such as BIONIC, Believe It or Not I Care, and FIDO, Forget It, Drive On.

Throughout his talk, the players sit in amazement, affected by his injuries and impressed by his cheerful outlook on life and his willingness to help others.

If nothing else, it puts tomorrow in perspective.

• • •

The flyers lying around the breakfast room on Saturday morning carry the following words:

THINK.

Mat Drills
Weights
Spring Practice
Summer Workouts
2-A-Days
Meetings
Treatments
How do you want to feel at 11:30 Saturday nite? More important . . .
Will you be feeling great at the 20th year SEC Championship reunion?

Breakfast is quiet. Many of the players come in and eat quickly, and relax in the lobby area and listen to music or talk on their cellphones. VanGorder sits by himself in a meeting room, watching film. The special teams meeting is slated for 11:55, and those not involved return to their rooms or hang out with teammates, waiting for the offensive and defensive meetings to start at 12:55. Richt makes his way downstairs around 12:30, finally out of his suit and into a black and red sweat suit.

"I don't care how long this takes," the coach says to start his meeting with the offense, "we need to get it right. You have to keep in mind when we played them we had 23 first downs and 411 yards of offense. We just didn't make the plays. We just need to make the plays and win the SEC Championship."

The meeting is labeled the "Blitz Meeting" because that is what the coach is focusing on. He shows film of LSU blitzes against certain offensive formations. The offensive assistant coaches—Callaway, Mike Bobo, Ken Rucker, David Johnson, and John Eason, most of whom arrived late Friday night or early this morning—sit near their players to add comments.

While Richt has the group watching film, VanGorder has his troops standing in the ground-floor atrium, walking through defensive calls. Ignoring the onlookers hanging over the lobby-level railing, VanGorder makes sure every movement is exact.

The pregame chapel is packed at 5:30 p.m. Virtually every player is there as well as the assistant coaches, Richt, now back into his suit, the police escorts, and Richt's father. Kevin Hynes's theme follows up on Richt's from yesterday—second chances. He relays the story of Jonah from the Bible, how God allowed him to have a second chance. Turning to the second chance at hand, Hynes says, "God has honored us by allowing us to get to the SEC Championship game. Let's honor him by playing hard." Hynes is followed by video coordinator and former coach Joe Tereshinski, who not only puts together the motivational videos to show before the games, but also has a few words for the players. The video is all about the *Rocky* saga, and so are his words.

* * *

The Georgia Dome locker room is not very big. There is a training room, a shower area, a bathroom. There is also a third dressing room for the trainers and equipment personnel. The coaches dress in a small, narrow space, with their attire hanging in lockers with their names written on tape posted above. Their space is not more than four feet wide. Above the locker room exit to the field is a sign brought from Athens. It reads, "Finish the Drill!"

The players dress and walk to the field in groups for pregame warm-ups. They are greeted by both cheers and boos. Richt remains in the coaches' room, wearing tan pants, a black and red Georgia pullover, and Nikes, and sits in a folding chair, looking over his handwritten call sheet one more time. He is interrupted by the game referee and umpire, who ask for the numbers of the captains and for Richt's help in "maintaining sportsmanship." The coach gets to the field with 40 minutes to go until kickoff, just as the entire team is stretching in lines. He walks to every player on the first two rows, shaking their hands and wishing them luck. He walks to midfield, where Nick Saban is watching his team warm up, and shakes Saban's hand and wishes him luck. He then assumes a position behind the quarterbacks, who throw passes to receivers as the team goes through its usual routine.

The Dome is not yet full but it's loud. There are many more fans dressed in black and red, occupying almost two-thirds of the seats, but the LSU contingent in purple and gold is vibrant and vocal. Its student section is directly behind one end zone, on the side of the field where Georgia is warming up. The LSU band is in full game mode, belting out songs, while its Georgia counterpart on the opposite end of the field does the same.

Back in the locker room, with 20 minutes left before kickoff, the players gather in a large shower. Together, they pray, as they do before all games. "If God is with us, then who can be against us?" they ask in unison. The players take seats in the locker room and there is silence. Neil Callaway sits in the coaches' room with an arm around one of his teenage sons. Richt sits in his chair, still reviewing the call sheet.

"Well, we're in Atlanta," he starts his pregame talk, with the players on knees around him. "This is where you wanted to be. As long as we're down here, we might as well win."

• • •

LSU wins the coin toss and defers the ball until the second half. As Georgia prepares to receive the opening kick, the Dome noise reaches a deafening pitch. Georgia's Tyson Browning returns Chris Jackson's kick 12 yards from his goal line to the Georgia 12. David Greene jogs onto the field with the offense, which faces a deep hole right away. But the game starts well for the Bulldogs, as Greene hits Fred Gibson on a nine-yard pass. Gibson is playing with a broken ring finger protected by a cast on his left hand. On the next play, running back Michael Cooper is smothered by the LSU defense for a loss of three and, as Georgia faces a third and four, they use an early time-out as the play is not sent in fast enough. Greene hits Gibson for a first down. Perhaps Gibson will be the difference that gives Georgia an edge?

A few plays later, the Bulldogs have a third and eight and Richt makes a gutsy play call, correctly assuming an all-out LSU blitz, and Greene fires a perfect pass to a very wide-open Kregg Lumpkin down the middle of the field. If Lumpkin hangs on, it is a sure touchdown. He drops the pass. Running backs coach Ken Rucker walks over to Lumpkin on the bench and tells him to forget about it. A few seconds later, Richt turns around to the bench and starts to walk over to Lumpkin, then stops and turns back around.

The LSU offense, led by quarterback Matt Mauck, has great field position, starting from Georgia's 46. Over the next seven plays, LSU can get no farther than the 31. The field goal unit is deployed with just over five minutes gone in the game. The Bulldogs' Sean Jones leaps and blocks LSU kicker Chris Jackson's attempt. Tony Taylor scoops it up and returns it to LSU's 31. Last year's SEC title game started with a Decory Bryant blocked punt and it set the tone. Will Jones's block do the same?

On the very next play, Greene throws toward tight end Ben Watson at the LSU eight, but the pass is picked off by LaRon Landry. It appears to the Georgia sideline that Watson was knocked down before the ball arrived, but neither Richt's protest to the officials nor the Georgia fans' boos results in a change of call. Richt walks back to the bench and asks Greene what happened. Watson, sitting nearby, motions for Richt to come over. "He waited too long," is all that Watson says.

LSU's freshman running back Justin Vincent did not play against Georgia the first time around because he was buried in the depth chart. But after injuries to others, Vincent became a go-to guy for Saban and offensive coordinator Jimbo Fisher. The 5'11" running back hails from Lake Charles and chose the homestate school over Wisconsin. Now Vincent has gone from an unknown to a star in just weeks. Injuries to Alley Broussard and Shyrone Carey cracked the door open and Vincent took full advantage. In the first six games of the season, he had a total of 30 carries for 132 yards. In the last six games, he has had 90 carries, 551 yards, and 5 touchdowns. For a young man who enjoys deer and rabbit hunting, it was open season on defenders.

Vincent has just eight yards on his first three carries 10 minutes into the game. But on his fourth, he picks up 87 yards and scores a touchdown, breaking tackles and outrunning the Georgia secondary. It is the longest run in SEC title game history. The air comes out of the balloon on the Bulldog sideline and the LSU fans explode. But there is a bright spot for Georgia, as Jackson's PAT hits the crossbar, leaving LSU ahead 6-0.

The Georgia offense cannot answer and, backed up near his own end zone, punter Gordon Ely-Kelso fumbles the punt snap and takes a safety, putting LSU ahead 8-0 and giving the ball back to the Tigers.

As the defense steps onto the field, Richt removes his headset, walks back to the benches, and calls the entire offense over to him. "Let's settle down and play football," he says. "After everything, it's only 8-0. Let's get the ball and put up some points." But nothing so far indicates that Georgia is ready to do just that. Dropped passes, quarterback sacks, and little running room are all they have seen. The coach paces up and down the sidelines wearing his headset, talking frequently with quarterbacks coach Mike Bobo up in the coaches' box.

Georgia almost creates a break for itself when Mauck is sacked by Robert Geathers and coughs up the football. Tackle Darrius Swain has a chance to fall on the ball but tries instead to pick it up and run with it. The ball is knocked out of bounds and LSU retains possession at its own 23. Richt simply bows his head and takes a breath. With the reprieve, Mauck leads LSU on a charge into Georgia territory as the first quarter comes to a close.

The first quarter stats are not good. Georgia has had four possessions, resulting in two punts, an interception, and a safety. They have rushed for *minus* 23 yards.

On the first play of the second quarter, Mauck drops back and throws a 43-yard touchdown pass to receiver Michael Clayton, who beats defender Bruce Thornton to the ball. Unbelievably, Jackson's second PAT attempt is blocked, this time by Kedric Golston. LSU leads 14-0. The Georgia sideline is stunned. There is desperation and there is anger. Callaway tries his best to encourage the bunch. Richt offers support to Greene, as the quarterback plays with a ball in his hands on the sideline. Neither coach nor quarterback shows any outward signs of concern.

The offensive drive again starts deep in Georgia territory, and an illegal procedure penalty backs the Dawgs up to their own 15. After a no-gain pass to Lumpkin and incomplete pass to Gibson, Greene goes down again, this time at the hands of Randall Gay for a 10-yard loss. Callaway stands by himself, headset on, arms crossed. Since Richt does the play calling, Callaway's focus is on the play of the offensive line. On the sideline, the Georgia defense is not thrilled with the offense's lack of movement. Not only are they failing to put points on the board, but their quick drives are keeping the defense on the field. A 42-yard punt by Ely-Kelso and a 10-yard return by Skyler Green give LSU great field position at Georgia's 37. Mauck gets the Tigers down to the 17, where LSU's Ryan Gaudet hits a field goal, increasing the lead to 17. (Saban replaced Jackson with Gaudet after Jackson's failed PATs.)

Georgia's best drive of the night so far comes in the middle of the second quarter, when they manage to go from their own 21 to LSU's 34. Facing a fourth and 20, Richt calls time-out to think it over, then sends out the field goal unit and kicker Billy Bennett, the same Bennett who missed three field goals in the loss to LSU in October. He calmly nails a 51-yard kick. On the ensuing kickoff, Bennett drills a touchback and as he sprints off the field, he shows more life than any Georgia player has shown on the night. His energy is infectious and, though it is just three points, the field goal shifts momentum on the field and in the stands to Georgia. The players stand up and the defensive captains pound fists on their hearts.

The Bulldog defense comes up big again and stops LSU, but after Greene throws three straight incomplete passes on Georgia's next offensive drive, the momentum sways once more to LSU. The teams exchange punts and the first half is over.

• • •

Things could be much worse. Georgia could not run the ball, catch the ball, or hold on to the ball, and yet they are down by only two scores. Most of the players are already back in the locker room as Richt enters. He walks straight back to the players' room and says, "We've been here before. Auburn last year." He turns and makes a loop around the locker room as the incensed voices of VanGorder and Fabris echo from the defensive room. Richt walks back to the coaches' lockers and takes a seat in a folding chair. His offensive assistants gather around him, including Bobo, who was watching from the box. They talk about what worked and what didn't.

"It seems like they're [LSU] listening but I know they're not," Richt says, frustrated that the LSU defense seems to be everywhere. The group decides to throw more screen passes to escape the blitzes and to allow Greene to work from the shotgun.

Richt can't stay still for long, making his way across the hall to the equipment room, then wandering into the locker room before returning to the coaches' room. With exactly nine minutes to go before the second half, he walks into the locker room. His team kneels before him. "We've been here before. Against Auburn last year, we're down 14-3. Now it's 17-3, there's really no difference. That team fought back and we won. Will you fight? We have never had a team die on us—don't be the first." Richt grows more emotional as he talks, his voice gets louder, his arms move more violently. "They get the ball first. We need the defense to get a stop. The offense get a score and we're just one play away." The coach continues, "We need to get the momentum. I saw what happened after our field goal, that's three points, but the momentum changed."

Richt gets his wish just two minutes into the second half. LSU starts with the ball and manages 14 yards when Matt Mauck's pass attempt to Michael Clayton is deflected and intercepted by Bruce Thornton at the LSU 44. The momentum shifts. There is new life for Georgia. But on their first offensive play of the half, Greene is sacked by Eric Alexander for a five-yard loss. The Georgia offense cannot add points to the board before punting. The defense keeps shutting down LSU, highlighted by an Odell Thurman sack of Mauck, and the Bulldogs get the ball back. With 7:46 remaining in the third, Billy Bennett nails a 49-yard field goal, and the score is 17-6.

The Georgia defense has been playing well all night, except for the long touchdown run by Vincent and the pass to Clayton. For the most part, they are able to slow the LSU attack. One thing they didn't deal with in the first half was Mauck's athleticism. In the third quarter, the quarterback scrambles for gains, but LSU is still forced to punt. On the Georgia sideline, the players seem to be waiting for someone to step up or for something big to happen. Their superstars, Greene and Gibson, are not having good nights, and their defense has been on the field far too long. They are searching.

Georgia has the ball deep in their own half and Greene drops back to pass, not seeing LSU defender Lionel Turner. Turner steps in the line of the ball, intercepts it, and runs 18 yards for a Tiger touchdown. If there was any hope and fight left in Georgia, it seems to go away with Greene's pass. 17-3 at half was one thing; 24-6 late in the third is another. But the Dawgs *do* keep fighting and on their next possession, using a 35-yard run on a reverse by Reggie Brown, a personal foul face-mask penalty on LSU, and an 18-yard touchdown catch by Ben Watson, they pull back to within 11. The Georgia fans grow loud and the players on the sidelines encourage them.

With 3:18 left in the third quarter, Mauck throws an out route pass to Clayton, who appears to be out of bounds when he catches the ball, right in front of Richt and the Georgia bench. The official rules it a catch. Richt is not happy. He tears off his headset and runs to the side judge who declared it a catch and who is adamant and confident in his call. Richt tries to no avail to get the call reversed and walks away, mumbling, "That's just embarrassing," out of earshot of the official. LSU's drive moves into the fourth quarter and on the first play of the final stanza, Vincent scores on a three-yard sweep to make the score 31-13.

There is no letup, no surrender, but it is clear who is the better team on this night. Working from his own 14, Greene hits Watson and Brown for two long pass plays and Lumpkin gobbles up yardage on the ground. Before they know it, they have their best field position of the night, facing a fourth and two on the LSU six. Kick the field goal or go for the first down? It doesn't take Richt long to make the call. A field goal does little in the way of a comeback, but a touchdown could at least make it a possibility. The coach calls for a trick play—a throwback to the quarterback. Greene hands the ball to back Michael Cooper, who runs to his right. Greene takes off wide to the left and waits for Cooper to pull up and throw the ball back across the field to him. But the quarterback is matched every step of the way and Cooper has no choice but to tuck the ball and try to run for the first down. He is stopped four yards behind the line of scrimmage.

LSU takes over and on first down the star of the game, Justin Vincent, breaks free and runs 62 yards to Georgia's 28. The LSU fans begin a chant familiar to fans everywhere: "Nah nah nah nah . . . Nah nah nah nah. . . . Hey, hey, hey, good-bye!" When LSU gets to a third and goal at the Georgia eight, Richt looks up at the scoreboard. He knows the second chance has passed. LSU settles for a field goal but it means little at this point. Arnold Harrison, a junior linebacker for Georgia, throws down his cup of water and becomes emotional. "It's about this now," he says, pounding his heart with his hand, repeating the phrase up and down the bench area. "It's what's here what we're playing for!"

With just over five minutes to go, Greene is sacked again on a fourth and eight. Close to two minutes later, a pass by the quarterback is intercepted by LSU's Jack Hunt at the Georgia 44. Saban elects to simply run out the clock. Running back Alley Broussard does the work, running for 30 yards over the next three and a half minutes to end the game.

Richt waits until there are just 10 seconds left on the clock before removing his headset and calmly jogging to midfield, where he shakes Saban's hand and congratulates him, surrounded by a throng of cameramen and reporters. The coach seems a bit confused, and is pointed to the correct tunnel by the patrolman with him. He answers a reporter's questions as he walks off the field.

The LSU defense, ranked first in the nation heading into the game, showed its toughness tonight. The Tigers held Georgia to just 50 yards rushing and allowed Greene to pass for 199 yards while sacking him five times. (The Georgia defense returned the favor, sacking Matt Mauck four times.) The Tiger offense amassed 444 yards, including 201 on the ground by Justin Vincent. Turnovers especially hurt the Bulldogs—they gave up three to LSU's one.

The locker room is silent as the players shuffle in. Some immediately take off their jerseys and pads, some sit and stare into space. A few shed tears. Richt walks in and waits for everyone to come in. "I am proud of everyone in this room. We got beat by a better football team tonight. They were better on offense, on defense, and special teams." Then, he looks forward. "Our season is not over yet. We've got a bowl game. Maybe it's Peach, maybe Citrus, we just don't know." He encourages the players to take the next week to focus on their schoolwork and upcoming exams. The coach's voice grows softer with each sentence.

Claude Felton reads the names of players wanted for interviews in the concourse just outside the locker room and the team then says a final prayer, led by Richt. The coach is taken to the press conference area. He is as calm as he was before the game, as knowledgeable as a coach as he was leading Georgia to a 10-2 record prior to kickoff. He got his second chance, but his team could not take advantage. Some coaches and players would rather not get to the "big game" than get there and lose it, but Richt would never buy into that line of thinking. His team overcame much in the last four months and a return trip to the SEC title game was sure worth the effort.

Nick Saban and LSU now must wait until tomorrow to find out if indeed, they will play for the national title. Tired as they may be, it will be a long night.

CHAPTER 11

Eliminating the Clutter

BCS National Championship Game/Nokia Sugar Bowl

#2 LSU vs. #1 Oklahoma
New Orleans, Louisiana
December 18–January 5

• • •

It wasn't until 7:30 a.m. on the morning of Thursday, December 18, that the Oklahoma Sooners truly became the center of attention for the LSU coaching staff. What had mattered since they clinched a berth in the national title game with a win over Georgia in the SEC title game two weeks before was the future of the program, not the future opponent. Immediately after the win over Georgia, Nick Saban and his assistants spread out across the country making home and school visits with coveted recruits. It helped that when they walked into a family's home they were a team headed for the title game—a fact that they emphasized. Saban was busier than his assistants, making home visits around the country, hosting groups of official visits on the weekends in Baton Rouge, flying to New York and Orlando for award ceremonies, and answering lingering questions about his future.

To get familiar with his title game opponent, Saban watched Oklahoma game film on his portable computer on airplane flights and in his hotel room at night. LSU had exchanged a season's worth of film tapes with the Sooners a day after the BCS match-ups were announced. Most of the assistants had watched some, if not all, of the Sooners' 2003 games over the past two weeks. On Sunday, December

14, when all of the staff was back in Baton Rouge for the weekend, they gathered for six hours to watch film together. By the time the defensive and offensive staffs met at 7:30 a.m. on Thursday, they had a pretty good idea of what to expect.

Defensive coordinator Will Muschamp wears jeans and a casual shirt, and the assistants in the meeting room—Travis Jones, Kirk Doll, and Tim Walton—look refreshed and ready to go. The practice plan for the next two weeks is simple: four practices of fundamentals, three practices on Oklahoma, four days off for Christmas, then six practices in New Orleans the days leading up to the game. All in all, there will be nine practices devoted to the game. The four fundamental practices will take place on Thursday, Friday, and Saturday. These sessions will resemble a fall camp workout more than a late-season one.

Though they know the "official" game planning won't start until Sunday night, the defensive staff is already well into it, watching film and creating a tentative game plan. In front of them on the conference table are Oklahoma offensive personnel charts, complete with color photos of the starters. Muschamp points out that Tiger opponents Mississippi State and Alabama ran offenses somewhat similar to Oklahoma's. He walks into his adjoining office and returns with pages of handwritten notes on those two SEC teams. In watching the film, the staff is amazed at how far apart the offensive linemen for the Sooners line up, and how quickly they release their blocking assignments.

The LSU defense is ranked #1 in scoring defense in the nation and #2 overall—behind Oklahoma. LSU improved as the season progressed, led by All-American defensive tackle Chad Lavalais, end Marquise Hill, and corner Corey Webster. Oklahoma's offense is not its best face, though by no means is it poor. Quarterback Jason White threw for 3,744 yards and 40 touchdowns and was the top-rated passer of the season, and for his efforts, won the Heisman Trophy. Wide receiver Mark Clayton put up strong numbers and garnered national attention. The Sooners played consistently and used multiple formations to try and throw off defenses. But will that be enough to beat LSU? "I don't think they've seen guys like Chad [Lavalais] and the speed we got," Muschamp remarks.

Down the hall, the offensive staff watches tape of Oklahoma's defense. Here, indeed, is Oklahoma's best face. The Sooners dominated their opponents and drew comparisons to the best defenses of all time. Linebacker Teddy Lehman won the Butkus and Bednarik

Awards, defensive lineman Tommie Harris won the Lombardi Award, and cornerback Derrick Strait won the Thorpe and Nagurski Awards. "They are good, real good," comments running backs coach and special teams coordinator Derek Dooley.

Offensive coordinator Jimbo Fisher is just as impressed, but indicates that the Oklahoma opponents this season were not that strong. "I really don't know how good they are," Fisher says, leaning back in his chair with his feet resting on the conference table. "It's just one of those things where I can't tell."

Meanwhile, in the staff meeting room, the lights are dim and the video is frozen. At one end of the long conference table, Nick Saban sits and writes on a white legal pad. In front of him are two cups of coffee and stacks of papers. He has been in the room for hours, watching film, planning out practice, and considering all of the options for the bowl week, including practice times, travel plans, and curfew. He gets up at 10:15 and pops into the staff meeting rooms to let them know what he wants out of practice today, including which personnel groups he wants to get the bulk of the work. Even though the practices will be fundamentals, there are ways to get in teamwork that will be used for the Oklahoma game.

"I've got to talk to the juniors. Got to do it today," Saban says at the start of the 10:30 a.m. staff meeting. There are five juniors on the LSU squad, led by receiver Michael Clayton, who are contemplating leaving school early for the NFL. The media is pressing them hard for information and Saban wants to end the discussion now. At least until after the bowl game. Agents have always been a problem for college coaches, calling players at home or on cell phones, perhaps telling them they are better than they are or what they should work on in practice or games. That advice may be divergent from what is best for the team. Players cannot accept anything from an agent or sign with one and remain eligible. Coaches don't even want the temptations thrown out and do their best, often unsuccessfully, to keep agents away.

Saban and the staff take 30 minutes to review the status of recruits—who is leaning toward LSU, who may be a long shot, etc. There is also discussion of bowl week. The coach is trying to decide whether time or location is more important for practices. The Tigers can practice every day at the Superdome at 2:00 p.m., except for the day they arrive, Sunday, and Wednesday of bowl week. Or they could practice earlier every day in Metairie, Louisiana, at the New Orleans Saints' practice facility, but without locker rooms. His inclination is to practice in the Superdome, even though two practices will have to be moved, because he wants the players to become acclimated to the dome. He chooses location over time.

Assistant Athletic Director Sam Nader talks about NCAA forms that the players need to fill out and the per diem money to be distributed, how the school can give players money to travel home for the holidays. Saban does not want to be bothered by the details. "Let's eliminate the clutter," he says.

At 11:20 a.m., 10 minutes before Saban is scheduled to meet with ABC broadcasters in his office, the coach finally gets around to Thursday's practice. Practice will last approximately two hours and include one team period and ten 40-yard sprints, as part of conditioning at the end. In a moment, Saban is off to his interview.

• • •

"I've got to bring this up, even if it is difficult for you," ABC's Brent Musburger says to Saban. "How do you handle the distraction of your name being out there for NFL jobs?"

Every year, it seems that Saban's name is thrown out by reporters and unnamed "sources" as a candidate for open NFL head coaching jobs. But he hasn't gone anywhere. "I have not contacted anyone and no one has contacted me," the coach responds to Musburger. "The team has worked all season to get here and this is not about me." It is a question the coach will surely get again leading up to the game.

Joining Musberger are Jack Arute and Gary Danielson, and the three spend 20 minutes with Saban in his office, asking about the coach and his relationship with Oklahoma coach Bob Stoops more than about the LSU players or the game itself. At noon, Sports Information Director Michael Bonnette, who is sitting in on the meeting, puts an end to the talk. Saban is already late for his press conference on the fifth floor.

• • •

"Let's eliminate the clutter," Saban tells his players, who are seated in front of him in the Bill Lawton meeting room for the first time in two weeks. Over the past 14 days, the players had no classes but many chose to stay on campus and work out. Today is the first time the team has assembled since immediately after the Georgia win. The clutter Saban is referring to is the set of distractions unique to big-time bowl games and the Christmas holiday season. "Agents, it ends now," Saban sternly demands. "Juniors looking at the NFL, it ends now. Buying your girlfriend presents, ends now." Saban points out that he is so focused he hasn't had time to buy his wife, Terry, an anniversary present, as the Sabans were married 32 years ago today.

After congratulating the players who were named All-American and Chad Lavalais, who was just named SEC Defensive Player of the Year, Saban humbly acknowledges the honor that was bestowed upon him last week—the Associated Press Coach of the Year. "It's all the hard work and effort that you put in—the players, coaches, trainers, sports medicine staff, weight staff. I'm just the driver of the bus."

Turning to Oklahoma, the coach plays the role of underdog. "It's their team. The media's team. Chad and I went to Orlando [for the Home Depot Awards] and they had seven guys and it was just me and Chad. We weren't going to pick a fight. They [the media] want them to win. But don't think about it." The coach slides off his glasses. "They are good, but we can beat their ass. I'll tell you this. Forget about the national title game and other stuff. You will be facing the best football player you have ever played against. You have to focus on that."

Finally, to conclude his seven-minute talk, Saban sets the tone for the next two weeks. "The game is going to be won over the next two weeks. Not on January 4, but for what you do over the next two weeks. Starts today with practice."

* * *

The national title game will be held inside, so it is only fitting that Saban decides that the prebowl practices will also be held indoors. There are a number of visitors to the 4:30 p.m. session, including top recruits, a few media members, friends of the program, and an ABC television crew. The crew attaches a portable microphone to Saban's black pullover and the cameras tail him for the first four periods of practice, capturing the sights and sounds of Nick Saban at work.

For the first practice after a two-week layoff, the players look sharp and well rested. The first four periods are designated for individual drill work, but during Period 5, the offense and defense come together in three different drills on three parts of the field. Jimbo Fisher and Saban run one of the drills, and on most plays, one, if not both, have someone in the doghouse. Through the early scripted plays the sounds of pads colliding echo through the indoor facility. As usual, Saban throws passes in individual drills, gets in the face of a few players not paying attention in a secondary drill, and enthusiastically encourages his players as they run the 10 sprints at the end of practice.

"That was a good start, a good start, men," the coach says to the exhausted team in front of him. "Now we need three more and then the Oklahoma practices start Sunday."

• • •

There is no rest for the weary. Friday morning, the coaches are back at it at 7:30, this time working on the day's practice scripts. But today is unusual. Saban has decided to conduct two practices, one in the morning at 10:30 and one at night at 7:30. Each practice will be preceded by a 15-minute special teams meeting and 30-minute position meetings. Saban, who constructs all of the practice schedules, informed Will Muschamp and Jimbo Fisher last night of the morning practice plan to give them time to prepare. Focus on the morning practice will be first and second downs. All along, the coaches are putting things in the practice plans that they know will be used against Oklahoma, without pointing it out to the players.

Before the first Friday practice, Derek Dooley works on kickoff coverage and kickoff return before a packed crowd at 9:15 a.m. Saban sits front and center and makes notes of four late-arriving Tigers. Dooley uses the 15 minutes to review film from the win over Georgia two weeks ago. He has not had time with the players since then to do it. Using a red laser pointer, and stopping when Saban injects a comment, Dooley points out the good and the bad. It is a quick meeting, as the position meetings are only 30 minutes and position coaches are very protective of their time.

"Blue personnel, zone pressure, flex fire Z trap man." The verbage coming from Muschamp's mouth to the defense seated in front of him is a mess of sounds, unless you know what the hell he is talking about. It is an impressive review session that lasts just minutes, with the fiery young coach pausing every few seconds to ask, "Any questions?" before hurriedly moving on. After the defensive line and linebackers are excused, Saban is left in the meeting room with his corners and safeties.

"Good start yesterday," he begins. He reviews practice film with the players, getting up from his chair more than a dozen times to demonstrate a positioning move, to make eye contact with a particular player, or simply because he can't sit still. He enjoys working with the secondary and is by far the most qualified on his staff to do it. "I've been doing it 32 years. Buddy Ryan told me once that when he became a head coach, he lost his best assistant—himself." The point is taken: Saban's best defensive coach is Saban.

After a brief walk-through and stretch period, it is full speed ahead for the morning practice. There are four quarterbacks dressed in red jerseys, three of them wearing #18. One is starter Matt Mauck. The other two are the scout team QBs wearing Oklahoma quarterback Jason White's number—also 18.

In the early position drills, offensive line coach Stacy Searels is already soaked in sweat. "You knock his ass through the wall," Searels says to an O-line starter. Across the field, Dooley is enraged when one of his backs, running sideline routes and catching passes, catches a ball and runs directly out of bounds. The usually even-keeled coach turns red and gives the player an earful. Stan Hixon works the receivers hard just yards away.

When practice ends, Saban returns to something he told the team in their first-team meeting yesterday afternoon. "You are going to be facing the best players you have ever faced. You have to dominate your opponent." It is becoming a mantra as game day approaches. Then, turning a bit more intense, Saban asks, "How many of you were late for the 9:15 special teams meeting?"

A few brave souls raise their hands, some hidden behind teammates.

"Four," Dooley blurts out.

"And what's going to happen to them?" Saban asks.

"Run with me after practice," Dooley responds.

Saban is peeved but sarcastically says, "And some of you who were late, I'm surprised you didn't say you were late because of class."

The players and coaches crack smiles, knowing that classes ended two weeks ago.

● ● ●

The first sign that things will not go well at the Friday night practice is the late arrival of the players' buses. Forced to wait, Saban cannot stand still. He paces back and forth, peeking at the entrance and looking at the turf. The players finally show, but the mood is already dampened. Then things go from bad to worse. On the offensive side, there are missed tackles, poor blocks, dropped passes, and incorrect routes. On the defensive side, things heat up as Saban does, and he and Muschamp even exchange a few words with one another. It is the end of a long day, and practice is not going smoothly. The coach tells the team as much before sending them back to the buses around 9:30 p.m.

Watching practice on Friday night are some valued guests. The head coach of Middle Tennessee State, Andy McCollum, is there to observe, as is Warren Rabb, the quarterback from the 1958 team, the last LSU squad to win a national title. Standing against a wall is Lonny Rosen, a psychiatrist on staff at Michigan State University. The tall, thin, bearded Rosen is not in town just to watch practice. He got to know Saban when the coach was at Michigan State and worked with Saban's players, as well as with Saban himself. He's not a sports psychologist—a guy who comes in and talks to a team to motivate them. Rather, he spends one-on-one time with players and then gives Saban and the coaches a report on what he finds and he spends time with the head coach, giving him suggestions. Rosen comes down three times a year, during spring practice, fall camp, and now, around bowl game time.

With so much at stake, Saban wants everybody focused on the task at hand, including himself, and is willing to take suggestions from a doctor.

• • •

Saturday morning is more film, more meetings. Saban spends over an hour with assistants going over special teams. Jimbo Fisher and Stacy Searels break down film of the Big XII Championship game between Oklahoma and Kansas State—the Sooners' only loss of the season. Can they learn something from what Kansas State did to blow out Oklahoma? It is clear by this point that the LSU offense is up for a big task. The Sooner defense is the best in the nation because they play aggressive, physical football, just like LSU. Scoring points will not be easy, and scoring the magic number of 25—a plateau that has thus far guaranteed Saban-coached LSU teams a win—will be difficult.

As this is the last of the four fundamental practices, a huge crowd gathers inside the practice facility, including close to a hundred members of the LSU Gridiron Club, as well as recruits and their parents or coaches.

The coaches notice a major turnaround from last night in the players' attitudes. Even Saban seems to be a little loose. Throughout the individual drills and team periods, the staff is setting the players up for the Oklahoma game plan.

The fundamental practices are over. It's Oklahoma time.

• • •

As usual, the coaching staff works on Sunday, with practice in the afternoon. The men have Sunday, Monday, and Tuesday to formalize the game plan and put it into action with the team before they break on Tuesday morning. Saban has given the staff off on Wednesday, Thursday (Christmas Day), and Friday. They will meet all day Saturday before leaving for New Orleans with the team on Sunday.

Over the next three days, the plan for winning the national title takes shape. They meet longer as staffs and in position meetings; practices are more specific and intense. Monday's practice is held outside on a beautiful day in Baton Rouge. By Tuesday, both coordinators have 90 percent of their game plan set. For the defense, the plan includes stopping the yards after catch, as Oklahoma throws many short passes and screens, and the LSU defenders keeping the ball in front of them. The Sooners' rushing game is not outstanding, and Muschamp thinks the LSU line, especially Lavalais, can get to Jason White and force him into bad decisions. The defensive staff works hard on calls that might give Lavalais a one-on-one. Fisher and his boys figure the best way to score on Oklahoma is to establish the run and convert passes against the Sooners' zone defense, particularly on third downs.

The clutter that so concerns Saban has not been eliminated and, in fact, continues to grow. Ticket requests from players and coaches grow to the point of absurdity—then lead to the inevitable. Despite warnings from Saban, two LSU players—running back Shyrone Carey and long snapper Steve Damen—are caught attempting to sell their complimentary bowl game tickets and are declared ineligible for the game. They can practice in Baton Rouge and travel with the team but not suit up, nor can they receive any of the assorted bowl game gifts, including rings, watches, etc. Carey was the starting running back when the season began but after a knee injury, was relegated to a backup role behind the sensational trio of freshmen. But Damen is the starting snapper on punts, and teaching a player long snapping and blocking is not an easy task.

On Tuesday, the Governor-elect of Louisiana, Kathleen Blanco, stops by at the end of practice and speaks to the team for a few minutes. She wishes them luck and tells them how proud she—and the entire state—is of their accomplishments, on and off the field. The team captains even give her an LSU jersey with "Blanco" on the back.

And the clutter is not limited to the players and visitors. There are media reports that parties on Saban's behalf have had preliminary discussions with the New York Giants about their head coach opening.

Finally, Christmas Break is upon the men of LSU. The coaches have three consecutive days off for the first time since July. Time will be spent with families, although thoughts of Oklahoma will never be far from their minds. On Tuesday night, Saban and Terry host the staff at their spacious home just minutes from campus for a Christmas party. Coaches, trainers, strength staff, and others join the family for some holiday cheer, and Saban even presents many guests with Christmas bonuses. The bonus for Saban will come in less than two weeks in New Orleans. He has already earned six figures in postseason bonuses and if he wins the BCS title, his contract stipulates that he is to be paid at least one dollar more than the highest paid college coach in America—Oklahoma's Bob Stoops. That's over $2.3 million.

Of course, winning the game is a big if and the Sooners will do everything they can to make sure Stoops remains at the top of the pay scale.

• • •

The buses roll up to the Marriott Hotel on Canal Street in New Orleans precisely at noon on Sunday, December 28, in front of a throng of LSU supporters, cameras, and the 3rd Line Brass Band. The players and coaches are escorted up an escalator to the second floor, where their room keys await. Michael Clayton, Matt Mauck, Rodney Reed, and Marcus Spears stand in front of Sugar Bowl banners and are swarmed by media. The rest of the players grab their bags and check into their rooms before coming back down for lunch.

The second floor of the Marriott will be home to LSU football for the next nine days. The floor has an expansive lobby area and over a dozen meeting rooms, many already set up for player position meetings. One room is designated for the video crew and they have reassembled their impressive computer complex in it. One room serves as a training room, complete with tables and a full supply of medicines. At the end of the wide hallway flanked by the meeting rooms, a staff room is arranged. Just outside the rooms are weights for those players interested in beefing up or toning during the stay.

"I'm not here to give you all sorts of warnings like your parents and coaches," a New Orleans judge and member of the Sugar Bowl Committee says to the team, seated in a banquet meeting room on

Sunday. But indeed, the judge is on hand, along with a police captain and Sugar Bowl officials, to give advice to the young men of LSU about the dangers of the Big Easy. Pick-pockets, prostitutes, scam artists, and fans looking for fights line the streets of the famous—and infamous—French Quarter. The guests hand out "LSU Cards," which the players can present to any police officer if they find themselves in "a situation." By presenting the card, the police know who to contact and how to proceed. It does not give the player free reign. Nick Saban keeps it simple: "Don't do anything to hurt the team."

When all of the officials and guests walk out, Saban has a message for the team. "We have all been about one word—dominant. We don't talk about wins. We want to dominate. We have climbed the mountain and we're near the summit, and we want to stick a flag at the top." He continues, "They are a good football team and they are used to smacking around teams and watching them quit. They will smack us around but it's going to take them three hours to beat our ass." Then, giving them a final reminder about treating this game like all the others, Saban looks up from his notes and says, "And I don't want to hear the word championship from anyone."

• • •

As soon as Saban walks into the New Orleans Saints' practice facility on Sunday afternoon, he is concerned about the lights and the height of the ceiling. The illumination is much different than the LSU indoor facility and the ceiling is not very high, prohibiting punts inside. There is nothing he can do about it either. Practice will be approximately 100 minutes and begins, as usual, with media allowed in for the first 15. In individual drills, the defensive backs, watched by Saban, do an open-field tackle drill. Each back faces a runner with the ball, 20 yards away, who sprints at him. The defender must track him down and wrap him up, but not tackle him.

The two-minute drill near the end of practice begins with the offense on their own 25, trailing by seven with two time-outs. There is 1:30 left on the clock. The offense struggles to move the ball and they turn it over on downs. Saban wastes no time, calling for the second team to do the drill, but the second-stringers produce similar results.

"We need to stick the flag in the summit," he tells the players, kneeling around him after concluding practice with ten 40-yard sprints. "You need to be business. When you are on the field and in the meetings, you need to be totally focused."

But these days are not *all* business. The activity for the night is a two-hour boat ride on the *Creole Queen*, with food and music. The players are required to attend, but few coaches appear. Director of High School Relations Charles Baglio escorts the players, and Saban does appear, swarmed by autograph seekers, many of them Sugar Bowl officials and their guests. He is not happy, as he wasn't expecting an autograph session, but he does manage to get in a little "James Brown dancing"—much to the delight of his players. Soon the young men have other things on their mind, as they have a night on the town with bed check not set until 3:00 a.m., as suggested by the seniors.

• • •

Seven thirty on a late-December Monday morning in a hotel in New Orleans is much like a mid-September Monday morning in Baton Rouge. The coaches split into offense and defense and watch Sunday's practice. They regroup a little after nine all together, at which time Saban sets the practice schedule and discusses the players' lifting schedule with strength coach Tommy Moffitt. Special teams present a final issue. Long snapper Steve Damen is ineligible and Gant Petty has been getting reps. Petty is the snapper on field goals and PATs but not punts. Saban is concerned about his blocking after snaps on punts, especially since Oklahoma has a strong punt rush.

Later in the day, special teams is a hot topic once more, as the coaches must make the decision of who is going to kick field goals, Ryan Gaudet or Chris Jackson. Both have been mediocre in recent games. The AstroPlay® surface at the Superdome is also a concern, since many college and NFL kickers have had trouble kicking on the surface. Dooley pays a great deal of attention to Petty in the meeting, as some players in the back fight off sleep after a very late night.

The three team buses wait outside in the rain for Saban to finish his meeting with the defensive backs so they can depart on time at 1:00. The first bus is for the starters, Saban, Fisher, Muschamp, Doll, and Hixon; the second is for the backups and the rest of the assistant coaches; the third bus is for the scouts, trainers, and anyone else. The bus ride to the Superdome takes just six minutes, and the team is in the Tulane football locker room by 1:15. The facility is plain and dated, but it will do.

The players quickly tape and dress in full pads, and are eager to take the field for the scheduled 1:40 walk-through. Saban is dressed in his normal black pullover, brown pants, and Nike sneakers. But instead of taking the field at 1:40, the players sit in the concourse outside their locker room. Why? Oklahoma, which was scheduled to practice from 11:00 to 1:00, was still on the field. Saban is not happy but takes it in stride—for a while. With Sugar Bowl officials and LSU administrators trying to get the Tigers on the field, the Sooners remain. Saban sits in a chair on the sideline, fuming as the last remaining Sooners depart. Finally, at 2:23, LSU takes the fields and a Sugar Bowl official apologizes to Saban.

The players seem to take the delay out on each other in an intense, full-contact practice. The offense works on screen passes and reverses. In the 9 versus 7 period, they go against the scouts for six minutes and the first-team defense for six. The minutes are hard hitting and emotional. There is work on blitzes and red zone plays, and Saban sees a lot to correct with his secondary. At the end of practice, Saban apologizes to his team for the delay in starting practice and reminds them of the goal. "Remember we are looking to plant the flag on the summit. All you have to be focused on is playing your best against the best player you've faced."

The coaches and their wives join Sugar Bowl officials for an invitation only dinner at the Bon Ton Café downtown, where a multicourse meal is served as committee members welcome LSU to the Big Easy. The players bus 10 minutes to nearby Lake Pontchartrain for a seafood dinner on the dock while being entertained—and humiliated—by a hypnotist. Players Melvin Oliver, Barrington Edwards, and Eric Alexander among others are put under a spell, and slow dance with one another, put on makeup, and act like Miss Piggy, Kermit the Frog, or MC Hammer while under hypnosis. Their teammates roar with laughter. Curfew is at 2:30 a.m. tonight, so most of the players go out again, headed for Bourbon Street or the nearby Harrah's Casino.

• • •

The schedule for Tuesday was changed late last night, after Monday's disruptive delay. Everything is moved back 45 minutes—but that doesn't mean the staff starts late. They watch parts of Monday's practice as a group, drills where the first teams face off, while Saban continues to fume about yesterday's delay. Jimbo Fisher and his assistants see plenty wrong with Monday's effort—wrong receiving routes, missed blocks, bad passes. They are already feeling the pressure knowing that the LSU offense must put points on the board if the team is to have a chance to win, and having mistakes in practice this late in the season further weighs on the coaches.

By Tuesday's practice, Saban and Dooley still have not decided on a placekicker. There is also the challenge of stopping Oklahoma kick returner Antonio Perkins, a deadly combination of speed and skill. Can the LSU coverage hold? Should the punters kick the ball out of bounds and away from Perkins? The concern is a credit to Oklahoma's explosive personnel. After all, Dooley has at his disposal all of the best athletes—all but one of the starters on offense or defense starts on at least one special teams' unit.

"You don't want to be the guy who has to face his teammates after the game who didn't dominate," Saban begins a brief team meeting in a banquet room at the Marriott. "Everybody has a different role. Some are big, some are small. But you don't have to win the game. The quarterback doesn't have to win the game. The defensive line doesn't have to win the game. All you have to do is dominate your player." But Saban has even more than this on his mind—in particular, the disrespect that he felt Oklahoma showed by straggling off the field. "But we're not going to confront them. Not out on the town or at the team functions. You know how you get to them? When you knock down the quarterback, offer your hand to help him. Congratulate him on the Heisman and tell him his offensive line is not helping him out today."

The players chuckle.

"We will handle ourselves with class," the coach concludes.

There is no delay at the Superdome on Tuesday. When the team arrives, the only Sooners left on the field are a few placekickers and some equipment managers. Practice is based on a typical Monday practice, which means the players wear shells and practice is light. Blitz drills and special teams dominate the day, with twenty-five minutes devoted to the kicking game. During seven-on-seven drills, long-snapper Gant Petty works on snaps and blocks off to the side. The battle between the offense and defense gets heated in drills, but in good fun. Saban even gets in the act, talking a little trash with receiver Michael Clayton, who proceeds to make a remarkable one-handed catch on the very next play. The coach smiles and says, "I can't talk anymore."

Players' parents, bowl officials, and television star and New Orleans resident John Goodman are on hand for practice. Two unwelcomed visitors are pointed out by Saban. They are sitting in an upper deck, apparently taking notes. Saban immediately summons security.

The two men quickly put away their papers and hurry off as security approaches. They are tracked down moments later. Oklahoma scouts? Media? No, two Superdome cooks making lists of food inventory while catching some of practice.

The linemen and skill players go upstairs to the Superdome weight room to get in a short lift after practice, while the kickers and "hands team" remain on the field to work on onside kicks. Saban walks off the field to a crowd of parents and takes Clayton's two-year-old daughter from her grandfather's arms. He walks across the field while Clayton receives punts and allows his star player a kiss from the adorable girl.

It is the side of Saban that most never see.

• • •

Like many 15-year-olds, Jonathan Clark watches sports on TV and imagines himself down in the count in the bottom of the ninth in Game 7 of the World Series or taking snaps during the final seconds of a tied Super Bowl. A fan particularly of college football, Clark has a notebook full of sketches and scores, and for the bowl season, he has listed every game and fills in the result as December progresses. But Clark is different from most teenagers in that he watches bowl games from a sixth-floor hospital bed at New Orleans Children's Hospital. Clark has an incomplete left lung and a tracheotomy that makes his adolescent voice sound like the voice of someone much older. He is not always in the hospital, but a stomach flu has brought him back in.

"I watch you on TV," Clark says to Nick Saban, head coach of Jonathan's favorite team, as he enters the boy's hospital room on Wednesday afternoon. "I'll blame you if we lose," says Jonathan, teasing the coach.

Saban spends a few minutes with Jonathan and his younger brother and mother. Close to 30 players, along with Saban and Terry, opted for the voluntary team trip. The players split into five groups and hit dozens of patients throughout the facility, signing autographs, taking pictures, and handing out LSU Sugar Bowl T-shirts.

Saban is at ease talking with Jonathan, as he was moments earlier with a six-year-old boy with severe asthma who has visited the hospital 23 times in the last three years. Room by room, child by child, the coach shakes hands, obliges autograph seekers, and signs memorabilia for the upcoming fund-raising auction for the hospital. The 45 minutes go by quickly.

It is New Year's Eve, and the staff calls it a day at 4:00. Along with their wives, they spend New Year's down the street at the Hilton Hotel on the Riverwalk. The coaches look like different men, dressed up in their coats and ties. Saban and Terry are there, as is Saban's sister, Diana, in from West Virginia, and his mother, Mary, visiting from Myrtle Beach. There are bands playing, a bar sculpted out of ice, artists drawing guest portraits. The coach looks anxious as he sits at his table, often finding himself alone, and exits by 9:30 p.m. His assistants follow a half hour later. There is work to be done.

• • •

Things are different on Thursday. The coaches' faces are drawn a little tighter in the early morning meetings; the players are more prompt; fewer jokes float through the rooms. For the first time all week, a meal is quiet, as only hushed conversations are heard at breakfast. Saban, dressed in a checkered sweater and slacks, sits at the end of the conference table in the staff meeting room by himself. He drinks coffee from a Styrofoam cup as his right leg shakes uncontrollably.

At practice in the afternoon, things are different, too. The coaches unanimously agree it's the best practice all week. The kids are simply more focused.

But it's not all good news. Backup receiver Junior Joseph breaks his collarbone going up for a ball. He is out for the game. At the end of practice, Saban lets loose on the team because a player arrived 15 minutes late for curfew last night. "I don't like talking about it, but I'll send your ass home," he says, referring to any further offenders. The culprit himself will sit out the first quarter of the game and do sprints after practice.

The staff watches film of practice back at the hotel until 7:30. The look of fatigue that usually sweeps across a staff room by Tuesday night has finally overcome the group on Thursday. As the offense watches practice film and tape of Oklahoma, GAs pop in or call in with the updated score of the USC-Michigan game, whose outcome is of interest to the LSU assistants, though they won't admit it. Stan Hixon points out just how many plays are in the offensive game plan. "If I'm going to a shoot-out I want full ammo," Fisher says without missing a beat. In fact, there are close to four hundred various plays at Fisher's disposal, many of them offshoots of the same basic formations.

"There are pluses and minuses to have so much time to prepare for a game," he says. "You can overprepare and start seeing ghosts. I'd rather play right away."

. . .

The players and coaches are at last struck by the magnitude of the weekend when they ride down the escalators to leave for Media Day and practice on Friday. Before they can even see the hundreds packed in the lobby, they can hear the cheers and chants. "LSU! LSU!" It is a mob scene. Outside, it is even more of a crush. Police try their best to hold back the throngs as the team climbs onto the buses. Tens of thousands of LSU and Oklahoma fans have descended on the town. Because the city is just an hour from Baton Rouge, there is a decidedly pro-LSU attitude, indicated by the outsized L-S-U on a side of a nearby building, the purple and gold lights illuminating the night, and the police officers on patrol stopping to give a cheer.

In the locker room at the Superdome, immediately before the players and coaches face the media on the field, Saban tries to prepare his players. "Look, guys, I'm proud of who you are and what you are. They're [media] going to ask you about USC. That has nothing to do with us. The 500,000 on Bourbon Street, the parades, the lobby when we left the hotel—it doesn't change who we are." The coach scans the crowded locker room. "You are good people, you're good football players. We're playing in the national championship game. The BCS selected us as the two best teams in the country. We're still the same people."

Assembling the players, coaches, trainers, and managers for the team picture proves more difficult than one might think but eventually they get it. When the media is allowed in, Saban, Jimbo Fisher, and Will Muschamp sit behind raised podiums on one sideline while selected players including Matt Mauck, Michael Clayton, and Chad Lavalais take positions in front of Nokia Sugar Bowl banners on the field at various yard lines. Crowds of press members surround the coaches first, then the players, dressed in game jerseys. For the majority of players and coaches, Media Day is nothing more than the team photo. They take seats in the lower sections of the Superdome and watch the craziness from afar as ESPN News carries the proceedings live.

Just as they had done on their first day in the Big Easy, LSU practices at the New Orleans Saints facility in Metairie on Friday. The players change and get taped at the Superdome, then bus to the practice complex, where a crowd of more than 200 awaits them—to the dismay of Saban. Though practice is closed, friends, family members, and high school coaches all make their way inside. Among the group are six former LSU players, two of them current NFLers. But even they have a hard time identifying the players. As has become tradition on the last practice of the year, the players swap jerseys. So big man Lavalais wears cornerback Corey Webster's #13.

Senior captain and punter Donnie Jones recites a limerick during stretching, as is Thursday tradition (even though it is really Friday). Kickoffs, punts, and field goals are the focus. Of particular interest to Saban and Dooley is the kicking battle between Ryan Gaudet and Chris Jackson. During field goal drills, Jackson does not help his cause by having three of his kicks blocked. But he is not the only one to have a bad day. The starting defense repeats multiple plays against the scouts at the insistence of Saban. And the offense fairs no better in the two-minute drill. Starting on their own 35, trailing 6-0, with one minute left and one time-out remaining, they struggle to move the ball at all, let alone score a touchdown.

It doesn't matter at this point, as even a perfect practice wouldn't give the coaches 100 percent confidence in the readiness of the team.

"Remember what we talked about," Saban says in a hushed voice at the end of practice, as if the players have no idea of what comes next. "You need to dominate your opponent, who is the probably the best player you ever played against. Do not worry about the national championship."

In the late afternoon staff meeting, a kicking decision. Dooley clearly favors Gaudet, especially after Jackson's dismal practice performance. Saban agrees. "Now the only thing," says Dooley, "is when do we tell them?" After back and forth between coach and assistant, they decide to say nothing until right before the game. Why get Gaudet anxious? Why disappoint Jackson, who will still handle kickoff duties? They will wait until Sunday and tell the media it will be a game-time decision.

• • •

Across from the Marriott that the Tigers have been calling home is the Sheraton. It is a massive structure forged of steel and cement, but on Friday night, the fifth floor weighs more than usual. Thousands of LSU fans have gathered for live airings of Nick Saban's television and radio shows. Saban, Matt Mauck, Jack Hunt, Marcus Spears, and Rodney Reed are escorted across Canal Street by a phalanx of police officers and taken through the delivery entrance and up the service elevator. They are greeted by what is best described as pure pandemonium. LSU fans young and old stand in the large ballroom, holding signs and pom-poms and sporting painted faces. The Tiger mascot runs through the crowd as the LSU band plays. A spontaneous cheer erupts from the mass of fans. It is a message for the coach: "Ten More Years! Ten More Years!" As he does during his weekly radio show, Saban uses the commercial breaks during the television show to work the audience, shaking hands, signing autographs, and smiling big and wide. When the television show ends, the coach walks from the television stage to the radio stage set up some 40 feet away. For the next hour, he fields phone calls during segments and signs autographs between them.

The coach is warm and excited throughout the two hours. He agrees to appear on ABC at halftime of the Fiesta Bowl, so he is driven to Jackson Square off Decatur Street, where John Saunders and Terry Bowden sit behind the ABC set. The crystal bowl national championship trophy is in the foreground and Bowden hecklers are seemingly everywhere. The coach answers questions about the success of defensive-minded head coaches, the emergence of Jimbo Fisher, and the play of Matt Mauck. The segment is taped to be aired less than 20 minutes later and after Saban leaves, Bob Stoops arrives for his segment as well. For Saban, a long day is complete.

Sunday, game day, will be even longer.

* * *

It is a bit awkward at the Hyatt Hotel on Saturday morning as Saban poses for pictures with Bob Stoops in between the coaches' press conferences. They share a handshake and stand behind the championship trophy as photographers snap away at the only photo op with both head coaches. As for the press conference itself, the questions are the same and so are Saban's answers.

After joining some of his players at a YES Clinic for youngsters at Tulane University, Saban is back in front of his group at the Marriott. Dressed in a light blue sport coat, a blue shirt, and slacks and wearing his black-rimmed reading glasses, he is at his most intense. "We have to be focused. Right now. I just went upstairs and told my wife, 'You're on your own 'til after the game.' Forget your girlfriends and family. Focus on dominating your opponent." At the end of his talk, he raises his voice, removes his glasses, and says, "I am proud of everyone in this room."

The final walk-through at the Superdome takes less than an hour and after dinner the team makes its way to a movie theater at 6:45, as many of the assistant coaches use their cell phones to make recruiting calls.

The Last Samurai is the story of an ex-American soldier, played by Tom Cruise, who travels to Japan to help defeat the Samurai insurgents, only to end up joining them in battle and in their way of life. There are graphic battle scenes, which seem to pique the interest of the players, and an underlying message of courage and honor, which seems to please Saban.

By the time the buses return to the hotel, the crowds downtown have swelled and, in a moment that says a lot about the devotion of LSU fans, two middle-aged men remove their baseball hats as the buses roll by and hold their right arm across their chest, to pay their respects.

• • •

Game Day.

The last time the LSU staff and players awoke on a game day was almost a month ago, hours before they humbled Georgia in the SEC Championship game in Atlanta. After weeks of practice, thousands of questions from the media, hundreds of ticket requests, and all the infamous clutter—it is time to play the game.

Will Muschamp is downstairs early, a little before 9:00, watching tape, alone in the defensive meeting room. Nick Saban comes down closer to 10:00, dressed in a coat and tie, and sits alone in the staff room. Before long, the two men are together, reviewing the game plan one more time. Before a game, the Tigers traditionally take a walk outside as a team just after breakfast, but the crowd situation in New Orleans poses problems. The solution? A walk around the outdoor pools on the fifth floor of the Marriott. So security shuts down the floor and the players, wearing bright purple warm-up suits, relax on poolside chairs, waiting for the walk to begin. Onlookers peek out from the windows of their rooms. Saban arrives, takes note of the wind, and says to a few assistants, "Do you think the wind will be a factor today?" It takes them a moment to remember the game will be played indoors and Saban cracks a smile. Then, following Saban, the entire group makes two large laps around the two pools. "Be focused," the coach tells them, "and be who you are."

Shortly after the pregame meetings and team meal, the staff meets one last time. What if the first- and second-string quarterbacks go down with injuries? Which end of the Superdome should they elect to kick off from if they win the coin toss? Is there enough space in the locker room to meet as a team? When these issues are resolved, Saban addresses his staff for the first time about what they need to do—not what the players need to do. "We just have to coach. Just like we've been telling the players, we don't have to do anything but what we've been doing all year. We need to put the players in the best position to win. And don't be afraid to try stuff. Don't get scared. You can't coach out of fear."

• • •

It is bedlam in the Marriott lobby and outside on the sidewalk as the team boards the buses. Earlier, Saban's teenage daughter, Kristen, handed her dad three good luck pennies, two more than she usually gives him. Fans line the street en route to the Superdome. Even with the police escort, the buses are slowed near the Dome when the Sooner Wagon, a horse-drawn covered wagon that is part of the Oklahoma pregame rally, makes its way slowly toward the Dome.

Once the team is inside, Saban takes a walk to the field. Posted in the entranceway of the locker room since Wednesday are four pieces of paper, printed-out downloads from *soonersports.com*, the official website of Oklahoma. On the site, they started offering the National Championship sweatshirts, T-shirts, and other apparel, days before the game.

Just before 6:00, the officials meet with Saban, who has been spending time in his personal dressing room with longtime friend and former coaching colleague Dennis Fryzel. Fryzel was the defensive coordinator under Earle Bruce at Ohio State when Saban was an assistant there. The two have remained close and Fryzel has spent time with Saban over the past few days. He is a calming influence and will be on the sidelines, as well.

During pregame warm-ups, kicker Chris Jackson misses a few kicks while Gaudet is solid. Dooley gives them the news. As the Tigers warm up, many of the LSU GAs carefully watch the Sooners do the same, looking at who is out there and what personnel groupings the team is running. Back in Saban's dressing room, barely big enough for him, let alone the entire staff, the coaches meet one last time. "They're running a lot of Silver," says a GA, indicating a personnel group that Oklahoma had not used much this season. Dooley lets Saban know that, though Gaudet is the man, the coach may want to think hard about attempting any field goal from 30 to 35 yards out or more. The coaches walk across the hall to a steamy and packed holding room.

"Remember your family and remember J.B.," Saban tells the team, referring to Jeff Boss, the former equipment manager who died of cancer earlier in the season. "We need to dominate the opponent," the coach says one last time. Then, seeming to think of a truer note to end on, he says, "Be who you are."

• • •

For all the purple and gold, the atmosphere does not belong to LSU alone. There are thousands of red-and-white-clad Oklahoma fans inside the Superdome, part of the largest crowd ever to gather in the facility. Both student bands are loud and the cheering doesn't stop. At kickoff, smoke from the pyrotechnic displays used during player introductions still hovers over the field. Oklahoma wins the coin toss and elects to kick.

On the first play from scrimmage, Justin Vincent takes a handoff from Matt Mauck at his own 20, breaks a tackle, finds a hole over right tackle and sprints into the open field. Only superb speed by the Sooners' Derrick Strait saves a touchdown, as he chases down Vincent after 64 yards at the Oklahoma 16. The LSU fans go crazy, as does the bench. Players hug each other, jump up and down, and some even run down the sidelines as the freshman makes his scamper. It's first and 10 from Oklahoma's 16. After a one-yard run by Joseph Addai and a four-yard pass to Michael Clayton, Mauck hits Clayton for an eight-yard gain and is knocked down in the process, resulting in a roughing the passer penalty on Oklahoma, setting up first down and goal from the one. Mauck fumbles the snap and Strait recovers. What looked like a sure seven ends up a very sure zero. The Tiger sideline is stunned. Mauck jogs off the field shaking his head. Saban simply claps his hands and pats Mauck on the rear as he passes by.

One of the themes that Saban had been using all week is resiliency. He had warned the players that the game would not be easy, that Oklahoma would come out fired up and that they would make plays. How LSU responds will dictate the game. Two minutes in, the team has their chance.

On Oklahoma's second play from scrimmage, Heisman-winning quarterback Jason White drops back and attempts to hit Mark Clayton on a deep pass, but safety Jack Hunt and corner Corey Webster converge on the ball. Hunt tips it, Webster intercepts. He runs back 18 yards to the Oklahoma 32 and the momentum lost just two plays earlier comes right back to the Tigers. As the LSU offense takes the field, Saban speaks into his headset, telling offensive coordinator Jimbo Fisher up in the coaches' box, "Let's just settle down." But he is hardly one to speak. Saban does not settle down during games. He does not perch himself at the line of scrimmage as many head coaches do. He walks, turns, and walks back, never stopping for more than a second.

Saban is 20 yards behind the ball when Vincent takes a handoff and fumbles it. The ball is recovered by Oklahoma's Donte Nicholson. But OU jumps offsides and there is no play. Two plays later, Mauck is late getting the play call and is forced to take a time-out before the play clock expires. When play resumes, receiver Skyler Green takes a handoff on a motion speed sweep and runs 24 yards to the outside for a touchdown. The run is set up by an impressive block by Joseph Addai.

The teams trade punts on the next two drives, as both defenses step up. While the LSU offense is on the field, Muschamp and Saban draw on a wipe board for the secondary. Saban pulls aside safety Jack Hunt and explains positioning. Then, while Muschamp draws on the board, Hunt turns to freshman safety LaRon Landry and explains it to him. From coach to upperclassman to freshman. This kind of awareness at every level has helped the Tigers' defense all year, and it's helping them again tonight. When the defense is on the field, they seem to have a sixth sense. It comes from their coach. As Oklahoma lines up to run a play, Saban is on the sideline motioning wildly with his hands and screaming, warning his players what is about to happen. And it does, just as he says.

After the opening run by Vincent and the touchdown by Skyler Green, the LSU offense struggles to find its groove. Mauck is picked off by Brando Everage but Oklahoma is called for holding, erasing the pick. On the Tigers' first possession of the second quarter, they go three and out again. This time, Saban takes off his headset and walks back to the benches. He claps his hands and says, "Let's get something going out there!" On their next possession, Mauck is sacked two plays in a row and, again, they go three and out. With the ball on their own 21, punter Donnie Jones's punt is blocked by Brandon Shelby and recovered by Oklahoma's Russell Dennison. The LSU special teams—particularly the punt coverage—have been playing well, containing dangerous punt returner Antonio Perkins. But this breakdown in protection gives the Sooners a golden opportunity to tie it up.

It is another chance for LSU to step up to adversity, and they appear to do just that. They stop Oklahoma from scoring on three straight plays but on the third down stop, LSU is called for offsides. The very next play, running back Kejuan Jones scores from one yard out.

LSU responds. Mauck leads them on a nine-play, 80-yard, three-minute drive that culminates in an 18-yard touchdown run by Vincent, putting LSU ahead 14-7. The drive is sustained by passes from Mauck to Clayton, Addai, David Jones, and Devery Henderson, supplemented with rushes by Vincent. The Tigers have a chance to add to the lead late in the first half when they have the ball inside Oklahoma territory. As they huddle before taking the field, Saban sticks his head into the huddle and reminds them they have no time-outs left. It doesn't matter. Mauck is intercepted by Perkins deep in his own territory and the Sooners elect to run out the first half clock.

• • •

In the first half, LSU had the ball eight times, resulting in two touchdowns, four punts, and two turnovers. Oklahoma's offense was not much better, forced to punt five times, scoring just once, with White throwing an interception. The Tigers had a three-minute time of possession advantage.

The entire staff, coaches and GAs alike, squeeze into Saban's dressing room upon entering the locker room. The head coach is calm and reassuring. He wants returner Skyler Green to catch more punts instead of letting them drop and he wants Jimbo Fisher and the offense to "keep mixing it up," trying different formations and blending passes with runs. "Guys, we're playing well. We had a great drive after the fumble. Resilient."

The offensive coaches bolt the room while the defense stays behind. Within minutes, both coordinators and Saban are addressing their respective players in the meeting room. It is hot and crowded, and players must focus on their coach to drown out the other voices.

"We are right where we want to be," a sweat-soaked Fisher tells his offense. "We have to play what we can control. Don't think of the outcome." In motioning to the offensive line, he says, "We can never lose the line of scrimmage."

Though halftime is 22 minutes, it moves fast and Saban barely has time to talk to the team. "Never look at the scoreboard," he begins, pointing with his hand at an imaginary scoreboard. "Dominate for 60. Offense, great job responding to their score. For 60 minutes, there is no score. Reset the tempo of the game. Defense, dominate their ass." Then he says it again, that thing he has been saying all week. "All we got to be is us. All we got to be is believing in us."

* * *

The first play from scrimmage in the second half for Oklahoma? Jason White is sacked by Marcus Spears for a loss of three yards. Second play from scrimmage? Spears intercepts White's pass and returns it 20-yards for a touchdown. That's a pretty good start. With the score now 21-7, it looks like LSU is firmly in control. But like Vincent's run to start the game, Spears's pick comes almost too soon. There is a lot of football left.

On the Sooners ensuing possession, White is sacked again, this time by Lionel Turner for a 17-yard loss, forcing an OU punt. Starting on their own 17, Mauck leads the Tigers down the field until they have a first and goal from the Oklahoma five, set up by a 23-yard catch by Green. Vincent is stopped for no gain on first down. Mauck is sacked by Teddy Lehman on second down and by Dan Cody on third down.

After having a first and goal from the five, LSU now faces fourth and goal from the 10. Saban has no choice but to call in Ryan Gaudet for the field goal attempt. Gaudet's kick is good. Wait. Penalty flags on the play. When referee Dennis Harrington sorts it out, LSU is called for holding and for a personal foul. The kick is no good and now the Tigers face fourth and goal from the 35-yard line. Gaudet lines up for another attempt, though Saban knows it is out of his range. He calls for a fake and holder Blain Bech takes the snap and throws to his right to a wide-open David Jones who runs 29 yards to the Oklahoma six. It's not a first down but as good as a punt. It was a chance to blow the game wide open. 28-7, or even 24-7, would have seemed insurmountable. As it is, we've got a game.

As the third quarter ends, with LSU driving on Oklahoma's 31, Saban, along with the players and coaches, raises four fingers on both hands and holds them high in the air. Trainer Jack Marucci and his staff are busy, as many of the players begin to cramp up in the second half, with the temperature rising inside the Dome. Smoke left over from the halftime pyrotechnics do not help the cause. The cramping leads to three players receiving IVs in the locker room: Clayton, Marquise Hill, and Spears. The defensive coaches, Saban, Muschamp, Travis Jones, Tim Walton, and Kirk Doll substitute more than they'd like, as players catch breathers on the bench.

The LSU Tigers are 15 minutes from the national championship. Can they hold on? On the first play of the fourth quarter, Mauck drops back to pass and is intercepted by Brodney Pool, who returns it 49 yards before being tackled from behind by Michael Clayton. Mauck is enraged as he jogs off the field and a few of the players on the sideline look confused. The offensive line sits in front of line coach Stacy Searels and he reminds them to "keep that eye of the tiger" look. On the field, Jason White takes the Sooners to third and goal from LSU's one and Kejuan Jones scores his second touchdown of the game and the lead is back to just seven, 21-14.

Saban appears confident that the Tiger offense will come right back, but they don't. LSU goes three and out. On the sidelines, you can feel the momentum shift. You can see the faces twisting. You can hear the silence growing. The Tiger defense returns the favor and forces an OU punt and, as the LSU offense takes the field, Saban is fired up, screaming encouragement at Clayton. But it's not enough. LSU punts again.

With 5:45 left in the game, LSU leads 21-14. The Heisman winner is at center stage for the #1 ranked BCS team, a team that lost once all season. They didn't get here by being timid, and they show no fear now, trailing late in the game. Starting on his own 39, White runs and passes the Sooners into LSU territory as the clock continues to move. On third and five from LSU's 19, White's pass to Mark Clayton is incomplete with Corey Webster covering, but Webster is called for pass interference, setting up an OU first down on LSU's twelve. White's next three pass attempts are all incomplete. On fourth down, White throws to Clayton in the end zone, but the ball hits his hands and then hits the ground. The LSU sideline is shielded from the ball and there is a brief second of silence before the back judge signals incomplete.

The game is not over yet with 2:46 remaining and LSU deep in its own territory. The LSU offense manages to move the ball just seven yards and after Donnie Jones's first punt is nullified by penalties, his second one travels just 33 yards. Saban runs to the defense on the bench before they enter the game. "Two minutes! Two-minute defense!" he shouts up and down the bench as he holds up two fingers on each hand. With 2:09 left, Oklahoma has no time-outs, having used two on LSU's offensive possession to stop the clock, and the Sooners start on their own 48. White passes to Kejuan Jones—incomplete. White passes to Brandon Jones—incomplete. White passes to Will Peoples—incomplete. On fourth and ten, White doesn't pass at all, as he is sacked viciously by Lionel Turner. The LSU sideline erupts as coaches try to hold players back from entering the field.

There is 1:51 remaining and OU has no way to stop the clock. Mauck takes the first down snap and moves back five yards and then falls on the ground. Saban is incensed. "What are we doing, Jimbo?" he shouts into his headset. "He's got to go forward!" Saban is astute enough to know that there is too much time for LSU to simply fall on the ball. He would have preferred Vincent carry a few times and, if he did fall on the ball, that Mauck not pop up from the ground so quickly, allowing the officials to restart the play clock so fast. On the next two plays, Mauck again moves back and falls on the ball. With nine seconds left, the Tigers face a fourth and 22. Saban calls time-out. While the fans celebrate and players jump excitedly on the side-line, Saban and Derek Dooley discuss what to do. Take a snap and fall down? That would stop the clock on the change of possession. Have Mauck take the ball and run around for nine seconds? Too risky. Saban decides to punt. OU sends everyone to block the kick but Jones gets it off. It lands, bounces around and the clock reaches 0:00.

Saban takes off his headset and thrusts both hands in the air as chaos consumes him. Photographers surround him as his police escort attempts to maintain space. Somehow, he reaches Bob Stoops near midfield and the men share an embrace and Stoops congratulates him. Saban then turns around and immediately begins searching and shouting for his 17-year old son, Nicholas. He won't go up on the podium until he finds him. Sure enough, they find one another and share a hug, and Saban's eyes water up. The field is bedlam, as players, coaches, family members, press, and even some fans converge. Within minutes, the coach, his captains, and seniors are atop the presentation podium holding the crystal ball. When Saban finally makes his way off the podium, he gives Terry a kiss and takes his young daughter, Kristen, into his arms.

The locker room is rowdy but not out of control. The team sings the LSU fight song. "Character" is why they won, Saban tells the play-ers. He acknowledges the guys leaving the program and welcomes them back and reminds the returning players just how hard it was to get here. The postgame interviews keep Saban and a few of his play-ers, including game MVP Justin Vincent, at the Superdome until well after midnight. They return to the hotel and are greeted by thousands of LSU revelers in the street. Saban and his family and friends cele-brate in the hospitality suite on the 38th floor for about an hour be-fore the coach finally heads to bed after two.

• • •

The clutter that so concerned Nick Saban from early December on was real, not imagined. The ticket requests, the parties, the fans, the media, the hotel lobby, the families, the hype. What won the game for LSU was its ability to eliminate the clutter, for coaches and players. Saban had a vision three weeks ago and the message did not get lost on the team. They won 13 of the 14 games they played. They won the SEC Championship. And now they are National Champions.

EPILOGUE

So much can happen in a week, let alone in a season. Crushing defeats, upset wins, injuries, suspensions. Match-ups that looked meaningless in August become must-sees in November and big-ticket games become inconsequential.

My stay at each school was but a snapshot. What happened before that week and after might have been vastly different from what I observed. But since most programs run the same week to week, what really changes are the moods and the meaning of games. When I selected the nine schools in the summer of 2003, eight of the teams were ranked in the Associated Press Top 25 preseason poll, Boston College the only exception. Here is how the Associated Press polls looked before the season started with the nine teams, and how the AP poll had them in the end:

Associated Press (August 24)		Associated Press (January 4)	
#11	Georgia	#2	LSU
#12	Tennessee	#7	Georgia
#13	Florida State	#11	Florida State
#14	LSU	#15	Tennessee
#15	Maryland	#17	Maryland
#21	Wisconsin	NR	Boston College
#22	Arizona State	NR	Wisconsin
#23	Colorado State	NR	Colorado State
NR	Boston College	NR	Arizona State

Who could have predicted that Arizona State, a PAC-10 favorite with a Heisman candidate at quarterback, would have such a miserable season? Or that Maryland would have lost to Northern Illinois? Or that Sonny Lubick's team, which could have gone undefeated, struggled to finish above .500? Here is a look at what happened to the coaches and schools after my visits.

Colorado State

The loss to Colorado in August was not the way Sonny Lubick wanted to start the season. "It was a heartbreaker," he recalls after the season. "I thought it would have had a more devastating effect, but we went out the next week and beat Cal on the road. We came out of it okay." After the upset of Cal, the Rams defeated Weber State in their home opener to move to 2-1. When Miami of Ohio came to Fort Collins the following week, CSU played ugly, losing 41-21. A loss to Utah followed. "The loss to Utah really took the wind out of us. We had six turnovers. Never done that before." But the Rams were resilient, defeating Fresno State at home, crushing BYU on the road on national television, and beating Air Force at home.

Losses to Wyoming and New Mexico followed and Colorado State was out of the conference race, just trying to win their last two to ensure a bowl game. They beat San Diego State and UNLV to end the season 7-5, and earned a berth in the San Francisco Bowl against Boston College, a game in which they turned the ball over six times and lost 35-21.

Quarterback Bradlee Van Pelt had a stellar senior season, but sat out part of the bowl game after breaking his hand against UNLV. He threw for 2,845 yards and 19 touchdowns and ran for 909 more, including three games with over 100 yards rushing. Marcus Houston rushed for 636 yards and nine touchdowns. David Anderson continued the torrid receiving pace he began against Colorado, finishing with 72 catches for 1,293 yards and nine TDs. Linebacker Eric Pauly's season ended after the fifth game with a knee injury and halfback Joel Dreessen missed four games with a lower abdominal strain.

"This was a year we hadn't experienced here in a long time," Lubick says. "Expectations were probably a little too high. Players read the clippings. The little edge was missing."

The expectations of a Mountain West title and of a possible BCS berth perhaps hurt the team from the start. Still, Lubick is one to take responsibility and points the finger only at himself. "Things are a little bit circular. But if you're well coached, you don't turn the ball over."

After the season, co-offensive coordinator John Benton left for the St. Louis Rams. In early January, Lubick and his assistants met for hours to review the year and, more importantly, suggest changes. Year 2004 is under way.

Georgia

After the seemingly easy wins over Clemson, Middle Tennessee, and South Carolina in September, the Bulldogs ran in to an equally tough LSU team in Baton Rouge. In a game that was decided in the final minutes, Georgia gave up a late touchdown and suffered its first defeat. They regrouped and stampeded through the SEC, crushing Alabama, Tennessee on the road, and Vanderbilt (and barely escaping University of Alabama at Birmingham), until they lost their second game to Florida in Jacksonville, 16-13. Again they rebounded, defeating Auburn and Kentucky to finish in a first-place tie in the SEC East with Tennessee and Florida. The three-way tie was broken by a series of tiebreakers and Georgia received the automatic berth in the SEC title game. They were outplayed in Atlanta in the rematch against LSU and settled for the Capital One Bowl in Orlando. They gave up a 24-point lead to Purdue in that game, but eventually won it in overtime.

Throughout the year, Georgia was plagued by injuries. Fred Gibson's leg never fully healed and the star receiver missed games. Star safety Kentrall Curry never made it back on the field at all and DeCory Bryant's career ended with an injured neck. "We finished sixth in the country (according to the *USA Today* poll)," Richt points out. He is disappointed in not winning the SEC and not playing in a BCS game, but he is proud of his coaching staff and players for overcoming adversity. "We didn't panic about the injuries. Injuries are a part of the complications that we faced but we never got to the point where we didn't think we couldn't win."

The Georgia defense was the key, holding opponents to an average of 14.5 points per game and 277 yards of total offense. For his coaching, defensive coordinator Brian VanGorder was awarded the Frank Broyles Award as the top assistant coach in the country after the season. David Pollack did not repeat as the SEC Defensive Player of the Year, but did cause havoc on opponents, making 92 solo or assisted tackles and registering 7½ sacks. Odell Thurman and Thomas Davis combined for 159 tackles. On offense, David Greene led the way, completing 60.3 percent of his passes for 3,307 yards and 13 touchdowns, though he did throw 11 interceptions. Michael Cooper rode his success in the South Carolina game to an impressive season, leading the team in rushing with 673 yards, followed by Kregg Lumpkin with 523. Not surprisingly, Gibson finished third on the team in catches, trailing Reggie Brown and Damien Gary.

Greene announced in November that he would return to Athens for his senior year and Pollack followed suit in early January.

"This was a rewarding year," Richt insists. "It was my most challenging as a head coach. We had more obstacles throughout the year and it took a lot of emotional energy. Our off-season was not great coming off the SEC Championship." To an outsider, winning 10 games, finishing sixth in the nation, and winning the SEC East would seem like a pretty good year. But to the diehards in Georgia, anything less than a national title and undefeated season seems inexcusable. But then, there's always next year.

Boston College

It was not the type of year that Tom O'Brien had hoped for, and more headlines were made for what Boston College did off the field than on it. Just over a month after their loss to Miami, media leaks began reporting that Notre Dame was headed to the ACC as their 12th and final team. But what happened when a deal could not be worked out with South Bend? Enter Boston College. Like O'Brien and Gene DeFilippo had predicted, the ACC came calling yet again, and again the Eagles were eager to accept.

The embarrassing loss to Miami at home on national television did not sink the Eagles' spirit. "I thought that the team would respond well [to the loss]," O'Brien says. "That was their shot. We searched for the right mix this season." They beat Ball State and Temple before losing on the road to Syracuse, a game played just hours after Boston College arrived in New York after airplane troubles caused a devastating delay. For the third year in a row, BC did beat its archrival Notre Dame and, after losses to conference leaders Pittsburgh and West Virginia, they defeated Rutgers on the road. They were 6-5 headed into Blacksburg to take on Virginia Tech in the season finale. "The Virginia Tech week, we played well considering all that was riding on the game. The string of five consecutive bowl games, playing the #12 team in the country. We needed a signature win." They got it. They played even better in their win over Colorado State in the San Francisco Bowl.

Derrick Knight finished his last season at BC with 1,721 rushing yards and 11 touchdowns. He used the winter to prepare himself for the NFL draft. Quarterbacks Quinton Porter and Paul Peterson split time behind center, and their statistics were quite similar. Porter had an efficiency rating of 128.95, completing 56 percent of his passes for 14 touchdowns. Peterson's rating was 134.30, completing 57.1 percent of his attempts and throwing for 10 touchdowns. On defense, Josh Ott led the way with 128 tackles.

The senior class won 40 games in five years, tying the mark from the Flutie era. It was the first time since 1977 that Boston College had five winning seasons in a row. But it doesn't mean it was easy. "This was most challenging for me," the head coach concedes. "Once you start to build a program, it's hard. We had a very rewarding season." O'Brien's secret to winning at BC and his teams' 4-1 record in bowl games? "Hire good coordinators," he admits. But I think O'Brien's discipline and spirit have something to do with it.

Things are bright for the Boston College program. The new football offices and team building will be complete in 2005. Recruiting went well and they are headed to the ACC officially in 2005. While they'll never forget Flutie, they might not need his miracles anymore.

Tennessee

The exciting overtime win over South Carolina propelled the Volunteers to 4-0, and it looked like they would be in the national title hunt. Phillip Fulmer saw signs in this team that he had last seen in the 1998 championship team. But the games are played, and some games are lost. The following week at Auburn, Tennessee failed in its comeback when Casey Clausen was intercepted late. "Auburn surprised us," Fulmer recounts. "Their defense whipped us in the front." The next week, the Vols were embarrassed at home, 41-14, by Georgia. "We had a great week of practice. We had lots of confidence going into the Georgia game. I think we matured after Georgia. We had an incredible amount of courage. Defensively, we grew up." They certainly did.

They went on to defeat Alabama and Duke, and then went into Miami and beat the Hurricanes. They kept on winning, beating Mississippi State, Vanderbilt, and Kentucky. They tied with Georgia and Florida for first in the SEC East, but Georgia got the bid in the SEC title game. That wasn't the worst of it. Tennessee was still a very viable candidate for an at-large berth in the BCS, but was passed over for Ohio State and Oklahoma. On top of that, Florida was selected for the Outback Bowl ahead of the Vols. When the dust cleared, Tennessee played Clemson in the Peach Bowl and lost.

Clausen was consistent all year, leading Tennessee to an average of 28.1 points per game. He threw for 27 touchdowns and ran for two more, and fell 32 yards shy of 3,000 passing yards on the season. Cedric Houston scored just two touchdowns on the year, though he led the team in rushing with 744 yards. James Banks, the hero of the overtime win against South Carolina in September, led the team with 621 receiving yards and scored seven times. All-American punter Dustin Colquitt averaged an impressive 45.3 yards per kick and pinned the opponents inside their 20-yard line 20 times. The defense was led by Gibril Wilson, Kevin Simon, and Robert Peace, who among them had 282 tackles and 9½ sacks.

"In the short term, is it very disappointing," Fulmer reflects on the bowl game loss. "But we had an incredible group of seniors. Two 10-win seasons while they were here. I was proud of them. I enjoyed being around them." For his efforts, the coach was rewarded with a contract extension through 2010 with a raise of almost $140,000 a year. He is rejuvenated and ready for spring ball to do it all over again. "I get excited every week. There is a new challenge every week. I do what I do."

Running backs coach Woody McCorvey accepted the offensive coordinator position with Mississippi State.

Maryland

It could have been a disaster. Having lost to Northern Illinois and Florida State early in the season, the Terps could have folded. But they rebounded with wins over The Citadel, West Virginia, and Eastern Michigan, then headed into the Clemson showdown. In their next seven regular season games, Maryland lost just once—at Ralph Friedgen's former employer, Georgia Tech. "We had a good week of practice before Georgia Tech," Friedgen says. "We came close. When we lost to Tech, I was pretty upset. They just outplayed us." They beat Duke, North Carolina, and rival Virginia at home and North Carolina State and Wake Forest on the road. The Terps finished 9-3, second in the ACC, and played West Virginia (again) in the Gator Bowl. They blew the Mountaineers out, 41-7.

The Maryland offense averaged 31.2 points per game, outscoring their opponents 406 to 206. Oft-injured running back Bruce Perry played in 10 games, rushing for 713 yards and six touchdowns. Josh Allen fell just shy of 1,000 yards. Scott McBrien enjoyed a solid senior season with 19 passing touchdowns, six on the ground, with just 6 interceptions, averaging 205.5 passing yards per game. On the receiving end of 39 passes was Latrez Harrison, who led the team in receiving yards. But Harrison had company as nine different Maryland players amassed over 100 yards receiving on the year. D'Qwell Jackson led the way on defense with 132 tackles and Shawne Merriman finished with 55 tackles and 8½ sacks.

"This was the toughest season we've had," the coach insists. "I didn't think we played as a team, especially early on. Defensively, we played well all year. Offensively, we clicked on and off. I told the guys not to worry about things." The coach continues, "It was hard."

They finished the season ranked #17 in the Associated Press poll—not high enough, in Friedgen's estimation. Maryland has won 31 games in the last three seasons, unparalleled in College Park and in most college towns. The coach's vision of putting Maryland football in the elite is almost realized. But as the coach says, "We are about 40 percent of where we want to be."

Wisconsin

The game of college football is all about momentum, and Barry Alvarez's group learned that lesson in 2003. After the loss to UNLV, they climbed to 5-1 and then stopped Ohio State's win streak at 19 in the most memorable game of the year. "The Ohio State win was the highlight of the season," Alvarez reflects. "We had to find a way to win. They had the winning streak and were ranked #3." But the following week, the Badgers had a letdown, losing to Purdue 26-23 on Homecoming, then falling on the road at lowly Northwestern and on a last-second field goal at Minnesota. Wisconsin went from 6-1 and leading the Big Ten to 6-4, in the middle of pack, in just three weeks.

They finally broke out of the losing streak with a thrashing of Michigan State but lost the season finale to Iowa. Against Auburn in the Music City Bowl in Nashville, the Badgers lost by two touchdowns, finishing 7-6. Wisconsin's season was about streaks: win streaks of two and four games, and losing streaks of three and two. Anthony Davis never really recovered from his early-season ankle injury and played in just eight games, and quarterback Jim Sorgi was injured and missed the Purdue game. "We had a very frustrating year," the veteran coach says. "We had injuries and tough losses. It was one of the more frustrating seasons we've had."

Sorgi threw 17 touchdowns with 9 interceptions, five of the TDs going to Lee Evans in one game against Michigan State. Evans had a tremendous senior season with 1,213 receiving yards, averaging 19 yards per catch and scoring 13 touchdowns. Backup quarterback Matt

Schabert, the hero of the Ohio State upset after the Sorgi choking incident, played in 12 games, completing over 50 percent of his passes. On the ground, Dwayne Smith and Booker Stanley combined for over 1,300 yards and 14 touchdowns. In the eight games he did play in, Davis rushed for 682 yards and scored seven touchdowns. Linebacker Jeff Mack and safety Jim Leonhard each had 98 tackles, followed closely by Alex Lewis. Leonhard had 7 interceptions.

After the season, defensive coordinator Kevin Cosgrove accepted the same position at Nebraska under new head coach Bill Callahan.

LSU

Auburn played LSU at the wrong time. After the loss to Florida at home, Nick Saban and his staff worked even harder as the Tigers defeated South Carolina and Auburn. And that was the start of their remarkable run. LSU's defensive domination continued through the season, as the Tigers beat Lousiana Tech, Alabama, and Ole Miss (in a showdown for the SEC West title) and tacked on a win over Arkansas. "I think the turning point was losing to Florida," Saban says. "And the Auburn game, everything came together. We kept talking about playing hard every week, being consistent." As described in previous chapters, LSU won the SEC Championship and then the national title.

"Oklahoma is like any good football team with tradition," the coach insists. "We had so many opportunities to put the game away. They showed resiliency as competitors. It can get you frustrated, not putting the game away." Saban acknowledges that the Tigers ability to "eliminate the clutter" helped bring them victory in New Orleans. "No question about it. We played well in the game. We did the things we emphasized. If there was ever a situation that could have affected us, it was the Sugar Bowl. The fans, the streets. Our guys did a great job going about it."

They won this season with defense, leading the nation in rushing yards allowed and points allowed per game. In fact, LSU outscored its opponents 475-154, allowing an average of just 11 points per game and an amazingly low 67 rushing yards per game. There were so many stars on defense—from Chad Lavalais to Corey Webster (who had seven interceptions), from Jack Hunt to his freshman counterpart LaRon Landry, from Marcus Spears to Marquise Hill. The entire defense was dominating.

On offense, Michael Clayton was superb, scoring 10 touchdowns and catching 78 passes for 1,079 yards. Devery Henderson was not far behind with 11 TDs and 861 yards. On the ground, Justin Vincent exploded onto the national scene with 1,001 rushing yards and 10 touchdowns. Matt Mauck completed 64 percent of his passes and threw for 2,825 yards and 28 touchdowns with 14 interceptions. Kicker Ryan Gaudet finished 7 for 12 while Chris Jackson went 5 for 8.

LSU's success resulted in numerous postseason awards, and not just for the players. Saban was named the National Coach of the Year by the Associated Press and by many other organizations. He was rumored to be first in line for a number of NFL jobs, including the Chicago Bears, but opted to stay in Baton Rouge. He was rewarded in February with a seven-year contract escalating from $2.3 million a year.

A title does not guarantee that a staff stays intact. Assistant coaches Lance Thompson and Tim Walton left for other college jobs while veteran coaches Stan Hixon and Kirk Doll moved on to the NFL. Despite the prospect of losing up to seven players early to the NFL draft, Saban lost just three, Clayton, Hill, and Mauck. The losses were softened by yet another top-rated recruiting class for LSU.

"When you have success like this," Saban says, "and I've been around, it creates opportunities for a lot of people. Coaches leave, guys go to the draft. I'm proud of the team. The biggest thing is how proud the state is and the supporters. I am proud of the way we competed." Then, predictably, "But we can't get complacent."

Florida State

The win over North Carolina State clinched the outright ACC title and the automatic BCS bowl berth for the Seminoles who closed the regular season by defeating rival Florida, 38-24. Craphonso Thorpe was out for the year after breaking his leg against the Wolfpack. FSU played Miami in the Orange Bowl, despite public pleas by Bobby Bowden for a Rose Bowl trip. He and his players did not want to stay in state and play such a familar opponent.

"Miami was the last opponent we thought we'd draw and we never thought we'd be in the Orange Bowl," he says. "It was a bit disappointing we went in Florida. Most of our kids are from Florida but we didn't let it bother us." Maybe it didn't, but they lost the bowl game, 16-14, to finish the season 10-3.

Chris Rix's numbers were not stellar, but he got the job done on 10 occasions. His efficiency rating was 137.93, throwing for 23 touchdowns, over 3,100 yards, rushing for five more TDs but throwing 13 interceptions. His backup, Fabian Walker, played in seven games, throwing just 50 passes. Greg Jones led the running backs with 618 yards and 7 touchdowns but Leon Washington and Lorenzo Booker added an unexpected punch, rushing for over 700 yards and four TDs combined. Thorpe would have surely broken 1,000 yards receiving if he had played the final two games; he finished with 994 yards and 11 touchdowns. On defense, Michael Boulware stepped up, as expected, and led the team with 111 tackles and 2½ sacks.

After the season ended with the Orange Bowl loss, Walker left Florida State to play at Valdosta State and receiver P. K. Sam declared himself for the NFL draft a year early.

"We set such a high standard before this season," Bowden laments. "Ranked in the Top Four for 13 years. Everybody expects it every year to win the title." Everybody includes the Florida State fans, who have come to expect 12-win seasons. "The biggest mistake that fans make is that they have built-in tunnel vision. They see us make a mistake and assume we are the only people making that mistake."

After 28 years at Florida State, how did the season rank for the coach? "Challenging but enjoyable. We didn't have the off-the-field distractions that we've had in previous years."

Arizona State

"It was a huge win over Arizona," Dirk Koetter explains after the season. "Our fans are always telling me, 'You can lose all your games, just beat Arizona.' It would have been difficult if we didn't win."

The victory salvaged part of the disappointing season for the Sun Devils. Arizona State finished 5-7, including a four-game losing streak late in the season. There would be no bowl game. "Last year, we lost to Kansas State in the bowl but had a great season. This year we beat Arizona, then had to watch the bowl games."

Walter did not have a Heisman-worthy season, but it wasn't as bad as it could have been. He completed 52 percent of his passes for 3,044 yards and threw for 24 touchdowns with 10 interceptions. Derek Hagan and Skyler Fulton caught 128 passes combined for just under 2,000 receiving yards and 19 touchdowns. Loren Wade led the charge on the ground with 773 yards and five rushing touchdowns. Jason Shivers had 104 tackles and one sack.

"By far, this was the most challenging, frustrating, and disappointing year of my head coaching career," an obviously downtrodden Koetter says. "When you can see things as a head coach and the team is in a downward spiral, you can see things go wrong but can't fix it. The majority of our problems were between the ears." So now what?

"Players learn from our mistakes and move on," Koetter says, "but the negatives stay with you when you are a coach and can stay with you a long time. It is one of the things that drive you in the off-season."

Three days after the Arizona win in which the ASU secondary did not play well, defensive backs coach Kevin Ramsey was fired and replaced by former All-American and NFL Pro Bowler Mark Carrier. In February, offensive line coach Jeff Grimes moved on to Brigham Young University.

● ● ●

December and January means recruiting, so the coaches hit the road in early December to make home visits. Even while preparing for bowl games, the staffs fanned out around the country for one final push—head coaches included. In the first week of February, Signing Day was held, the earliest date on which prospects can sign National Letters of Intent with schools. All of the schools signed solid classes.

Of course, recruiting scandals rocked college football. Allegations of sex parties for recruits, visits to strip clubs, rape, and underage drinking at the University of Colorado. But the Buffaloes were not alone. Indiscretions by players and recruits at campuses around the nation have led to the creation of an NCAA task force and a more watchful eye by college presidents.

Late winter and early spring are used for evaluating next year's recruits on videotape as well as reviewing the past season and looking ahead to the next. It is also a time when many head coaches speak to booster clubs and charity organizations. Though the hours are shorter, there is still work to be done. For the players, they are well into their off-season conditioning programs, which many coaches point out is the most critical component to success. Before they know it, spring practice is here in March and April.

In late April, 33 of the players from the nine teams were selected in the NFL's seven-round draft, including first-round picks Lee Evans from Wisconsin, Ben Watson from Georgia, and Michael Clayton from LSU. LSU led the way with six draft picks followed by Florida State with five. Among the players selected in late April were quarterbacks Bradlee Van Pelt from Colorado State and LSU's Matt Mauck, both picked in the last round; Badger quarterback Jim Sorgi, selected in the sixth round; and despite their disappointing season, Arizona State had Mike Karney and Jason Shivers selected in the fifth round. Many more players from the teams signed free agent contracts shortly after the draft.

With NCAA rules permitting players to stay on campus during the summer and be on scholarship, the teams condition and work out together and the players take one or two courses to make their fall class load lighter. Coaches find the time in late June or early July for vacations with their families. By mid-July, staffs are well into scouting their upcoming opponents and preparing for fall camp, which starts in early August. So much for the off-season.

The journey begins again for the coaches and players, and for the millions of fans who follow their every move. The 2004 season will bring its share of drama, heartache, and triumph. Some coaches will lose their jobs, some will jet to greener pastures. There will be injuries and scandals, blown chances and comeback victories, long hot practices and freezing December games.

It is college football, after all, and every week *is* a season.

AFTERWORD

"The more things change, the more they stay the same," someone once muttered. Long after I began my journey in August of 2003, college football is still packing stadiums every Saturday, coaches are still staying up past midnight to watch game film, and players still have dreams—some realistic, some unrealistic—of playing on Sundays.

It is now August of 2005, and a season has gone by since *Every Week a Season* was originally released. As the games of 2004 played out, I watched the book's nine teams with more than a passing interest; I was curious to see how they fared, knowing the coaches and many of the prominent players. I know the feel of victory and I know what a locker room is like after a devastating loss. My own journey gave me a unique perspective, a way to watch Saturdays just a little bit differently.

Unlike at the end of the 2003 season, there was no doubt at the end of this one as to who was the national champion. In 2003, LSU won the BCS title while USC took home the Associated Press #1 ranking. There were screams for one final game between the two, which, of course, never materialized. In 2004, The Trojans were the preseason #1 team and never lost a game en route to a blowout of Oklahoma in the Orange Bowl. There were still critics of the BCS, as Auburn finished undefeated and felt shut out from the title picture, and BCS commissioners promised yet more changes to the formula.

At the University of Colorado, head coach Gary Barnett survived the scandal that engulfed the program and, in fact, took the Buffalos to the Big XII title game. But the big story in 2004 was not scandal or rankings; it was the coaching carousel. It started midseason with the letting go of Florida's Ron Zook, followed by the unexpected firing of Notre Dame's Ty Willingham; the hiring of Steve Spurrier at South Carolina; openings at Washington, Stanford, and Illinois; and the departure of Nick Saban from LSU to the Miami Dolphins. All told, twenty-one jobs changed hands.

So what about the nine schools profiled in *Every Week a Season*? Some had better seasons than 2003, some failed miserably. Surprisingly, considering the turnover in coaches, just one of the nine coaches—Saban—is gone. Players who moved on to the NFL met with modest success, if any, and a new crop of rising stars took the spotlight. A brief look at the nine schools:

Colorado State

If 2003 was a good season for Sonny Lubick at 7-5, than 2004 was horrible at 4-7, including blowout losses to Air Force, Minnesota, and #1 USC. To begin with, the season opened with another crushing loss to rival Colorado. In the absence of Bradlee Van Pelt, who is on the practice squad of the Denver Broncos, Justin Holland attempted to lead the team, but met with little success. Lubick's team was young and struggled against a tough non-conference schedule. On the bright side, eighteen starters return for 2005.

Georgia

Many members of the media believed that 2004 was the year of the Dawgs. Mark Richt's team was loaded on both sides of the ball, led by David Greene at quarterback and David Pollack at defensive end. Greene threw twenty touchdowns and 2500 yards, and receiver Fred Gibson caught seven touchdowns for 801 yards. The emergence of freshman running back Danny Ware gave Richt yet another weapon. But it wasn't meant to be. An upset loss at home to Tennessee ruined their chance at the national title, and a loss to Auburn made it two too many. They salvaged the season with a gutsy win over Wisconsin in the Outback Bowl. Greene, Pollack, and many teammates are headed to the NFL in 2005, leaving quarterback D. J. Shockley as the go-to guy. Acclaimed defensive coordinator Brian Van Gorder moved on to the NFL's Jacksonville Jaguars.

Boston College

It's not surprising that Tom O'Brien's Boston College team was competitive in 2004, but it is astonishing where they finished. The Eagles beat Pittsburgh, Notre Dame, and West Virginia to tie for the Big East championship in their final season in the league. They won their fifth bowl game in a row, the longest streak in the country, with a win over North Carolina in the Continental Tire Bowl, and finished #21 in the AP poll at 9-3. Paul Peterson emerged as a solid signal caller and Mathias Kiwanuka anchored a strong defense. Last year's running back star, Derrick Knight, is currently out of football. The new football facility opened in 2005 as O'Brien and his team head to the ACC.

Tennessee

Off-season suspensions changed the Volunteer lineup, but the biggest concern was who was going to replace QB Casey Clausen, now headed to NFL Europe. It turns out that it takes two people to replace him. A pair of freshmen quarterbacks, Brent Schaffer and Erik Ainge, took the state by storm, alternating snaps and games before injuries took them both down. The Volunteers were humiliated at home by Auburn but then turned around and beat Georgia on the road. They won the SEC East and lost a rematch against Auburn in the SEC title game. A win over Texas A & M in the Cotton Bowl left the Vols with a 10-3 record and left coach Phillip Fulmer, who himself had endured threats of lawsuits and accusations resulting from an Alabama recruiting scandal, with a good feeling.

Maryland

Fans of Maryland worshiped at the feet of coach Ralph Friedgen, who had led the Terps to three straight ten-win seasons in College Park. Though he would be without QB Scott McBrien, Maryland was loaded at many positions and prepared to compete for the ACC title. But the offense never got the message. The Terps struggled to a 5-6 record and endured an embarrassing three-game losing streak in which the offense scored just 17 points *total*. The highlight of the season was an upset home win over Florida State. Though it would have been unthinkable just a year earlier, Friedgen came under fire from fans and the media.

Wisconsin

Lee Evans, last year's star, has emerged as a standout receiver for the Buffalo Bills in the NFL, while leaving a hole on the 2004 Wisconsin team. But not all that much of a hole. Barry Alvarez's team exploded out of the gate, going 9-0 and climbing into the Top 5 in the polls. They had to beat Iowa and Michigan State to run the table, win the Big Ten, and have a shot at the national title. They lost both games and settled for the Outback Bowl. It was the Badger defense that led the charge, anchored by four linemen with outstanding ability. There was a new defensive coordinator, Bret Bielema, as Kevin Cosgrove had left for Nebraska. Oft-injured running back Anthony Davis showed flashes of brilliance in running for 973 yards and eleven touchdowns but was never 100 percent healthy. QB John Stocco threw nine TDs and seven interceptions.

LSU

How could anything compare to the magical 2003 season, when LSU went 13-1, won the SEC, and captured the BCS national title? Receiver Michael Clayton was busy catching eighty passes and seven touchdowns for the Tampa Bay Buccaneers and the big question mark heading into 2004 was behind center, as Matt Mauck had moved on to the NFL and senior Marcus Randall and red-shirt freshman JaMarcus Russell took turns as signal-caller. Justin Vincent, the freshman star of 2003 at running back, did little in his sophomore season. LSU escaped the opener against Oregon State but did not look good, then suffered a one-point loss to Auburn and a humiliating defeat on the road at Georgia. Nick Saban's team showed promise, getting to 9-2 before losing on the last play to Iowa in the Outback Bowl. After Dave Wannstedt was fired by the Miami Dolphins, the Saban Watch began. On Christmas Day, Saban announced he was leaving LSU for Miami.

Florida State

Bobby Bowden's team lost the Labor Day opener to Miami and never fully recovered. They were upset on the road at Maryland and beat by Florida at home. Star QB Chris Rix was injured midway through the season and then benched after throwing just three touchdowns and seven interceptions. Wyatt Sexton filled in admirably (eight TDs/ eight INTs) until Bowden decided to go back to his senior for the final games. The Seminoles finished at 9-3 with a win over West Virginia in the Gator Bowl. Criticism continued to mount as FSU was a nonfactor again in the BCS, and in the offseason Bowden made changes to his offensive staff, including the demotion of his son, Jeff, from offensive coordinator.

Arizona State

What a difference a year makes. Dirk Koetter's team beat Arizona in the last game of 2003 to get to 5-7 and salvage a disappointing season. With virtually the same personnel returning—but with a new attitude—the Sun Devils were a surprise in the nation, going 9-3 with losses only to USC, California, and—stunningly—Arizona. Andrew Walter regained his status as an elite quarterback, throwing thirty touchdowns and passing for over 3100 yards. Koetter was suddenly a name being mentioned for the top jobs in the country. ASU beat Purdue in the Sun Bowl to cap off a remarkable season.

2005 will, of course, bring more story lines. Stars will emerge and coaches will be fired. But every week, a new season emerges—a new chance for redemption, a new game with which to stake your claim. And I will be watching.

BRIAN CURTIS
New York
August 2005

INDEX

BRIAN CURTIS's first book, *The Men of March: A Season Inside the Lives of College Basketball Coaches*, was released in the spring of 2003. Curtis was a sports reporter and broadcaster for Fox Sports Net based in Los Angeles. He was a features and game reporter for the *Regional Sports Report* and contributor to the *National Sports Report,* primarily covering college basketball and football. He was nominated for two local Emmy Awards. Curtis worked as a sports reporter for a local television station in Ohio, covering basketball and football in the Mid American Conference. He hosted a call-in sports radio talk show, *Sports Conversation,* in Virginia and covered ACC basketball on radio.

He is a contributor to *The Jim Rome Show,* Fox Sports Radio, ESPN Radio's *GameDay,* and ABC Sports Radio. He has been a guest on *The Best Damn Sports Show Period* and has appeared on hundreds of radio and television stations around the nation as well as websites including sportsillustrated.com, sportingnews.com, msnbc.com, and foxsports.com.

He is a member of the Football Writers Association of America and the United States Basketball Writers Association. He holds a Master's Degree from Ohio University in Sports Administration and a Bachelor's Degree from the University of Virginia in Government. He currently resides in Los Angeles, California.